Camilla Fitzsimons

Community Education and Neoliberalism

Philosophies, Practices and Policies in Ireland

palgrave
macmillan

Camilla Fitzsimons
Maynooth University
Maynooth, Kildare, Ireland

ISBN 978-3-319-45936-3   ISBN 978-3-319-45937-0 (eBook)
DOI 10.1007/978-3-319-45937-0

Library of Congress Control Number: 2016958755

Cover illustration: © Thomas Northcut / Getty Stock Images

Printed on acid-free paper

This Palgrave Macmillan imprint is published by Springer Nature
The registered company is Springer International Publishing AG
The registered company address is: Gewerbestrasse 11, 6330 Cham, Switzerland

FOREWORD

Community Education and Neoliberalism: Philosophies, Practices and Policies in Ireland is essential reading for everyone working for equality and social justice. Camilla Fitzsimons is one such worker. Her work takes place at political, civil society and community levels. And, crucially, she also works at academic level. This scholarly context provides an essential reflexive space, the room to think and theorise on practice and activism. This book succeeds in spanning these domains. As well as looking at the practice and practitioners in her research, Camilla focuses her attention on the strata underlying the causes of the deep divisions in society, divisions which deepen in a neoliberal economic environment. These divisions ultimately destroy the human spirit. With her studies, her practice, her activism and now, with this book, Camilla rekindles hope as resistance to the onslaught of neoliberalism.

The values of classical liberalism with its guarantees of freedom of speech, freedom of the press and religious freedom and so on, as well as free trade and free markets, have been used as the Trojan Horse of neoliberal economics. Yet we know from social movements, particularly feminism and the LGBT movement, that liberalism did not deliver equality in any real sense of the word, quite simply it granted greater autonomy for powerful people and groups, and the subsequent weakening, exclusion and/or exploitation of everyone else. In this context, education could play a crucial role in disrupting that seamless takeover, as well as revealing and analysing the disparities.

However, unfortunately, education has been instrumental in supporting the status quo, or worse, in furthering the ambition of inequality.

In particular, education has emphasised individualised agency, while occluding the structures that constrains and marginalises agency, such as class, gender, sexuality, as well as race, ethnicity and ability. This means that education ignores the real impact of the big picture, the social categories that divide and segregate. It also undermines the communities that could heal those divisions, isolations and segregations. When Freire critiqued mainstream education as "banking education", he was most prescient about the ways in which it performs as the instrument and tool of neoliberalism.

Community education emerged as a model of resistance when Ireland was in the maelstrom of the deepest depression. Camilla Fitzsimons has provided a keen i`nsight into the origins and practice in the field. My recollections from those early days when women, in particular, organised their own education and development in the community, were full of hope and imagination. It was an era when women were increasingly subject to the backlash against equality. In addition, unemployment figures rose exponentially and vast numbers of people emigrated, draining the country of youth and vitality. The new waves of neoliberal economics was nurtured by the political will of Thatcher and Reagan, ultimately facilitated by the economic globalisation, which we can see now as the latest version of colonisation and imperialism.

The impact of this political will was profound, with the undermining of collective action, organised labour, privatisation of public resources and social housing in particular. It was the birth of the conditions that led to the collapse of 2008 with the resulting homelessness, unemployment and poverty that we can see all around us in Ireland, and in Spain, Portugal and Greece but also in the widening divisions between rich and poor all over the world. It is breathtaking to think that we have experienced at first hand a complete meltdown of the neoliberal economy in 2008. Yet as a society, we have been convinced and persuaded that it works, that it may need a bit of sacrificial tweaking and a bit of judicious regulation but fundamentally, it works.

This book helps us to see the ways in which social processes become the conduit for the doctrine of neoliberalism. Within democratic politics, of the people, for the people, by the people, the market economy prevails, with the commodification of representation, such that votes are bought and sold. There now seems to be no difference between political campaigning, lobbying and marketing, with the messages reduced to simplistic bargains and deals.

Community education, adult education, higher education, lifelong learning, training and so on, all of these have been drawn into the limelight in these critical times of austerity. And all have been framed in the context of neoliberalism, that is, that the only way to social cohesion, equality and democracy is through serving the economy. Meanwhile, the poor must suffer; the poor will always be with us. Thus, the very institutions that ought to protect us from poverty, marginalisation and the vicissitudes of economic boom and bust, are, instead, bent on convincing us that *there is no alternative.*

For Camilla Fitzsimons, there *has* to be an alternative. There must be hope. She has continued her work for equality and social justice with this book. She has explored the meanings of community and the ways in which it becomes shorthand for society or for minority groupings, obscuring the complexity and multifaceted nature of community. She has examined the practices in community education in Ireland in order to reveal the underpinning philosophies, especially feminist, critical pedagogy, democratic integrated group work, experiential learning, reflexivity, discussion, dialogue, the creation of "really useful knowledge", perspective transformations and consciousness raising, to name a few, while not fully capturing the scope of these underlying principles. In her practice, she has been inspired by educators as activists, critical educators who embed and embody emancipatory processes. She has scrutinised the policies on community education and the ways in which those policies subtly change the meanings and outcomes of the practice. Thus, in this volume, Camilla draws on her deep scholarship to investigate what has happened in this context and to open a new conversation on the future of Irish society and the alternative to destructive inequalities.

The potentiality for community education to create a just society remains. As it emerged in a dark era, it can also be rekindled for a more optimistic future. But we have to join in the conversation in a thoughtful way, to inform ourselves, to engage with complex ideas, to listen to the voices of those who are silenced, to build an aspirational, imaginative and creative environment, for ourselves and our children. And this book provides the wherewithal to participate in this vital discussion.

Maynooth University   Bríd Connolly

ACKNOWLEDGEMENTS

Thanks to the many participants of community education, the community educators who took part in this research and who work for social change.

Thanks to my family and colleagues who assisted along the way.

A special thanks to Peter Dorman who drew the illustrations that open chapters 1–7.

Contents

1 **Introduction: Community Education in Neoliberal Times**   1
  What Is Community Education?   3
  Assessing the Neoliberal Turn   6
  Ireland's Neoliberal State   11
  Neoliberalism in Crisis   16
  Neoliberal Resistance and Pockets of Difference   25
  About the Book   29
  Part I – What Is Community Education?   31
  Part II – The Neoliberalisation of Community Education   32
  Notes   33

Part I   Community Education, Philosophies and Practices

2 **Models of Community Education**   37
  The Dubious Nature of Community   38
  About Education   43
  Involving Practitioner Voices   45
  What Is Community Education?   49
  Models of Community Education   53
  Identifying Models of Practice   60
  Conclusion   65
  Notes   66

3 Community Education in Ireland   69
   Sketching a History of Adult and Community Education   71
   Daytime and Evening Provision Through VECs
   and the Literacy Movement   73
   Women's Community Education   77
   The Spread of Ideas Through Training for Transformation   81
   The Wider Community Development/Anti-poverty Movement   82
   The Involvement of the Academy   87
   Research Findings on Contemporary Community Education   90
   Conclusion   101
   Notes   101

4 Critical Education and Community Education   103
   Theories of Learning   104
   Why Do We Need Philosophies of Education?   105
   The Benefits and Pitfalls of Humanistic Community Education   108
   Towards a Feminist Pedagogy   118
   Conclusion   129
   Notes   130

Part II   The Neoliberalisation of Community Education

5 Community Education and Employability   133
   What Is Social Policy?   134
   The European Lifelong Learning Agenda   136
   Ireland's Policy Reaction and the Implications
   for Community Education   141
   Community Sector Policy Developments   143
   Neoliberalism Takes Hold   144
   Practitioner Perspectives on Change   151
   Strategising Relationships with Policymakers   159
   Conclusion   160
   Notes   161

6 Community Education and Accreditation   163
   The Origins of Accreditation   165
   The Europeanisation of Accreditation   168

The Implementation of Qualifications Frameworks   174
Quality Assurance as a Process of Surveillance   178
Practitioner Thoughts and Experiences on Accreditation   181
Conclusion   192
Notes   193

7   **Insiders, Outsiders and the Professionalisation
    of Community Education**   195
*What's in a Word – Explaining Professionalism
and Professionalisation*   197
Precarity and Professionalism – A Contradiction?   207
Practitioner Perspectives on Professionalism and Precarity   208
A Culture of Volunteerism   221
Conclusion   223
Notes   224

8   **Rekindling Community Education in Neoliberal Times**   227
A Landscape of Community Education in Ireland   230
*From the Personal to the Political – Rekindling Community
Education*   237
In conclusion   243
Notes   244

Bibliography   247

Index   281

LIST OF FIGURES

Illustration 1.1	The scales of injustice	1
Illustration 2.1	Models of community education	37
Fig. 2.1	What is community education, participant responses	50
Fig. 2.2	Models of community education	54
Illustration 3.1	The heterogenity of community education	69
Fig. 3.1	Network membership amongst research respondents	93
Illustration 4.1	The limitations of humanistic approaches	103
Illustration 4.2	Code used with focus groups	126
Illustration 5.1	Community education and employability	133
Illustration 6.1	The impact of accreditation	163
Fig. 6.1	Three dimensions of accredited learning	192
Illustration 7.1	The Professionalisation of community education	195
Fig. 7.1	Highest qualifications held by researched community educators	212
Fig. 7.2	How community educators gained their initial qualification	213
Fig. 8.1	Quantification of philosophies and examples of practice	230
Fig. 8.2	Community education – triangle of involvement	232

LIST OF TABLES

Table 2.1   Overview of research participants by organisation type   47
Table 2.2   How community educators interpret their role   52
Table 2.3   Quantifying models of community education   61
Table 2.4   Who should community education target?   62
Table 2.5   Does community education reduce inequality?   65
Table 3.1   Summary of project outputs in relation to participation in,
             and content of training and education and social awareness
             programmes (1996–1999) (Nexus 2002: 35).   85
Table 3.2   Connections between the community sector and public
             provision   89
Table 3.3   Types of organisation participating practitioners work for   91
Table 3.4   Examples of practice quantified   95
Table 5.1   Attitudinal measurement on relationships between equality
             and political reform   152
Table 5.2   Attitudes on community sector cooption   155
Table 5.3   Strategic participation/non-participation   160
Table 6.1   Quantifying accreditation   181
Table 6.2   Attitudinal measurements on the benefit of accreditation   181
Table 6.3   Attitudes on the suitability of FETAC (now QQI)   183
Table 6.4   Attitudes on whether accreditation interferes with practice   188
Table 7.1   Attitudes on the need for formal qualifications   211
Table 7.2   Measurements of 'insider' and 'outsider' practitioners   212
Table 7.3   Attitudes on 'insider' versus 'outsider' suitability   215

Table 7.4   Cross-tabulation of socio-economic background and suit-
          ability community education work   216
Table 7.5   Number of community educators working outside of paid
          hours   222

CHAPTER 1

Introduction: Community Education in Neoliberal Times

Illustration 1.1   The scales of injustice

© The Author(s) 2017
C. Fitzsimons, *Community Education and Neoliberalism*,
DOI 10.1007/978-3-319-45937-0_1

At the 2015 autumn gathering of the AONTAS[1]-led Community Education practitioners Network (CEN) I was lucky enough to participate in invigorating conversations about the nature of community education in Ireland. Prompted by a pre-set agenda, these discussions included the work of the CEN as well as standards and quality within community education more generally. Given that there was a national general election on the horizon, we also made space for discussion on the network's pre-election strategy as was befitting of practitioner's historical and ongoing commitment to shaping domestic community education. The passion within many people's words reflected their commitment to the work but, alongside this passion, there was also a sense of anxiety about the future of community education in Ireland. One could argue that such anxiety is misplaced as there have been notable developments for those availing of community education since contemporary practice emerged in the 1970s and 1980s. These developments include State subsidy for attendance, greater opportunities to gain recognisable certificates and a more obvious progression pathway into further and higher education. For community educators, a more distinct occupational identity has been forged through specialist adult and community education programmes. In particular, a recent government-led realignment of community education providers alleges to have streamlined provision, thereby addressing a previous "absence of co-ordinated delivery" (SOLAS 2014a: 36).

That day, the most likely cause of collective anxiety was a growing mistrust in the government's motivations in pushing forward such changes. Many Community Education Network (CEN) members, most of whom were women, had already been affected by a similar realignment that began some years earlier in the grant-aided Community Development Programme. This realignment resulted in the non-negotiated merger of many independent organisations into the structures of the State and the closure of some community groups where State grant aid was suddenly withdrawn. There was also a sense that practitioners were finding it more difficult to maintain some of the traditional principles of community education such as its needs-based approach and its incorporation of a social analysis into everyday life. Instead there were reports of increasing pulls towards outcomes-based and conformist approaches to education.

Attendees at the CEN meeting were also likely to be feeling the personal effects of Ireland's programme of austerity which took hold some six years earlier. One of its many features was savage cuts to the community sector that were disproportionate to other publically funded entities (Harvey 2012).

The job instability this brought (as testified to later in this book) meant many community educators became part of Ireland's growing population of part-time and low-paid precarious workers, a situation that disproportionately affects women (Spillane 2015: 151). As well as austerity cuts to organisations providing community education, those in the room were likely to be experiencing the personal effects of greater indirect taxes and of reduced social services (Nagle 2015). Given that 19% of all residential mortgages are in arrears (Central Bank of Ireland 2015: 7–8) and that private rents are soaring, who knows how many were privately concerned about housing debt.

The reasons for these erosions in ordinary living standards and the ideological pulls on community education lie within Ireland's successful recalibration of its social, political and economic priorities towards a model of neoliberal free-market economics. Introduced in the main through macro- and micro-policy interventions, the resultant *neoliberalisation* has successfully infused business logic into public and community spaces (Lynch et al. 2012). This institutes a political system that prioritises the economy above everything else.

A core purpose of this book is to substantiate this claim with an emphasis on the impacts for community education. Although much of this book focuses on Irish experiences, a globalised and neoliberalised country (Coulter and Nagle 2015), I will also raise questions about neoliberalism more generally so that international comparatives can be drawn. This opening chapter will discuss a global turn towards neoliberalism sharing some of the many consequences of this market-led ideology. Congruent with an anti-neoliberal stance, I will outline a destructive process of neoliberalisation within community education that threatens to undermine its democratic foundations. I will also provide a summary of each subsequent chapter and explain how each contributes to this perspective. Before doing this, I will begin with discussion about *community education* itself and outline its connection to sociopolitical contexts.

What Is Community Education?

At its broadest, community education refers to any localised, structured adult learning that happens outside of traditional institutions such as schools and colleges. This can be within specialist adult education centres, in community buildings, literacy support centres, independent community sector organisations, charities, training centres, health centres, in churches, unoccupied social housing, people's homes and whatever other premises are available to providers and groups. Commonly, academic contributions go further by describing community education as not simply locationally based, but as an approach that is underpinned by egalitarian principles. Prominent contributor Lyn Tett (2006: 2) explains: "community education sees a community as a group of people who perceive common needs and problems, have a sense of identity and a common sense of objectives". Similarly Johnston (2000: 14) centralises its political potential proposing "community education provides a localised focus for a social purpose education whose key values are a commitment to social justice, greater social and economic equality, and a more participatory democracy". Community education prides itself on process as much as content with a commonly evoked mantra being the idea of starting *where the person is at*. This does not just mean accommodating the many practical challenges facing adults as they return to education, such as flexibility, affordability and childcare, it also means an awareness of the knowledge, skills and values a person brings to a learning experience. These factors determine subjects and modes of delivery with contents *uncovered* as much as *covered* through collective, politicising, bottom-up processes. Bríd Connolly (2008: 6) captures its spirit eloquently when she describes community education as not just *for* the people, but *of* the people.

In determining a history of community education in Ireland, (uncovered more comprehensively within Chapter 3) two distinct trajectories emerge. The first of these is through public provision which I will date back to the 1970s. A second arguably more political pathway is through locally established, independently managed community sector organisations, many of which were formed in the 1980s and 1990s. These bottom-up projects emerged from communities that were commonly referred to as "disadvantaged" and were certainly the neighbourhoods that experienced the harsh end of structural inequality (Kelleher and Whelan 1992; Connolly 2003). A 2002 government evaluation of these community sector projects reported that all projects "to a greater or lesser extent" are involved in "delivering training, educational or social awareness programmes within their own communities" (Nexus 2002: 33). These two strands – public and community sector provision, coalesced within these neighbourhoods forming a localised milieu that is often interpreted as not only extending educational opportunity beyond traditional settings, but as fulfilling important civic functions. One such function is its potential to actualise a range of citizen rights through collective, praxis-oriented approaches that encourage systemic change.

At one stage, such politically charged aspirations for community education were written into Irish government policy. *Learning for Life: White Paper on*

Adult Education (2000) describes community education as "a process of communal education towards empowerment, both at an individual and a collective level" and describes it as something that is intrinsically linked to "community development" (DOES 2000: 112).

When determining the meaning of *community development* (discussed in more detail in Chapters 2 and 3) most Irish accounts link it to international descriptions of locally based, bottom-up processes of collective action, underpinned by principles of empowerment, social justice, participation and equality (Lee 2006; Motherway 2006; CWC 2008; Crickley and McArdle 2009; Lloyd 2010; Fitzsimons and Dorman 2013). By its own admission, the White Paper's inclusion of what it calls this "second view" (DOES 2000: 112) (the first view presumably being individualised instructional learning) came about as a result of successful consultation with community sector organisations following a review of the proceeding *Green Paper: Adult Education in an Era of Learning* (Government of Ireland 1998).

Irish contributions to the ongoing development, implementation and documentation of community education have emanated from the academy (Connolly 1996, 1999, 2001, 2003, 2007, 2010, 2014; Keily et al. 1999; Feeley 2007; Fitzsimons 2012), from The Irish National Adult Learning Organisation which is called AONTAS (Basset et al. 1989; Inglis et al. 1993; AONTAS 2004, 2008; Bailey et al. 2010, 2011) and from practitioners (Cullinane 2003; Dorman 2006; McCallion 2009; Slevin 2009; Fitzsimons and Dorman 2013). There are also Irish produced how-to handbooks containing politicising, collective, dialogic and experiential exercises for practical use in community settings (Sheehy 2001; McNeill 2005; Sheehy et al. 2007; Collision and Ní Chasaide 2008; Crowley et al. 2015). A common trend across these varied publications; by academics, advocates and practitioners alike, is a starting point that interprets present-day capitalism as the cause of much of the social and economic inequality that many people who access community education are affected by. In response, community education seeks to offer equality-based solutions, both to individuals and communities. To demonstrate this perspective within practice, the AONTAS CEN[2] describes community education as "a process of personal and community transformation, empowerment, challenge, social change and collective responsiveness... grounded in principles of justice, equality and inclusiveness" and different from "general adult education provision due to its political and radical methodologies" (AONTASCEN 2008: 1). Another network, the Community Education Facilitators Network (CEFA) which is an association of

State (or publically) employed Community Education Facilitators (CEFs) concur. Research by CEFA claims that community educators "assert the social purpose, origins and meaning of adult and community education which is about empowerment of marginalized individuals and communities for collective social and economic transformation" and continues, "it is political and asserts democratic participation and focuses on social justice outcomes" (McGlynn 2014: 6).

ASSESSING THE NEOLIBERAL TURN

Any suggestion that community education can act as panacea for the woes of capitalism should be treated with considerable caution. During the same period when there was an expansion of equality-based community education, there was also a growing gap between rich and poor both globally (OECD 2011, 2014; United Nations 2014: 2, 2015: 8) and in Ireland (Allen 2003; O'Connor and Staunton 2015). This growth in income inequality has been presaged by a profound global shift to the political right as Keynesianism, paralysed by stagflation in the 1950s and 1960s, was strategically replaced with neoliberalism (Harvey 2005). Born out of the ideas of Chicago School economists and spurred on by Reaganomics and Thatcherism (Birch and Mykhnenko 2010: 3–5), neoliberalism encouraged a return to elements of classical liberalism's laissez-faire economics that would reinvigorate the accumulation of capital through specific political and economic actions.

Neoliberalism promised financial gain for everyone. Bhagwati (2004: 53) explains how "poverty is licked" by free-market economics and he proposes a simple "two-step argument; that trade enhances growth, and that growth reduces poverty". This conjecture is based on the assumption that deregulated entrepreneurialism at the top of society creates economic growth below that benefits all people through a downwards flow of widespread job creation. Concurrently, this drives consumer spending, the fulcrum of all capitalism. At the same time, individual freedom is protected through market freedom as prices independently adjust (including wages) in response to supply and demand (Duménil and Lévy 2004: 11).

Whilst governments are called upon to implement the neoliberal project, the relationship between the State and the socio-economic realm is revolutionised as the former is refashioned as a preserver of the free-market economy "at all costs" (Harvey 2005: 64). This is so that businesses and corporations can operate without restrictions and boundaries. *The Washington Consensus*, a policy convergence agreed in 1989 made neoliberal ubiquity inevitable when the World Bank, International Monetary Fund (IMF) and US Treasury agreed a set of policy directives; the tenets of which are described elsewhere as:

> tight fiscal discipline (with virtually no public budget deficit allowed); an end to subsidies and re-direction of public expenditure on basic health, education and infrastructure; tax cuts; financial liberalization; free-floating exchange rates; trade liberalisation and a unified low tariff; openness to foreign direct investment (FDI); privatization; deregulation; and secure private property rights. (Birch and Mykhnenko 2010: 9)

This consensus was later expanded to include other organisations, such as the World Trade Organisation, and a compliant global economy of capital mobility emerged which fed off a presumption of continued growth and was implemented through domestic attention to short-term market demands (Saad-Filho 2004; Nagle 2015).

With the market viewed as sacrosanct, another key feature of the neoliberal project is the transfer of public entities into private ownership. The logic of privatisation is that expensive and cumbersome State mechanisms such as schools, hospitals, prisons and transport services can be more efficiently managed and can also be a source of profit in their own right. Take schools as an example. A privatised model is argued as more efficiently run and less hamstrung by trade union legacy agreements. As they are no longer a drain on the public purse, people are asked to pay less tax on their income. Theoretically, this gives people more control over their money and more capacity to pay school fees. Parents and guardians can choose from a range of competing school when deciding where to educate their children.

Neoliberalism's Failed Agenda

In some respects, neoliberal claims of less tax, more jobs, more educational choice and greater opportunities in life concur with many of the aspirations of community education and with the needs commonly expressed within communities. The difficulty is that these equality objectives have not transpired with Harvey (2005: 21) noting "enough contradictions in the neoliberal position to render evolving neoliberal practices (vis-à-vis issues such as monopoly power and market failures) unrecognisable in relation to the seeming purity of neoliberal doctrine" (brackets in original). The notion of freedom through liberalised market economics is fictitious. To borrow the words of adult educator Ira Shor:

> The free market is not free ... [working people] don't control the job market, the housing market, the money market, the food market, the insurance market, the car market, etc. In reality, they are jockying for position, couple-by-couple, person-by-person, in a society where wealth and power lie in corporate hands. [...] Economic globalisation is ideal for big business but bad news for working people ... who are running faster merely to stay in place or to slow the decline in their living standards. (Shor 1996: 36)

Where often much lauded cuts to income taxes are introduced, these are frequently cancelled out through indirect taxes such as property tax, and charges for domestic services such as water and waste collection.

Rather than trickle wealth down, neoliberal systems "hoover wealth to the top" (Klein 2007: 86) as the lower and middle classes are economically squeezed. This is through so-called redistributive that policies allow the accumulation of capital by the minority, a persistent and dominating feature of this socio-economic model (Birch and Mykhnenko 2010; Chomsky 1999; Duménil and Lévy 2004; Harvey 2005; Allen and O'Boyle 2013; Giroux 2011, 2013; Coulter 2015). One Organisation for Economic Co-operation and Development (OECD) report *Focus on inequality and growth* (2014) claims that the richest 10% of the OECD population earns nine and a half times more than the poorest 10%, an amount that has grown from a seven to one ratio in the 1980s (OECD 2014; 1). To personify the extremes of inequality, the 2016 Forbes rich list cites the global top-earner Bill Gates, as having a personal net worth of some €75 billion.[3] Gates is one of the 1% that owns almost half the world's riches, an estimated $100 trillion (Oxfam 2014: 2). Oxfam (2014: 2) further catalogue increased wealth for the world's richest 1% since 1980[4] with the USA 1% capturing 95% of post-financial crisis growth. Simultaneously, the report claims that the bottom 90% became poorer. At the other end of the rich–poor spectrum, Save the Children (2014) has highlighted the preventable deaths of one million babies per year on their first day of their life. Stark claims are also made by the United Nations (UN) as part of a review of the Millennium Development Goals:

> About 800 million people still live in extreme poverty and suffer from hunger. Over 160 million children under age five have inadequate height for their age due to insufficient food. Currently, 57 million children of

primary school age are not in school. Almost half of global workers are still working in vulnerable conditions, rarely enjoying the benefits associated with decent work. About 16,000 children die each day before celebrating their fifth birthday, mostly from preventable causes ... In 2015, one in three people (2.4 billion) still use unimproved sanitation facilities ... Today over 880 million people are estimated to be living in slum-like conditions in the developing world's cities. (United Nations 2015: 8–9)

Neoliberalism seeks to reverse previous common perspectives that some countries are poorer because they do not have the same socio-economic resources as others. This is by framing accepted causes of poverty in a way that directs attention away from under-resourcing and seeks to blame "misconceived state intervention, corruption, inefficiency and misguided economic incentives" (Saad-Filo 2004: 113–114). This line of thinking conveniently absolves the global-North from its role in perpetuating poverty through unfair trade policies and asset stripping. There has also been a co-option of local elites within poorer countries through IMF and World Bank structural adjustment programmes that are entered into as part of much needed loan deals (Manfred and Roy 2010: 119). These images of inequity still tend to focus on country-to-country poverty where the global-North is interpreted as rich and the global-South as poor. Our understanding of poverty has since been expanded to include measureable differences across social class in life expectancy and infant mortality, physical and mental health, educational performance and imprisonment rates within so-called Western societies (Wilkinson and Pickett 2009).

In spite of these shortfalls in the neoliberal model, there has been rapid expansion of free-market economics made possible by a successful de-emphasis of inequality through a culture of wealth and a global illusion of shared economic prosperity. Firstly, this was through a reinvention of capitalist relations of production outside of the accrual of surplus value created by workers over and above actual labour cost. Capitalism was thus reimagined into a post-industrial, globalised and illusive knowledge economy with its previous dependence on manufacturing viewed as *passé*. A mirage of growth was created through high-risk financial transactions, an inflated property bubble, and the generation of shares (asset-backed securities) by bundling loans together (Duménil and Lévy 2011: 106). Despite the now obvious short-sightedness of this approach, some proponents declared an end to the boom-bust nature of capitalism with our "new economy" set to deliver only boom for the foreseeable future (Nagle 2015: 110).

The second illusion in capitalist growth was a shared veneer of middle-class comfort that was held in place through unprecedented levels of private debt. This dynamic plugged capitalism's chasm of inadequate basic income, with debt-money funding both subsistent needs and life events such as divorce, illness and/or unemployment (Soederberg 2013: 494). Rather than questioning the unsustainable nature of a credit-led accumulation of wealth and the folly of citizens kicking the can of day-to-day expenditure down an uncertain road, the response from governments was to transform themselves into what Soederberg (2013) describes as *debtfare* States. This was by validating and even lauding unsecure debt creation, including sub-prime mortgage lending, all of which was facilitated through a paralleling deregulation of financial systems.

A key factor in understanding why the neoliberal project is maintained lies in the common internalisation of a *neoliberal logic*. This hegemony, or consent by the majority to the general direction of society imposed by a minority (Gramsci 1971: 12), ensures sufficient levels of public compliance to allow certain policies to be advanced even when they are against most people's best interests. Increasingly, neoliberal logic takes root though a homogenised popular culture and centralised control of public pedagogic spaces (Herman and Chomsky 1994; Giroux 2013). These are powerful mechanisms in determining whose voices are heard, what counts as representation, what behaviours are considered normal and, conversely, what is thought of as subversive. The trade union movement has been a particular target for neoliberals as hard-line political tactics and media accounts portray strikers as deviant and as often to blame for national problems (Philo et al. 1995). This is alongside little reporting of the erosion of working conditions that commonly lead to industrial action in the first place. To give an example, in response to recent trade union-endorsed strike action within *Irish Rail* (undertaken to counter demands for increased productivity) the Irish Minister for Transport evoked business logic when he expressed dismay at such inflammatory actions "in the context of a company losing over €1.5 million per month" (The Irish Times, 17 October 2015[5]). When this neoliberal common sense is relayed through a globalised media in the control of a small number of individuals (Bagdikian 2004), this perspective becomes the dominant discourse and the only reasonable analysis. Remove the logic of business, and the conversation becomes a discussion on why essential transport services are not sufficiently funded through public revenue and how we are all entitled to decent pay and conditions.

As well as being promoted through public pedagogic spaces and a co-opted media, the logic of neoliberalism is deliberately spread through a process of *new public managerialism* (Clarke and Newman 1997; Chandler et al. 2002; Walsh 2006; Lynch et al. 2012). New public managerialism emerged as part of the devolved public expenditure policies of the UK Thatcherite rule of the 1980s (Clarke and Newman 1997) and reformed fiscal public sector management by introducing an accountancy discourse that demanded more accountability and transparency in spending. Rather than being led by social responsibility and public need, neoliberal managerialism is strict about its allotment of ring-fenced budgets which have to be justified through measurable outputs. This metamorphosis is said to tame previously unwieldy bureaucratic organisations making them more efficient and more user-friendly. New public managerialism claims to address duplication through rationalisation, to increase staff productivity through performance indicators, to improve standards through competition to enhance customer choice and, ultimately, to ensure a more efficient, rationalist operation. Clarke and Newman (1997: 22) also detail a more deliberate second phase of managerialism which more transparently reveals its neoliberal loyalties. This is a phase of marketisation through privatisation which commonly involves outsourcing and increased charges for use of public services. Privatisation undermines the concept of State subsidy of essential services and, in doing so, greatly alters public sector culture both internally and externally.

IRELAND'S NEOLIBERAL STATE

Though carrying many similarities with broader global events, Ireland's transformation to a "neoliberal State" (Allen 2007: 62) is worth considering in isolation. Its neoliberalisation was largely influenced by a Celtic Tiger economic growth period of the 1990s, a time during which there was rapid expansion of the community sector. On the world stage, Ireland boasted about an impressive national spreadsheet which was bolstered by an inflated and ultimately unsustainable property boom that relied on the American sub-prime market (Allen 2003). A domestic financial sector also grew, again reinforced by foreign investment that was attracted to our shores by a substantively unregulated banking system whose primary intention was to encourage market growth (Kirby 2010: 9; Tobin 2010; Allen and Boyle 2013). Ireland also became a tax haven for multinational corporations (McCabe 2015) through tax rates on profits that were lower than other base rates across Europe. Public support for light-touch financial regulation and a lower tax toll was sought through continued government emphasis on the mutually beneficial nature of such inward investment through job creation. Some multinational visitors deny their principal interest is our preferential corporate tax regime claiming they are attracted to our shores for our educated, efficient workforce and our geographical location within Europe. Whether such corporate giants as *Amazon, Apple, Google, IBM, Intel, E-bay* and *Yahoo* would have located their European bases in Ireland for these reasons alone seems highly questionable.

As with other global nations, the Irish State also adopted a debtfare approach when dealing with its own population which was once again supported by financial deregulation. At the height of the boom, Irish banks had lent out the equivalent of over twice the worth of the Irish economy, and an amount almost €200 billion greater than what they held in deposits (Allen and O'Boyle 2013: 3). Private debt rocketed during the Celtic Tiger period. In 2004, the Central Bank revealed outstanding personal debt of €85 billion, well above 100% of estimated disposable income at the time (Kelly and Reilly 2005: 85).

Another key feature of Irish neoliberalisation was the Trojan horse of corporatist *social partnership*. Ireland's domestic model of social partnership involved an initial ensemble of the State, trade unions, employer and farmer representative organisations who regularly met to determine social and economic policies. Following extensive lobbying by some within the community sector (Larraghy 2006), partnership participation was extended in 1997 to include a national *Community Pillar*, an amalgam of self-appointed community sector leaders, along with other chosen third sector non-governmental organisations (NGOs).

This model of governance did not happen in isolation but was part of a world-wide trend in "third way" politics. Largely credited to prominent sociologist Anthony Giddens, the third way claims a fusion of left- and right-wing political ideologies in a way that can harnesses the more extreme consequences of capitalism. Liberal democracy is reinvented into a "movement of double democratization" (Giddens 1998: 72) where civil society and government meet half way to agree the terms of social management. The first Irish partnership agreement *A Programme for National Recovery* (1987) was broadly welcomed. Trade union-endorsed strike action dissipated and a more sedate, post-partnership period emerged (Coakley 2012). The consensus model embedded within partnership became a key feature of Ireland's social, political and cultural landscape for over 20 years. Supporters of national partnership agreements claim that community sector representatives (along with the trade union movement) ensured a renegotiation of power that made sure justice and equality were key components (Nye 2001: 192; Hardiman 2002: 11; Fahey et al. 2007: 5; Larraghy 2014).

The difficulty with social partnership is that it did not tame capitalism. Instead, social partnership offered an illusion of compromise and shared decision-making that concealed the transfer of wealth from the lower tiers of society to the top (O'Hearn 1998; Douthwaite 1999, 292–4; Allen 2000, 2003, 2007; Kirby 2002; Coulter 2003). Allen (2000: 14) demonstrates how it was our first social partnership agreement that introduced three key features of neoliberalism namely cuts in public spending, tax breaks for private enterprise and the curbing of trade union activity and power. As will be demonstrated, social partnership was also to become an important feature in the depoliticisation of much community education.

The Neoliberalisation of Community Education

New public managerialist policies of outputs, rationalisation, transparency and accountability have impacted community education that is provided through the historical State network of Vocational Education Committees (VECs). McGlynn (2012) details increased pressure on CEFs within VECs to measure their work through outcomes approaches, most notably through certified learning. This is despite the way in which State-funded community education had traditionally offered both accredited and non-accredited programmes thereby addressing a range of community needs. This is coupled with increasing demands for financial accountability, which are deliberately set against performativity models (McGlynn 2012: 143–144).

The community sector's reliance on State funding has meant that it too has been transformed by new public managerialism. Although a spate of recent reforms are sometimes considered intrinsic to the recessionary period that began in 2008 (which I will return to in due course), a more accurate starting point is in 2002 and the shift of responsibility for the publically funded Community Development Support Programme (an amalgam of c150 Community Development Projects (CDPs) and c150 Family Resource Centres (FRCs)) into the newly founded Department of Community, Rural and Gealteacht Affairs (DCRGA).[6] One year later DCRGA announced a review of departmental programmes and structures so that they could measure the effectiveness of services and supports in local communities (Combat Poverty Agency 2003: 2). Terms of reference for this review included the core tenets of neoliberal managerialism namely an examination of perceived duplication, increased transparency in expenditure and rationalisation of administrative overloads (Combat Poverty Agency 2003: 7). The review also involved a parallel monitoring of community sector work as previous three-year funding cycles were replaced by annual reviews where work plans now needed to be endorsed by local government. These changes altered funder–funded relationships which, from this point forward, were shaped by the need to justify and quantify service delivery in terms of value for money and not to build capacity, promote empowerment and instigate social change as had previously been the case (Bassett 2007). Bissett (2015: 174) describes this new arrangement and subsequent review as a "strategic turn . . . which signalled a sharp authoritarian turn in the state's position vis-à-vis the community sector", he argues the most likely motivation was to suppress an independent and critical voice.

Co-option Through Social Partnership

Another, more stealthy neoliberalisation of community spaces was through the community sector's previously named involvement in the national structures of social partnership. Civil society organisations were never fully integrated into these structures and those directly involved in national negotiations describe the process as unproductive and of delivering only tokenistic gains (Murphy 2002; Meade 2005; Stafford 2011). Stafford (2011: 78) shares how those inside the Community Pillar felt their presence at the table was "merely a box-ticking exercise" and not the space for meaningful grass-roots engagement they had hoped for. There was also an incremental weakening of any limited influence the Community Pillar might have at first held. Where refusal to sign off on certain policies forced minimal concessions during early partnership deals, this changed in 2002 when some Community Pillar representatives rejected aspects of the national agreement *Sustaining Progress*. Their punishment for defiance was expulsion from the process (Larraghy 2006: 395–396). This starkly demonstrated the falsity of any notion of equal partnership.

There were other difficulties with social partnership. Divisions emerged between those inside the process and those outside the process with some on the outside believing those involved were compromised (Crowley 2013: 152). There were concerns about the unmandated nature of representation (Broaderick 2002: 13) and about how partnership detracted from grass-roots activism (Lee 2003: 55). There were other more politically charged criticisms also with specialist community development voices in the academy arguing its primary motivation was to protect the interests of the rich and simultaneously muzzle resistance from an oppositional community sector (Ó' Cinnéide 1998/1999; Collins 2002; Meade and O'Donovan 2002; Powell and Geoghegan 2004: 241, Kirby and Murphy 2011).

Much of the future of community education was also determined by local partnership structures. This was through a network of Local Area Partnerships (LAPs) that emerged as part of an European Union (EU)led renegotiation of State–civil society relationships (Harvey 1994). On foot of European grant aid, the State established a pilot programme of 12 partnership companies. The job of these partnerships was to address stubbornly high unemployment in targeted areas, to promote entrepreneurialism and business start-ups and, crucially, to support existing community development work (Walsh et al. 1998; Teague and Murphy 2004: 5). Harvey (1994) explains how local partnerships were again broadly welcomed as their understanding of poverty included a focus on human rights and on creating opportunities. They also insisted on co-operation between public and civil society organisations. Partnership numbers grew, first to 38 LAPs in 1994 and then to 94 partnership companies by 2008. This figure incorporates Urban Area Partnership and rural Integrated Local Development Bodies funded through the EU LEADER programme.[7] Many partnership companies became involved in providing education and training by forging close working relationships with both FÁS (the since disbanded National Training Authority) and with existing community sector organisations. Moreover, when community representation was sought, community sector organisations were often called on to fill seats at board of management level. By 2002, a State-commissioned national review of the Community Development Programme described social partnership structures as the space where community sector presence was "most evident widespread and sustained" (Nexus 2002: 46).

Whilst Lloyd (2010: 50) interpreted LAPs as interested in seeking representation so that they could "engage with and collectivise those experiencing social exclusion", some in the community sector voiced difficulties with these local structures. Questions surfaced about their democratic legitimacy through concerns about how management structures were formed and how they related to host communities (Sabel 1996; Crowley 1998; Walsh 1996a, b; Walsh et al. 1998; Zappone 1998). One 1998 review of LAPs expressed concern about how decisions were commonly dictated by central government, about poor, if any, structures of public accountability and about a lack of uniformity in coordinating relationships between LAPs and communities (Walsh et al. 1998). The same review also emphasised haphazard relationships with local and national policymakers and hugely diverse management practices across different community settings. Retrospectively, a certain naivety could be claimed about the community sector's involvement with social partnership as it was never a partnership built on democracy. Another way to explain participation is to examine the political establishment's way of doing business at the time. Stafford (2011) takes this position maintaining organisations had little choice. This was because consensus was reached by offering enough monetary incentive to community organisations to guarantee they toe the line with the alternative being financial penalties should they disengage.

The truth is, by the late 2000s community education providers; community sector and public sector alike, were caught up in a neoliberal embrace with the State that was so tight, its potential to nurture democracy from below was significantly diminished. When neoliberalism hit crisis point, there was little possibility for opposition.

NEOLIBERALISM IN CRISIS

According to Žižek (2009a: 9), the only surprising thing about the 2008 global economic crash was acceptance by so many that it was a surprise. Before this, economists and politicians who questioned market sustainability through asset speculation were repeatedly dismissed (McCabe 2015: 50–51) with the Irish Premier Bertie Ahern (speaking in 2007) infamously expressing bewilderment at how such sceptics "don't commit suicide", a comment he later apologised for.[8] The reality was that by 2008 re-engineered global capitalism had experienced a near disintegration of stock market values, bankruptcy of leading financial institutions and a worldwide collapse of property values. Birch and Mykhnenko (2010: 256) link the global downturn to "the shrinkage of money credit that began in 2007" claiming:

> The global financial and economic crises have painfully revealed that the long boom in the heartland of global financial capitalism was propelled by consumer led indebtedness. We can now see that global financial capitalism was the ultimate neoliberal innovation enabled by the proceeding waves of deregulation and liberalization.

Despite various stimulus packages and often crippling austerity measures, the anticipated recovery associated with the boom-bust nature of capitalism has been slow to emerge. In 2010, the US congressional research service described capitalism as "locked in a descending spiral" with conventional federal interventions failing to get the crisis under control (Jickling 2010: 4). Rather than let neoliberalism crash, responses to the economic downturn and indeed the bulk of conversation in the public domain were about managing this crisis and similar ideologies were espoused from both sides of the mainstream political spectrum.

One particularly potent way in which ideological hegemony has been maintained is through a strengthening and expansion of neoliberalism's imperialist logic which spread its principles to nation states presented as ostensibly non-democratised and therefore as problematic to Western capitalist value systems. Although the likely rationale for the spread of neoliberalism is to expand global market control, dominant nations, particularly the USA assumed, and still assume, a protectionist, global-policing role that is framed as necessary for domestic defence. Chomsky (2006: 3) describes this mentality as "a doctrine of 'anticipatory self-defence' with unstated bounds". An increasingly relevant feature of this imbuement is a greater than before militarisation of society. This can be understood as a situation where permanent military readiness becomes a normal and unproblematic cultural reality. Whilst this militarisation is most pronounced in the USA, American cultural hegemony also influences European behaviour (Stephen 2006; Storey 2010) with Irish society increasingly shaped by an omnipresent global military prerogative. Even though Ireland is a neutral country, its geographical closeness to the UK also exposes it to social militarisation. To give an example of what this looks like, plans for a Royal Air Force (RAF) "flypast" at the 2016 Gay Pride parade were criticised by some as "the militarisation of the event" and thus "against the spirit of the event" (The Guardian, 23 May 2016). There has also been a growth of militarisation into popular culture, a significant event when we consider how popular culture is a component part in creating oppressive narratives that help to maintain injustice (Žižek. 2009b: 71). By way of bringing this perspective to life, Chesterson (2011) remarks on the increasing military presence within popular culture observing:

> there are soldiers on talent shows, parading in sports stadiums and singing on daytime television [...] Britain has been drawn into a deep sleep about war and nowhere is this slumber more pernicious than in the militarisation of popular culture ... the debate about why they are still dying – and killing – in Afghanistan has disappeared from public life. Instead, an acceptance that the military is an agent for good has become the norm, and we are told to

love our soldiers as if they are members of an extended family. This year, from the The X Factor to football, from Radio 2 to the tabloids, we have been encouraged to welcome the military into our homes and hearts.

There has also been seepage of militarisation into seemingly innocuous spaces such as fictional television programmes, video games and films. To demonstrate, the 2014 Christmas day movie aired by the Irish national broadcaster Raidio Telilifis Eireann (RTÉ) was the animated film *Arthur Christmas*. This children's adventure story retells the story of Santa Clause with a pronounced militaristic undertow. Santa is portrayed as a general of an army and his elves, dressed in full army fatigues and associated military paraphernalia are presented as soldiers, rather than selfless gift-bearers and workers.

Behind this insidious pageantry, the creeping militarisation of society normalises such actions as drone bombings, torture, sleep deprivation and violence against women and children as just another part of the day-to-day fabric of our society. This normalisation of a military presence is combined with an equally ubiquitous terrorist discourse that is selectively appropriated to qualify certain acts of violence, yet utterly rejects other forms of violence, notably State violence, the violence inherent in economic sanctions such as those enforced on the people of Iraq during the Gulf Wars, or domestic violence such as gun crime. To borrow words from Kundnani (2014: 21) in his satirically titled contribution *The Muslims are Coming!*

> To designate an act of violence as terrorism is to arbitrarily isolate it from other acts of violence considered normal, rational or necessary. The term terrorism is never used to refer to the military violence of Western States, or to the daily reality of gender-based violence, for example, both of which ought to be also labelled terrorism according to the terms usual definition: violence against innocent civilians designed to advance a political cause (the maintenance of patriarchy is eminently political). (Brackets in original)

Some of you are no doubt wondering what soldiers on the X factor and debates about global terrorism have to do with community education. Militarisation matters for two reasons. Firstly it creates and perpetuates a *culture of fear* which redirects concerns with the structures of power to concerns about the preservation of so-called Western values (Giroux 2006; Linke and Smith 2009; Žižek 2009b; Kundnani 2014). This is an essentialist construct that is blind to the heterogeneity of any cultural context. The resulting othering of non-Western culture not only takes our gaze away from the institutions of power but also redirects this gaze onto "others", particularly domestic Muslim populations. Despite wide variances in nationality, politics and religiosity (Carr 2015) these communities are increasingly homogenised as both harbourers of Islamist terrorists and as spaces where all members are capable of being radicalised (Lynch 2013; Ali; 2014). Unless challenged, these dominant cultural values and beliefs outside of the classroom permeate and shape what happens inside of adult learning groups (Heron 1999).

A second reason why societal militarisation is important to community education is because of how it encourages a cultural acceptance of brutality on the most vulnerable in society (Giroux 2013: 80). This cultivates a Darwinian-style survival of the fittest mentality, a mentality that Giroux believes has a profound impact on the way we organise society. Domestic examples of brutality are all too easy to evoke. Those seeking asylum, displaced as a result of complex social and economic factors, are left for years in direct provision centres, there are increased levels of poverty for older people (CSO 2013b), growing homelessness, and premature deaths as a result of lack of access to basic healthcare particularly diagnostic procedures (O'Shea and Collins 2016). Many of those affected by this brutality are often also affected by disproportionate funding cuts to the community sector.

Ireland's Austerity Agenda

Where Ireland could have been used as "a textbook case for the failures of neoliberalism" (Allen 2012: 425) the post-2008 period became one of intensified neoliberalism. Deepened free-market economics is continually presented as logical through the need to safeguard our financial institutions, to further reduce expenditure by streamlining the public sector and to promote entrepreneurial endeavour as the only reasonable route to revival. Nowhere is this logic more obvious than in the management of Ireland's inflated banking system. Immediately following the crash of the late 2000s, much of the banking system was socialised, a contradictory, but predictable move given neoliberalism's ongoing business-friendly financial assistance programmes amidst rhetoric of laissez-faire economics (Lapavistas 2004: 34–35). Many Irish financial institutions became dependent on the State, most notably through a controversial government line of credit, or *bank guarantee* introduced in 2008 to protect the domestic banking system. McCabe (2015: 54) explains how this guarantee was interpreted as "extremely reckless" by other EU governments as it gave a clear competitive advantage to Irish banks over their European counter-parts.

There is little doubt but that the primary losers of the bank guarantee were the Irish people with the guarantee's ultimate survival depending on a foreign loan deal from the IMF, the European Central Bank (ECB) and the EU. This *Troika*, the term commonly used to describe the joint work of the IMF, ECB and EU, enforced repayment through public expenditure cuts and a strict programme of austerity that brought Ireland into the midst of a structural adjustment fiscal arrangement more commonly associated with industrialising nations. These measures were hegemonically framed in a way that ensured the burden of blame fell on everyone's shoulders, but the cost of repayment was carried by those with little or no involvement in creating the crisis in the first place (Carney et al. 2014; O'Flynn et al. 2014).

The impacts of austerity have been profound. For those in employment a series of pay freezes, income tax hikes and unpopular indirect taxes have considerably reduced consumer wealth. Youth unemployment has trebled under austerity politics affecting 75,000 of those under 25 years; a figure that does not capture those who emigrated or stayed in education (ICTU 2012: 6). By 2012, unemployment in general terms had reached 19% and, as well as affecting young people was also mostly affecting lone parents and those living in "unemployment black spots" (CSO 2012: 15–17). The Central Statistics Office (CSO) lists these "black spots" (CSO 2012: 162) as particular urban neighbourhoods as well as rural locations with poor infrastructure connections. Unsurprisingly, both the urban and rural areas named were the same communities engaging in community education.[9]

For those who depend on social welfare, the burden of austerity is captured by in-depth research on income adequacy across household types with just 22% of welfare-dependent households "with an income sufficient to meet minimum expenditure costs" (Collins et al. 2012: 154). Other stark impacts include claims by Social Justice Ireland (2014) that over 1.2 million people are forced to go without some basic necessities, with 750,000 living in poverty, an increase of 120,000 since the recession began. The same report notes 16% with an income below the poverty line are working, whilst 58% are either older people, have disabilities that render them unable to work, are in caring roles, or are students. Twenty-five percent are children (Social Justice Ireland 2014: 11). Eighty-two percent of households report spending less, most frequently on socialising, but also on clothing and footwear (cited by 65%) and groceries (cited by 51%) (CSO 2013a). This typifies the contradiction at the core of austerity by undermining capitalism's dependence on consumer spending. In light of these conditions, it is unfortunately unsurprising that connections have been made between deteriorating personal economic circumstances and increased rates of suicide (Arensman et al. 2012).

For the Irish community sector, measures were introduced to ensure compliance with public expenditure cuts that were demanded by the Troika. The government Central Expenditure Evaluation Unit[10] (CEEU) published a paper *Rationalising Multiple Sources of Funding to Not-for-Profit Sector* which made three interconnected recommendations, all of which pointed to a process of downsizing. The first of these was to reduce the number of transactions between the State and the "third sector", the second recommendation was to improve monitoring and streamlining of expenditure and, thirdly, that smaller groups merge with larger groups and that these larger organisations should compete for funding (CEEU 2011). New public managerialist motives were evident namely to prevent duplication of services, to improve systems for monitoring and measuring outputs so value for money could be ensured and so that excessive administration, such as double reporting to multiple funders, could be addressed (CEEU 2011). Ironically, there was no acknowledgement that it was successive government policies that created the situations described above; where projects managed multiple funding streams each with their own reporting structures.

Any opportunity for the community sector to object to realignment and funding cuts through social partnership channels were by this stage gone as these structures had effectively collapsed when the Troika arrived in 2009. As a consequence, the community sector co-option that began in 2002 was rapidly accelerated without consultation. In 2013, the Community Development Programme was forcibly absorbed into LAPs (itself reduced from 94 to 52 partnership companies) forming the since disbanded Local Community Development Programme (LCDP). Predictably, the overseeing Department of Environment, Community and Local Government (DECLG) justified these reforms so that they could ease administrative burdens, further streamline funding and reporting relationships and reduce duplication, all of which was alleged to be in the interests of service users (DECLG 2012: 3–8).

Above all else, these mergers and rationalisation processes ensured less money and less control for local communities who had previously been at the centre of community sector decision-making. For those at the coalface, the impacts are demonstrated by O'Byrne (2012: 22) when she quotes one CDP coordinator who describes "the heavy boot of the state on their neck through the use of economic violence". O'Byrne (2012: 14) interprets community development as "in crisis" believing it has been deradicalised with its social change ethos compromised. Although not apportioning all blame to government actions, she concludes:

> It [the State] has removed local management groups of CDPs; it has removed their support agencies; it has introduced managerial practices; and it has failed to understand the nature of community development. What seems certain, however, is that government has detected the growing power of CDPs, and that the demise of community development in Ireland may be due to, more than anything, a perverse response by the state to a growing political influence in the process. (O'Byrne 2012: 34)

Open competition for funding, as recommended by the CEEU, began in 2015 when the work of the LCDP was put out to competitive tender through the Social Inclusion and Community Activation Programme (SICAP). The Community Workers Cooperative (CWC), a national organisation of community workers which has since been renamed Community Work Ireland, objected to this change claiming "this opens up the possibility of the biggest social inclusion programme (the LCDP) being implemented on a commercial/for-profit basis" (CWC 2014: 19). In preparation for SICAP's open tender process there was a trimming at the edges with potentially unprofitable avenues such as projects for drug users, Traveller education, and other services for Travellers disproportionally affected by cuts (Harvey 2013).

The eventual allocation of SICAP contracts forced more closures, this time of some LCDPs and further expansion on this topic is contained within Chapter 5. Other community sector organisations such as FRCs and addiction supports, both of which are often providers of community education (Chapter 3) were also streamlined into State structures with FRCs instructed to take on a monitoring role as a condition of funding. Addiction supports, historically established and managed by community sector organisation, have too been consumed into the structures of the Health Service Executive (HSE). Typical of the usual touchstones of new public managerialism, *The National Drugs Strategy 2009–2016* (DCRGA 2009) approaches problem drug use through a value for money over a needs-based perspective and sets out key measurable performance indicators which projects must comply with.

There has also been a deepening of neoliberalism for public providers of community education. This is through a substantial restructuring of State provision via a non-negotiated merger of 33 VECs and FÁS (The National

Training and Employment Authority) into 16 Education and Training Boards (ETBs) which was completed in 2013. Predictably, this reform was packaged as crucial in tidying up a disparate sector, and within "the need for efficiency, effectiveness and value in the deployment of public funding" (SOLAS 2014b: 6). These ETBs, themselves managed by a new national authority called SOLAS,[11] hold responsibility for public community education. Although SOLAS (2014a: 144) acknowledge a "range of providers including independently managed not for profit groups and statutory organisations" it parcels community education and its multiplicity of approaches within Further Education and Training (FET) and as a gateway to employment for those most distant from the labour market. FET is packaged as a vital ingredient in reinvigorating Ireland's economy (SOLAS 2014a) with little regard to the way this limited interpretation negates the breadth of provision historically catered for within public community education contexts.

Whose Recovery?

The Irish government's Spring Statement of 2015 was one of positivity with an overriding message that Ireland was in recovery and that citizens could look forward to a steady, stable economic growth period and higher quality of public services.[12] This perception of recovery is important to engage with as the emerging Ireland is fundamentally different to pre-neoliberal situations, not least given the absence of an independent community sector. Ireland's recovery is an ideological recovery for neoliberalism (Allen 2012) and not one that substantively improves the lives of ordinary citizens. The Think Tank for Action on Social Change (TASC) report *Cherishing All Equally: Economic Inequality in Ireland* (2015) confirms continued growth in the rich–poor divide post-recession measuring Irelands gross-market income inequality as highest in the OECD where the top 10% get 34% of all taxable income, up from 27% in 1970 (O'Connor and Staunton 2015: 8).

Another hallmark of "Ireland in recovery" is a growing housing crisis and what the well-known social justice campaigner Fr Peter McVerry has described as a "tsunami of homelessness" (The Irish Times, 18 May 2015). In the first two months of 2016, 206 families including 363 children became homeless[13] through a combination of bank repossessions and of ordinary people being priced out of a largely unregulated private rental market. Most people in State funded, but privately owned, emergency accommodation have never experienced homelessness before.[14] Public health services are also faltering. A recently published European Health consumer index ranks Ireland's healthcare system as 21st out of 35 countries examined, down seven places from 2013 (Björnberg 2016).

Meanwhile Ireland continues to champion neoliberal free-market economics through its ever present dependence on foreign direct investment enticed to our shores by our continued light-touch approach to corporate taxation. This has sometimes been against the tide of wider global opinion. A 2015 merger between US pharmaceutical giant *Pfzeir* and the Dublin-based company *Allergen* was sharply criticised for tax avoidance through corporate inversion across the US political spectrum (The Irish Times, 24 November 2015). This was predictably rejected by the Irish government who, somewhat unconvincingly, claimed "lots of reasons" for this relocation including that English is our primary language.[15] In 2016, a US Treasury crackdown on corporate inversion abruptly halted this merger and Pfzeir was eventually forced to withdraw. This is not the first time outside influences have challenged Ireland's tax relationship with multinationals. In 2014, the European Commission (EC) announced an investigation into relationships between global corporation *Apple* and Irish Authorities to examine whether EU rules had been deliberately contravened through Ireland's transfer pricing and profit allocation arrangements (DDCI 2015: 2). In August 2016, EC competition watchdogs ruled against Apple ordering them to pay €13 billion euro in unpaid taxes to the Irish government. This was to compensate for previous periods of time where they had paid as little as less than 1% despite a domestic tax rate of 12.5%. Much to the dismay of some citizens the Irish government has appealed the ruling arguing that to accept such a refund would in some way damage competitiveness and dissuade corporate investment in the Irish economy. Whilst successive governments deny secret tax arrangements they offer little transparency through blanket refusals to disclose their arrangements with multinational to the general public, despite the fact that it is public money they are negotiating with.

Other attempts are also continually made to preserve Ireland's questionably tax laws. Within a week of Donald Trump's surprise victory in the 2016 American presidential election, Michael Noonan the then minister for finance had held a private meeting with the president elect in a bid to dissuade any US reduction in corporate tax-rates; a move that would surely result in less multinational interest in Ireland. This admission undermines the argument that preferential tax-rates are not the principal motivator for foreign investment.

NEOLIBERAL RESISTANCE AND POCKETS OF DIFFERENCE

Any suggestion of a neoliberal turn should include an account of its opposition. Alongside perpetual militarisation and war, increasing income inequality, public sector shrinkage and the co-option of much civil society infrastructure, there has also been perpetual protest. The 1999 "Battle in Seattle" remains a noteworthy international example given its convergence of anti-globalisation movements including many community organisations from around the world. Anti-capitalist demonstrations did not just hit the streets of Seattle. During the 2000s, the World Bank and IMF were regularly accompanied by anti-globalisation protesters dissatisfied with international trade and tariff arrangements, but also with the banking system itself (Žižek 2009a: 9; Birch and Mykhnenko 2010: 256). Reactions to adversarial movements from second-wave neoliberal politicians were swift and decisive as political leaders turn to the coercive wing of the State and their relationship with the conventional journalistic press to keep such forces in check (Steger and Roy 2010: 121). Although occasional victories were enjoyed in the 2000s, the impacts of mass mobilisation were diminished. A key historical turning point was the way many government's disregarded the globally synchronised opposition to the invasion of Iraq in 2003. This undoubtedly gave confidence to neoliberal governments enabling them to push through further unpopular measures.

Protest movements rose again in the 2010s. The *Occupy Wall Street* movement of 2011 initiated a wider global *Occupy movement*[16] that popularised a 99% versus 1% income distribution rates through slogan such as "we are the 1%". There have also been mass mobilisations against austerity in Greece, Spain and many Latin American countries, accounts of which are sporadic in the mainstream corporatised media but readily available across online journalistic sites. Ireland's most prominent anti-austerity response came through an outpouring of discontent against the Troika imposed introduction of domestic water charges. In 2014, 100,000 people marched against these charges with this stealth tax interpreted as one step too far in the politics of austerity (The Irish Times, 11 October 2014). Similar street mobilisations were held in 2015 and 2016. Some community sector organisations were involved both in organising national protests and in mobilising people within their local communities by organising transport to these national events. Importantly, the anti-water charge movement also incorporated much local community activism. Meetings were held on local green areas, in people's homes and in community centres each of which built support for a national boycott and blockades were sometimes organised to prevent the instillation of water meters. In research examining the impacts of this community activism on some of the women involved, Lynch (2015: 61) concludes:

> Moving beyond the personal, the potential implications for communities, society and politics are even greater. Within their families and communities these women are educating and organising others, and encouraging active participation and collective action. By awakening others, a sense of community and community spirit is building in virtual and geographical locations. There is reclamation of community spaces and the foundations of new networks and relationships arising from the anti-water charges campaign. In these lie the potential for on-going consciousness-raising that could produce more community activists to affect social change locally in a meaningful and participatory way.

As a consequence of public non-compliance and high-profile demonstrations, water charges were suspended by the Irish government in the spring of 2016. In December 2016, The *Home Sweet Home* campaign with the support of *Housing Action Now* and trade unionists occupied a public building under the ownership of the National Assets Management Agency (NAMA) and converted it into a homeless shelter. High profile Irish entertainers with international notoriety (including the actress Saorise Ronan, Oscar winner Glen Hansard, director Jim Sheridan, singer Damien Dempsey and actor John Connors) openly participated in this initiative calling on the public to take control of our spiralling homeless crisis (discussed in more detail in chapter 5). Some well-known small business owners also donated beds and other requirements. This act of civil disobedience received support from some Homeless advocacy organisations, the general public and, according to campaigners, some Gardaí (Irish police force).

As well as local and national mobilisations, anti-neoliberal protest was increasingly organised through the Internet. To give an example, on the 30 November 2015, a twitter storm[17] with the hashtag #IrlRecovery was flooded with comments to counter government-led talk of recovery. These tweets included "how many people on trolleys in A&E today", "recovery for the banks and the elite while we pay for it" and "there are 40 shades of recovery in #Ireland but not 1 shade for the most of us". Others using the #IrlRecovery hashtag linked tweets to newspaper articles on newly emerging soup kitchens for the poor, on increases in house repossessions and on ongoing emigration. On the same day another the top national trends was #LivingWage.

As well as opposition through street protest and online activism, there has also been resurgence in trade union endorsed industrial action. In 2015, the

Irish Nurses and Midwives Organisation (INMO) voted for industrial action in opposition to persistent overcrowding in hospital emergency services. Government reaction was predictably against worker's rights to withdraw labour as a way to legitimately bring about change. The Fine Gael/Labour government of the time called for nurses to enter into "constructive engagement" with health service coordinators, a request dismissed by one opposition leader Mary-Lou McDonald who captured much national sentiment when she accused the government of having "some cheek". Describing nurses as "at the end of their tether", McDonald continued:

> They are stressed out of their minds and managing an impossible and utterly chaotic situation in our hospitals. It takes gall of the highest order for the Tánaiste [deputy prime minister] to appeal to them to be constructive. They are more than constructive. Every day they are managing the chaos the Government has caused in our hospitals.[18]

Industrial action by nurses is ongoing with predictions that other public sector workers namely teachers and university lecturers are both likely to instigate industrial action in search of pay restoration. LUAS tram drivers were awarded an 18% pay rise in a dispute with the private global transport organisation Transdev with whom the Irish government have a contract for services. There is also discontent within the private retail sector not least ongoing industrial action within the corporate giant Tescos. In 2015, the leader of the right-wing opposition party Fine Fail surprisingly supported strikers at another retail store Dunnes Stores calling on the company to engage with the trade union movement "in the name of decency" (The Journal, 2 April 2015).

This support from traditional opponents of trade union activism may well be an attempt to respond to the rise of the left at the ballot box. The Irish Spring election of 2016 left the combined votes of Ireland's two largest right-wing parties at 54%, a spectacular decline in these parties share of votes in the decades preceding this. At the same time there is a growing amalgam of anti-capitalist and anti-austerity politicians, many of whom are independents filling the political void. Ireland may seem out of step with international trends where a common hegemonic narrative is to present a radical rise in the far-right. This argument is often justified through the recent election of Donald Trump in the US as well as a UK referendum vote in favour of leaving the European Union (or Brexit). All too often these political victories are presented through a simplistic categorisation of Brexiteers and Trump followers as nothing more than xenophobes and nationalists. Whilst such voices certainly feature, another way to interpret these political turns is as grounds-well of dissatisfaction with the centrist vanguard of neoliberalism. In a speech to the Irish parliament made soon after the Brexit vote in June, 2016, left-wing politician Richard-Boyd Barrett remind us that the main funders of the UK campaign to remain part of the EU were not anti-neoliberal, social justice voices but were the financial powerhouses of Morgan Stanley, Goldman Sachs and a multitude of hedge-funders, each of whom are the significant benefactors of globalised free-market economics.

The 2015 election of Jeremy Corbyn as leader of the UK labour party is also worth emphasising. The growing popularity of this self-proclaimed democratic socialist and anti-austerity activist sends a clear message to labour Blairites that their third-way political rhetoric would no longer go unchallenged.

Community Sector Resistance

There is also opposition within the community sector. *The Spectacle of Defiance and Hope*, a broad-based alliance of community organisations, artists and trade unionists, is committed to creative resistance to community sector cuts and wider economic injustice. Its actions have culminated in the mobili-sation of 2,000–3,000 community members and workers in colourful street protests on three occasions. As part of this process, a Freirean[19]-influenced process of conscientisation was initiated through community education designed to raise political awareness (Fitzsimons 2012: 38). The spectacle has also produced photographic exhibitions of communities sharing grie-vances and hopes, and a stage performance *Songs of Grievance and Hope* outlining the impact of cuts to the sector and performed by community workers and unpaid local activists[20] A second collaboration between the community sector and trade unionism, the *Communities against Cuts Campaign* has also mobilised support, most significantly through a gathering of 12,000 people opposing cuts to the community sector in 2009. In February 2015, a rally in opposition to SICAP saw Communities against Cuts and The Spectacle of Defiance and Hope join forces with their demonstration attracting national media attention (The Irish Times, 28 February 2015). Additionally, the Irish Congress of Trade Unions has convened assemblies for workers, spaces where community workers can share information, validate experiences and organise responses to the challenges faced by the sector.[21]

Alongside perpetual protest, there have also been many acts of individua-lised and collective rebellion as well as the emergence of alternative forms of social relations, some born out of survival in negotiating the conditions of neoliberalism (Holloway 2010). Within his book *Crack Capitalism*, Holloway (2010: 72) suggests "not only a logic of capitalism but an anti-logic of humanity, of refusal, of movement in-against-and-beyond capital" and he cites increasing examples of miss-fitting elements. Holloway (2010) sees limits to protest claiming it is a reactionary activity that allows neoliberals to continue to set the agenda. In determining what can be done to halt neoliberalism, he calls for an expansion and linking of alternatives, or what he suggests are cracks that exist within capitalist society. The notion of working within the cracks, or the crevices, has been previously explored within writings on adult and community education (Shor 1996; Thompson 2007) and much influential theorising has been born out of significant struggle, for example Freire (1972) and hooks (1994).

More recently, there have been renewed calls for adult and community educators to reflect on neoliberal social relations and to consider how these shape power relationships (Kane 2001; Brookfield and Holst 2011). At the heart of such assertions is an ongoing belief that community education can be counter-hegemonic, not only capable of challenging the premise that there is no alternative to neoliberal global capitalism, but of advancing alternative notions of society. Community education can nurture personal capacity, build social agency and foster critical awareness in a way that supports politicised praxis (a cyclical process of action and reflection that is explored in Chapter 4).

ABOUT THE BOOK

The book offers an account of community education across Ireland that both explores the impacts of neoliberalism and contemplates ways it can be opposed. It doesn't just draw from existing literature but presents findings from research carried out in 2011–2013 that gives voice to over 220 community educators. The notion of *really useful research* (Connolly 2016) is supported where critical research forms part of counter-hegemonic actions to advance equality. The mixed-methods approach I use allows philosophical, theoretical and sociopolitical issues to be embraced in a way that draws from qualitative and quantitative methods as appropriate to the way in which the study unfolds (Biesta 2010; Green and Hall 2010; Tashakkori and Teddlie 2010: 8; Mertens 2012). Sometimes quantitative research can be dismissed by adult educators because of its association with positivism and its reluctance to incorporate subjectivism. I think we can benefit from both perspectives. Quantitative research helps us to capture the social structures of class, patriarchy and Caucasian supremacy. Qualitative research helps us appreciate the personal impacts of this structural inequality. The fight for social justice needs quantitative research if we are to differentiate between personal experiences and measurements of collective oppression (Oakley 1999). Although Oakley's contributions is now 15 years old and stemmed from an era that embraced concepts of multiple meanings, her words still resonate when she notes how unfashionable it can be to suggest social research is about approximating a sense of *what is really going on,* despite this being the thinking that drives our everyday lives (Oakley 1999: 252).

Neither the academy, nor policymakers hold monopoly in describing community education and the voices of practitioners bring an important layer of understanding. However, the voice of those engaging in community education are absent from this book meaning assumptions are made about practice without consulting the very communities it purports to support and at times represent. This is a limitation to this contribution.

Consistency of Language Amidst Community Education Restructuring

Notwithstanding the political significance of language in appropriating ideological stances (Murray 2014), the need to decipher the quagmire of terminology within community education can be an additional challenge when presenting work in this area. Not only are we swimming in a sea of acronyms that are littered throughout this book, it is not uncommon for seemingly different terms to be used interchangeably by some, and rejected by others. I have applied the same meaning to *State provision* and *public provision.* I also use both *radical/critical education* and *critical pedagogy* to describe the same thing; education that sees the world as distorted by unequal power relationships and as a way to challenge compliance with capitalist norms (McLaren 2009).

The timing of this book brings additional challenges as previously established organisations, namely Vocational Educational Committees (VECs), FÁS, Local Area Partnerships (LAPs), Community Development Projects (CDPs) and Local and Community Development Projects (LCDPs) all ceased to exist in the last four years. The VECs frequently referred to by community educators participating in this research are now merged within Education and Training Boards (ETBs) with the language of practice at times lagging behind policy and structural changes. This can also be said about FÁS, now too consumed into ETBs. These are more than simple name changes but signify major structural realignment. Similar difficulty arises with the LCDP. Again, this does not merely signify a name change from previous LAPs, but instead represents an immense reshaping of a core component at the heart of the community sector. The language of accreditation has also changed with FETAC and HETAC[22] now merged into Quality and Qualifications Ireland (QQI).

Signposting Chapters

The introductory chapter serves a number of purposes, to describe community education and its connections with community development, to introduce discussion on the global ubiquity of neoliberalism, to determine a process of neoliberalisation within community education and to introduce the inclusion of primary research. Beyond this, this book is organised into two distinct sections.

PART I – WHAT IS COMMUNITY EDUCATION?

The first half of this book explores an understanding of community education. This is organised over three chapters:

Chapter 2 – Models of Community Education explores the contested nature of "community" and questions the purpose of education. I discuss attempts to define community education and update a previous framework that differentiates between universal, second-chance and radical models of practice. Chapter 2 also gives the reader more information about research methodology and participant recruitment and begins a process where the contributions of research participants are shared through the publication. Participant contributions in chapter 2 focus on what practitioners' understand by community education as well as how they interpret their role.

Chapter 3 – Community Education in Ireland offers an account of the emergence and ongoing presence of community education in Ireland. It draws out four historical influences; day-time and evening courses organised through VECs, the women's movement and women's consciousness-raising groups, the Training for Transformation movement and the community development movement. I problematise the sectoralisation of community education by demonstrating strong ties, both ideologically and practically between public provision of community education, and that which stems from a once independent community sector. Chapter 3 showcases the work of community education by sharing examples of practice from the field.

Chapter 4 – Critical Education and Community Education makes the case for a radical/critical approach to community education. It shares established philosophies of adult education with a particular emphasis on humanistic approaches, the philosophy that is most influential within community education. Humanism is problematised through the key ideas of the educationalist Paulo Freire whose theories of critical education are built on to incorporate a feminist pedagogy. Doing community education is also discussed as Chapter 4 draws out the importance of critical group work as a way to support a dialogic, problem-posing approach to community education.

PART II – THE NEOLIBERALISATION OF COMMUNITY EDUCATION

The second half of this book is organised over four chapters. The first three focus more deliberately on how neoliberal managerial policies impact day-to-day practice and the final chapter summarises research findings and suggests ways forward.

Chapter 5 – Community Education and Employability is a chapter about the relationship between social policy and the sociopolitical context it emerges from. It considers the role of a European lifelong learning agenda that pushes community education away from its equality-based origins and pulls it towards a national labour-market activation agenda that benefits the economy above all else.

Chapter 6 – Community Education and Accreditation builds on a core theme to emerge from primary research namely the relationship between community education and accreditation (or certification). It explores the origins and meaning of accreditation as well as the right for the participants of community education to have their learning formally recognised. It problematises normative expressions such as qualifications frameworks, learning outcomes and quality assurance, again considering these within managerialist contexts. A culture of self-regulation is uncovered where locally implemented policies are at odds with the expectations of an accrediting body, in this case Quality and Qualifications Ireland (QQI)

Chapter 7 – Insiders, Outsiders and the Professionalisation of Community Education is principally about professionalisation and professionalism. Although both concepts are commonly interpreted as unproblematic and ostensibly positive, professionalisation is discussed in the context of inequality and social class. Relationships between insiders (community educators with local connections) and outsiders (community educators from other more affluent communities) are drawn out and an update of professionalisation of community education is presented. This includes the involvement of the regulatory body *the Teaching Council of Ireland*, an organisation traditionally associated with the school system. The precarious nature of community education is uncovered as practitioners share stories of redundancies, pay cuts, unstable contracts and other general concerns about their occupational well-being.

Chapter 8 – Rekindling Community Education reasserts an anti-neoliberal position, offers a summary of research findings and shares practitioner suggestions for change. It proposes a more deliberate integration of humanistic and critical characteristics and offers examples of practice that achieve this balance. It encourages practitioners to continue to seek out the cracks where counter-hegemony can be nurtured and to conceive of the principles of community education in non-traditional spaces.

NOTES

1. The Irish national learning Adult Learning Association, a State-funded member-led organisation of Adult and Community education practitioners.
2. The CEN is a practitioner network that has circa 200 members. It is important to distinguish the AONTAS CEN from the AONTAS umbrella organisation. CEN members do not have to be AONTAS members; there are no membership fees and no reporting structure to AONTAS.
3. Gates was also top of the rich list in 2014 and 2015. The source of his wealth is listed as "Microsoft". The full rich list is accessible at www.forbes.com.
4. This is reported as between 1980 and 2012 and in 24 out of 26 countries where data were available.
5. These comments are relayed in an article entitled "Donohue rules out intervention in Iarnród Éireann dispute" written by Martin Wall.
6. To this point the Community Development programme and the Family Resource Centre programme were managed within the Department of Social, Community and Family Affairs. The dismantling of this department split Community Development work from Family Resource work previously co-supported under the Community Development Support Programme
7. For further information on the Leader programme as part of the EU Rural Development programme see http://www.environ.ie/en/Community/RuralDevelopment/EURuralDevelopment/. Accessed 17 December 2014.
8. Bertie Ahern made this remark at a conference of the Irish Congress of Trade Unions in 2007. He later apologised for the remark. The full speech

and some media reporting of the event is available at http://www.rte.ie/
news/2007/0704/90808-economy/. Accessed 13 November 2015.

9. The highest unemployment rate named is within the electoral district
   "Johns A" in Limerick City, recorded at 56%. Ballymun in Dublin is listed
   as having an unemployment rate of 44% whilst in Kilanarden in Tallaght,
   South Dublin, unemployment is measured at 42%. The complete list is
   appendix 14 (CSO 2012: 162).

10. The CEEU was established was a unit within the Department of Public
    Expenditure that was set up to oversee expenditure review in response to
    Troika agreements.

11. Stands for the Gaelic An tSeirbhís Oideachais Leanúnaigh agus Scileanna.

12. Economic Spring Statement by the Minister for Finance Michael Noonan,
    available in full at http://www.finance.gov.ie/news-centre/speeches/cur
    rent-minister/spring-economic-statement-speech-minister-finance-mr-
    michael. Accessed 20 December 2015.

13. These figures are taken from Focus Ireland's homeless estimations for the first
    quarter of 2016 and were widely reported on radio, television and print media

14. One of the legacies of the Celtic Tiger years were a copious amount of hotels
    built by developers with the support of government tax breaks. Many of
    these are now ironically being used to house many homeless families in need
    of emergency accommodation. This unanticipated income from the State
    for hoteliers is no doubt enabling them to continue trading all be it in a very
    different way than they originally anticipated.

15. Simon Coveny Minister for agriculture speaking on national radio on the 24
    November 2015. Audio link at http://www.todayfm.com/Ireland-is-not-
    a-tax-haven–Coveney-. Accessed 25 November 2015.

16. This included a camp outside the Central Bank in Dublin before it was
    dismantled by police in March 2012.

17. A twitter storm is the expression used for a sudden and often coordinated
    spike in twitter activity using an agreed hashtag.

18. Taken from the Dail transcript of leaders questions from the 26 November
    2015. Retrieved from http://oireachtasdebates.oireachtas.ie/debates%
    20authoring/debateswebpack.nsf/takes/dail2015112600020?opendocu
    ment. Accessed 29 November, 2015.

19. This refers to the influence of educationalist Paulo Freire whose philoso-
    phies will be discussed in greater detail later in this book

20. Further information about the Spectacle of Defiance and Hope can be found
    at www.aspectacleofdefianceandhope.ie

21. Further information on this initiative is available at http://siptucommunity.
    blogspot.ie/2013/11/community-sector-assembly.html. Accessed 31 July
    2014.

22. The Further Education and Training Council (FETAC), and Higher
    Education and Training Council (HETAC), respectively.

PART I

Community Education, Philosophies and Practices

CHAPTER 2

Models of Community Education

Illustration 2.1   Models of community education

© The Author(s) 2017
C. Fitzsimons, *Community Education and Neoliberalism,*
DOI 10.1007/978-3-319-45937-0_2

When people talk about community education, one thing we can be sure of is that not everybody is talking about the same thing. There is no shared meaning that can be methodically learnt, a practice many of us have had to unlearn as we move away from the traditions of mainstream education. Differences are to be welcomed. Limiting meaning to one ring-fenced definition risks excluding innovation. It can also create a situation where strenuous efforts sometimes have to be made to shoehorn real-world events into distinct parameters. What about power at the point of naming a phenomenon such as community education? Some multidisciplinary fields of social studies can favour one meaning over another preferring the one that supports established academic knowledge, rather than the one that accurately reflects socio-economic and cultural circumstances. This is often compounded by the absent voices of people living the experiences under discussion (Lynch 1999; Shearad and Sissel 2001). A better way to think about definitions is to be open to the contested nature of many concepts at the core of sociopolitical thought. This does not mean abandoning attempts to explain foundational concepts; in fact, it is important to be clear about the principles that underpin our work. Otherwise, practitioners can unwittingly contribute to the co-option of practice by allowing those in powerful positions to have their version of community education culturally embedded within hegemonic logic. The preceding chapter has demonstrated how, under neoliberalism, this is towards market-oriented, instrumentalist perspectives that are interested in satisfying the demands of capitalism over the needs of people.

In an attempt to better understand community education and to clarify principles of practice, this chapter considers much debated concepts at the heart of discussions. It begins with debates on the contested notion of community and continues with discussion on the nature and purpose of education more generally. Previously established models of community development – a universal approach, a second-chance, compensatory model and a radical/critical approach (Martin 1987) are then updated. Given this book's ambition to give voice to community educators, this chapter also provides information on research methodology and shares practitioner accounts of the nature, purpose and philosophy of community education.

THE DUBIOUS NATURE OF COMMUNITY

At its most literal, *community* describes all elements of a geographical area regardless of the make-up of its population. Sometimes people talk about other types of community. Communities of interest can refer to people united by something of significance to them. A good example is the *Gaelic Athletic Association* (GAA), a national promoter of Gaelic games in Ireland that describes itself as a "volunteer-led, community based organisation".[1] There are also issue-based communities where people are united around a shared concern such as concern for the environment. Some communities are linked by identity like the gay or Muslim community whilst a feature of our globalised society is the prevalence of online communities where interactions between members are primarily through the Internet.

Whatever the shared characteristics or circumstance, use of the word community usually indicates positivity and well-being through relatively harmonious cohesion. Understanding community is however more challenging than this essentialist viewpoint suggests and there has been much discussion on a search for meaning. Over 40 years ago, Bell and Newby (1972: 21) describe attempts by sociologists to define community as "an occupational hazard" explaining:

> Most sociologists, no more than other individuals, have not always been immune to the emotive overtones that the word community carries with it. Everyone – even sociologists – has wanted to live in a community ... the subjective feelings that the term community conjures up thus frequently lead to a confusion between what it *is* (empirical description) and what the sociologists feel it *should be* (normative description).

Whilst Bell and Newby are correct to emphasise the emotive nature of naming community, their objective/subjective quandary, is in many ways, more symptomatic of wider philosophical tensions about the nature of reality, tensions that remain today. Do we name our world by emphasising how we interpret our experiences (interpretivist), do we name it as something that objectively exists outside of our experiences. Can we draw from both?

One commonly evoked starting point in understanding community is through the ideas of German sociologist Tönnies (1887/2002) who is noted for contrasting *gemeinshaft* (community) and *gesellshaft* (society) whilst considering them in tandem. Gemeinshaft relates to personal contacts that are private and intimate yet linked by spaces that share such characteristics as language, religion, cultures and beliefs. Gesellshaft "is public life – it is the world itself" (Tönnies 1887/2002: 33) thus a space characterised by urbanism, heterogeneity and impersonality. The track from gemeinshaft to gesellshaft was born out of prudence as societies began to modernise. Not dissimilar to Tönnies, David Clark (1996) also refers to community as a social system that is continually negotiating its relationship with wider society. In his book *Schools as Learning Communities*, Clark draws out the importance of people, place, relationships, beliefs and values. He suggests it is through the presence of three core feelings – (1) of *significance* – that I matter, (2) of *solidarity* – that I belong and (3) of *safety* – that I won't be harmed either physically or psychologically, that community is created. Along with these components, Clark (1996: 48) proposes a "communal dilemma" describing this as "the problem of how social systems can become more open to one another without weakening their own sense of community or destroying that of others". By engaging with this communal dilemma, communitarianism, or the interactions between individuals and their community, is developed in a way that ensures these interactions are respectful, nurturing and diverse. To give an example, if we take a newly built urban estate on the outskirts of an established town or city, the formation of community is by creating identities, cultures and practices amongst residents that promote feelings of safety, significance and solidarity. Addressing the communal dilemma Clark sets, is to be open to accommodating the identities, cultures and practices of other neighbouring communities as well as embracing identity-based communities within our new estate. This openness stops cliques and elites from emerging and prevents the isolation of certain groups so that communities can respectfully coexist.

Clark's ideas do help us to understand community but they are a bit idealistic and do not really address some of the controversies that can surround the expression. Closer examination of terms such as community, community development, community education and, the increasingly popular, community cohesion (Ratcliff 2012) reveal that these are all highly contested concepts. Often, the most influential factor is the political inclination of the user. Terms such as "strengthening community", "nurturing community" or "building community spirit" have all been used to justify a range of competing policy interventions both left and right of the political spectrum (Mayo 1994; Shaw 2008; Hoggett et al. 2009; Mayo et al. 2013). But if we a little more attention to who is being talked about when the expression community is evoked, conversations are invariably about areas where the working- and lower-middle classes live (Thompson 2000: 68). Sometimes, these communities are thought about as a drain on the rest of society and, more often than not, they are also described as *dis-advantaged*. There is little doubt but that certain communities do need more support than others. This is where there are higher concentrations of people who are unemployed, more people parenting alone, more living on low incomes and higher than average densities of immigrant populations. One reason for this consolidated demographic is bad government planning in the allocation in social housing (Fahey 1999; Drudy and Punch 2005; Norris and Redmond 2005). Take for example the "surrender grant" (as it was popularly known) of the 1980s where financial incentive was offered to those willing to vacate their social house and enter the private housing market. This grant was taken up by those with leadership and employment capacity who were replaced by those at the top of the housing waiting list therefore those "at high risk of poverty" and in urgent need of housing (Norris and Redmond 2005: 175).

Ill-conceived decisions on social housing are not only historical and are not simply bad judgement. Such initiatives are part of a growing dependence on the private market to address housing need, a dependence that is coupled with a minimisation of social responsibility for housing. One major intervention in marketising social housing was the *Housing (Miscellaneous Provision) Act* introduced into law by a Fianna Fail[2] government in 2009. This legislation replaced State responsibility for "social housing", to responsibility for "social housing *support*" (Government of Ireland 2009, Part 2: 10, my italics). This one word changed the State's relationship with its housing responsibility. Mass construction projects that had characterised national responses to housing need during the 1900s became a thing of the past as the State was legislatively encouraged to enter into long-term leasing arrangements with private landlords of between 5 and 20 years.

Some of you might think this arrangement is unproblematic because of its potential to stimulate private investment in the housing market and strengthen market values. The difficulty is that these schemes have not worked and have done little more than privatise social housing. This is because much investment by the State is no longer used to build-up the public housing stock but is transferred into the wallets of private property owners. Despite the potential for long-term rental schemes to guarantee a regular income for these private owners, there has been a shortfall in suitable housing entering the schemes and, according to government figures, 90,000 households languish on the housing waiting list (Department of Environment, Community and Local Government

2014). This has left many with no choice but to turn to the private rented sector, a sector characterising by virtually no security of tenure and inadequate rent certainty. This precarious situation creates *temporality* as people struggle to emotionally invest in their community because they live under the shadow that their housing circumstances could change at any time. For those fortunate enough to be renting from the public sector, inadequate funding for public housing authorities has perpetuated residualisation as the quality of social housing estates diminishes, the profile of tenants becomes more concentrated in terms of poverty and the stigma of living in certain areas increases (Fahey 1999: 20; Considine and Dukelow 2009: 337).

The communities most affected by residualisation and temporality are the same communities often engaging in community education and there is often intense interest in these so-called disadvantaged communities. Through the lens of structural inequality, there is little wrong with assigning a label such as this. The difficulty is how, often, speculation about the impact of clustered poverty favours the idea of a cycle of deprivation where these communities are themselves considered the locus for generating and reproducing the social problems they face (Hoggett et al. 2009: 38–39). Frequently, this is accompanied by an individualist discourse that claims people can lift themselves out of poverty through their own actions; actions that include engaging in community education. This individualism, an important cornerstone in neoliberalism, is increasingly cemented into hegemonic logic through the notion of *social agency*, or connections between ourselves and other community members. By improving social agency, communities can allegedly generate enough *social capital* (an interesting turn of phrase given its monetary comparative) to ensure greater community cohesion (Ratcliffe 2012). Reverse this, and the cause of social decline is because of deteriorating interpersonal relationships and broad disengagement from civil society spaces (Putnam 2000). I imagine most of us would welcome stronger connections between neighbours and more cohesive communities. However, claiming that social capital can reverse the complex causes of poverty and disadvantage does little more than blame the poor for the circumstances they find themselves in and expect them to overcome a milieu of economic and social difficulty. This is without acknowledging the social policies that create their living conditions in the first place.

There are other problems with the notion of community. What about its common presumption of homogeneity (or sameness), even within the conversation above. By assuming shared traits between neighbours and similarity amongst those of the same faith or those with shared interests or concerns, we can disregard many micro-economic, political and cultural differences as well as the individuality each of us hold. The structures of community can also be thought of as a way to maintain privilege, a privilege that is enforced through deliberate actions to exclude those considered undesirable (Mayo 2000: 41, Shaw 2008: 29). This underbelly of discrimination and banishment, sometimes with dangerous consequences, has forced identity-based communities, such as the aforementioned gay and Muslim communities, to emerge out of a sense of their own protection and to counter isolation within "acceptable" community. Conversations about desirable community are also commonly upheld through a nostalgic view of history, or "of praising the past to blame the present" (Bell and Newby 1972: 22). Such rose-tinted memories of contented, cohesive neighbourhoods usually revolved around a domestic role for women and a continual reinforcement of the idealised family through popular culture. Any veneer of historically contented communities also conceals a now well-documented bedrock of abuse within Irish State institutions, a situation that again mostly affected women and also children. Although carried in the experience of individuals, often with devastating consequences, the impacts of institutional abuse was in many ways silenced from the collective conscience of communities at the time.

ABOUT EDUCATION

Just like the term community, education is usually thought of positively and it is not uncommon for people to think that expansion and reform of formal education would be enough to deliver a more equal and just society. There is some truth in this. However, the level of reform most people envisage falls well short of the changes critical pedagogues argue are needed to create the emancipatory, democratic educational spaces this would require (Illich 1971; Freire 1972; Giroux 1983). Most discussions are not about such altered visions for education but are about tweaking the traditional school and college system; a system that is principally viewed as ostensibly neutral with meritocracy presented as the most effective way to ensure equality across experiences. Most people accept that the school system is not perfect and that there is some inequality. This inequality was first recognised by the State over 50 years ago within the joint Organisation for Economic and Co-operation and Development (OECD) and government report *Investment in Education*, which was published in 1965. Though mostly known as the policy document that introduced public secondary schools, *Investment in Education* also introduced a disadvantage paradigm described through OECD benchmarks of "family background, location and attainment" (Government of Ireland 1965: 110).

Since then, specialist schemes have been designed to widen access at each stage of the education system. These begin in early childhood with free pre-schooling and target early interventions and continue throughout the formal school system.[3] Fees for higher education were abolished in 1996 as part of attempts to address inequality (though it is hard to dispute that hikes in registration fees have effectively re-introduced fees in a different guise). Policy interventions have made a difference in improving equality of access and more people are certainly staying in school for longer. However, because the school system is deeply rooted in its socio-economic, cultural and philosophical contexts, the problem with education is not simply getting everybody into the system and keeping them there through to terminal examination. The real problem is persistent inequality of outcome as repeatedly, a person's performance at school has been linked to their socio-economic status (Boldt et al. 1998; Eivers et al. 2004, 2005, 2010; Fallon 2005: 289; Williams et al. 2009; McCoy et al. 2014). Poor school performance has a corresponding effect on access to university with wide discrepancies in attendance again linked to a person's socio-economic status (O'Connell et al. 2006; Higher Education Authority 2014).

Sometimes policymakers excuse these discrepancies believing it is little more than a normal feature of class-based society where different life expectations are inherent (Gaine 1998: 1–2). This sentiment often carries weight with the general public also. Yet if we examine the structures of our education system more closely, a different picture emerges. This begins by reminding ourselves that schools were not established to support individual well-being and intellectual capacities. Schools actually emerged during periods of industrialisation as governments sought to create an obedient workforce (Bowles and Gintis 1976; Coolahan 1981). Baker et al. (2004: 140) explain:

> School and Colleges were not principally designed therefore as institutions of liberation and enlightenment, although that was clearly one of their purposes from the perspective of egalitarian educators. They were primarily designed to be agents of social control, to regulate citizens, to socialise people into particular religious beliefs and into particular gendered, ethnic and sexual identities.

In post-Colonial Ireland, another deliberate function of the education system was to inculcate ideas such as nationalism and fixed Christian notions of human nature and destiny (Inglis 1998; O'Sullivan 2005; Walsh 2005).

Social control through schooling continues to manifest itself through what is sometimes referred to as a *hidden curriculum* that deliberately reproduces the inequalities of capitalism. This is by ensuring socialisation through a reliance on hierarchical relationships, a normalisation of inequality, an enforcement of civil obedience, a respect for authority and an alienating school curriculum (Bowles and Gintis 1976; Giroux 1983; Lynch 1989, 1999; Radner et al. 2007; Connolly 2008: 108–109). One way to expose the hidden curriculum is to think about Bourdieuan concepts of *habitus*, the alternative cultural inculcations of customs, tastes and attitudes that are determined by the lifestyle spaces a person occupies (Bourdieu 1984: 170). Now think about how schools largely dismiss any cultural incongruities beyond a dominant middle-class experience. The *othering* of the working class (Lawlor 2005) reduces a person's school performance to how capable they are of internalising and reproducing the dominant middle-class, capitalist-friendly culture. Derision of non-dominant culture is also compounded by a dearth of working-class and ethnic minority teachers whilst the large numbers of women in teaching re-enforce essentialist concepts of care. For the middle and upper-classes there is also a clear advantage paradigm. This includes the subjective expectations of teachers (Smyth and Hannon 2007; Radner et al. 2007), greater school choices for those with economic capital (Lynch and Lodge 2002: 40; O'Brien 2003) and a shadow system of private tuition for those with economic capital (Smyth 2009). Moreover, the way the formal school system measures learning advantages behaviourist philosophies, dominant cultural frames of reference, individualised learning and certain cognitive abilities (Garner 2006).

Involving Practitioner Voices

From this point forward, this book incorporates practitioner perspectives through the involvement of circa 226 community educators who participated in social research.[4] Their involvement helps us to get a sense of who community educators are, where they work, how they work, what motivates and frustrates them and what they understand community education to be. As indicated in the introductory chapter, the approach I take to social research is congruent with my stance on community education. I believe that it is by listening to the voices of those directly involved in delivering community education; we get a sense of what is really going on. The picture this paints can then be both problematised through theory, and made available to practitioners in a way that informs self-determination. Before presenting some of the findings from the field, I will clarify how participants became involved and what research methodologies influenced the process.

Research Methodology

The perspectives of community educators were gathered across three phases of a mixed-methods research project, undertaken from 2011 to 2013. The first phase involved qualitative in-depth one-to-one interviews with seven purposefully selected community educators all of whom shared a critical approach to community education. Throughout the text these contributors are identified as interviewee one through to interviewee seven. Following on from these interviews, the pool was widened through an online, imbedded (qualitative and quantitative) survey questionnaire. This was completed by 219 community educators who were recruited through non-random, "judgmental sampling" (Sarantakos 2005: 164) with dissemination organised through identifiable gatekeepers. Broad circulation was encouraged with eligibility limited to "those working as a facilitator/tutor role with adult groups in community settings (or who have done so in the last two years). This means working with groups outside of Higher Education and Further Education institutions and local to participants". Representativeness was strengthened through multi-indicator questions (Bryman 2004: 68). In the end, participants emerged from the community sector, within public provision (Vocational Education Committees (VECs)), from non-governmental organisations (NGOs), Higher Education Institutions (HEIs), from independent practitioners not affiliated to a particular organisation and from others eligible to participate though work within other organisations. A full breakdown of the types of organisations participants were drawn from is provided within Chapter 3, for the moment, the summary below gives you a sense of the makeup of participants.

One survey question invited people to put themselves forward for further involvement in phase three of the research through focus-group participation.[5] Thirty-five community educators participated in these focus groups which were held between July and September in 2013. These were geographically organised around emergent clusters and groups were held

Table 2.1   Overview of research participants by organisation type

Organisational type	
Community Sector Organisations	49% (n108)
VECs	31% (n67)
Higher Education Institutions	5% (n11)
NGOs	4% (n9)
Other State Providers (HSE and FAS)	1% (n3)
Others (inc. private provider)	4% (n8)
Independent practitioners	6% (n13)
Total	**100% (n219)**

in Limerick City, Cork City, Waterford City, Athlone Co. Westmeath, Naas Co. Kildare, south-Dublin, north-Dublin and central-Dublin. A further six community educators who were unable to attend focus groups were facilitated to participate via telephone interviews (tele-interviews). Throughout the text these contributors are identified as tele-interviewee one through to tele-interviewee six. When quoting from surveys and interviews I will name the type of organisation each person is working in as catagorised in Table 2.1. This is not done when quoting from focus groups as to do so could compromise a participant's anonymity.

This book cannot present an exhaustive overview of all comments made by each participating community educator as there simply would not be space to incorporate everything that was said. What it does do is make sure to draw from each phase of research and to present an integrated analysis that incorporates every theme to emerge.

This book also provides statistics which have been generated from phase two (survey participation) only. Where statistics are presented, missing values (where a question has not been answered) are specifically named when there is a greater than 5% (n11) non-response rate. Where missing values are less than 5%, valid percentage[6] is reported. Statistical analysis is contextualised through findings from open-ended survey questions and from responses to a final survey question which asks – "have you any other thoughts or views about community education that you would like to share (including any thoughts on matters already raised such as accreditation, co-option, disadvantage, working conditions etc.)".[7]

Whilst both qualitative and quantitative research brings strengths, both also bring weaknesses. We know from other studies that all human surveying is problematic. People do not always tell the truth, sometimes do not understand the question, can forget details when relaying past events and can answer questions in the way they think a researcher wants them to answer (Dockery and Bedeian 1989; Lohr 2009: 10). De Vaus (2002: 59–60) demonstrates how, within any sample, those with post-level qualifications and those who share the same first language as the researcher are more likely to participate. Beyond the research itself, Ball and Drury (2012) effectively demonstrate how the political inclination of the interpreter can conflate statistics to satisfy their own ideological leanings. It is also difficult to ignore the power of the quantitative researcher who introduces the hypothesis to be tested (Valsiner 2000: 14) and subjectively shapes quantification (De Vaus 2002: 100; Sandelowski et al. 2009).

Notwithstanding these trepidations, there are advantages to quantitative research. Surveys help us find out about the composition, traits and attitudes of a larger number of community educators in a way that qualitative research alone would not allow. It also offers anonymity to participants not keen to participate face-to-face. Moreover, analysis of survey findings allows previous assumptions about the nature of community education to be tested within the field and enables dominant trends to emerge through quantification (Seltzer-Kelly et al. 2012).

As with quantitative research, qualitative research also has weaknesses. It is an approach that heavily relies on personal interpretations, both by the researcher and the researched, something Granek (2013) describes as an intersubjective exchange where each are epistemological co-creators. Additionally, the purposeful selection of a small number of potentially like-minded participants can shield a researcher from competing sentiments. The key strength of qualitative research is how those researched have the power to determine what is discussed and to provide context. This is both in relation to hypotheses posed and through open questions. Using focus groups brings additional richness to social research. This is by creating a more interactive encounter than one-to-one and survey methods allow as participants reflect on their opinions in the company of others which further contextualises their own involvement.

Now that you have some information of the background to the research, findings and analysis will be infused throughout including information on which research phase contributions are drawn from. This starts within discussion on what community education is, before moving on to distinguishable models of community education.

WHAT IS COMMUNITY EDUCATION?

The introductory chapter of this book claims governmental interpretation of community education as principally about employability, a theme examined in depth in Chapter 5. To get a sense of how practitioners understand community education, one open-ended survey question asked "When you see community education in action, what is happening that causes you to say 'Now that is community education'". Repeatedly, research participants describe a process-oriented, multilayered approach that is underpinned by equality. To share some typical examples, one community educator who works as an independent practitioner, and is therefore paid by the organisers of local education programmes, describes community education as having "a number of components" continuing:

It is genuinely participative and delivered in engaging learning environments in which the traditional teacher/student dichotomy doesn't exist; responsive to the needs of learners and their communities, underpinned by critical pedagogy; concerned with social justice, change and equality, not about equipping people with specific technical skills to enable them to respond to the demands of the economy. (Survey respondent, independent practitioner)

Such a layered response is not an isolated opinion. The educator quoted below names four levels – "personal, community, political and wider society" continuing:

It is individual and collective transformation. It captures participant's interests and passion on posing issues and problem solving solutions collectively. Participants learn to analysis, cause and effect and to develop their own critical analysis and theories. (Survey respondent, community sector)

An employee of a Family Resource Centre (FRC) puts it like this:

When people begin to take responsibility for changing their situation; when they take on statutory bodies; when they develop critical social analysis; when they are able to delay a process when they see it is to their advantage; when they trust their own cultural insights. (Survey respondent, community sector)

Similar descriptions are shared from those working within State structures. One Community Education Facilitator (CEF) believes community education happens when people come together through shared interest in such things as art or cookery classes explaining how this commonly evolves into something more politicising and group led. This, she claims happens as a result of the educational approach which is one of "listening to each other, supporting each other, identifying what they would like to do together" adding:

> ... then as the class progresses, the conversations that happen and are facilitated, can lead to stronger bonds being created and further support for each other. The group may then decide to work together to create something for the community or to resolve some issue in the community. Sometimes, where a group have formed as part of a CDP or women's group, there is a more explicit community education/development agenda and the group may work to develop their capacity to collectively address issues that affect their community. (Survey respondent, VEC/Education and Training Board (ETB))

As well as these qualitative, multilayered descriptions, quantification of survey findings (Fig. 2.1) gives us an overall sense of the dominant interpretations shared. Measurements are made on the basis of whether

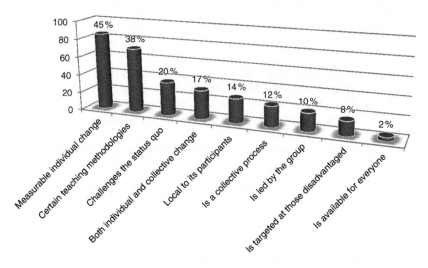

Fig. 2.1   What is community education, participant responses

a particular feature is "mentioned" or "not mentioned" within responses to the survey question "When you see community education in action, what is happening for you to say *now that is community education.*"

In total, n315 elements are named as many participants cite more than one feature. For example three people who believe community education should specifically target those who are disadvantaged, also believe both individual and collective change should be present. Twenty-one people who are keen to see certain teaching methodologies also seek individual change.

As Fig. 2.1 depicts, individual change is the single biggest characteristic, cited by 45% of participants. Some qualitative comments help us to understand what practitioners mean by this. One women speaks of community education like this:

> People are seeing their own gifts and resources and those of others and believing that change is possible. The process of learning individually and communally begins to replace the notion that learning is about acquiring lots of knowledge. People see themselves as knowledgeable and capable of generating knowledge. (Survey respondent, community sector)

For those to emphasise teaching methodologies, many compare community education to traditional education especially that which people encountered in school. Across community sector and public provision there is a sense that community education is different. This is due the way people are invited to become involved in course design and because of the participatory approaches employed. This educator with almost 30 years of experience and currently working on a voluntary basis illuminates this well through her comment:

> Its emphasis is process (including group-work, check-ins, consultation, supports, childcare etc.), and never letting a pre-written syllabus dictate how it should be done (Survey respondent, brackets in original).

The Role of the Community Educator

Survey participants were also asked to rank a list of five statements designed to describe how they mostly interpret their role. Some respondents equally ranked more than one option. Table 2.2 measures where

Table 2.2   How community educators interpret their role

Please rank the following statements describing how you "mostly" interpret your role when tutoring/facilitating	Mostly accurate (%)	Least accurate (%)
To respond to the issues and needs of the group regardless of the demands of the course descriptor/programme.	30	36
To introduce groups to knowledge and theories that I am familiar with thereby sharing my expertise.	11	22
To build the self-confidence and knowledge base of individuals enabling them to avail of a range of opportunities.	57	6
To encourage the groups that I work with to collaborate with each other and to together, take action to address issues that affects their community.	17	21
To up-skill individuals so that they are better equipped to compete against others in getting a job.	8	45

respondents prioritise, or de-emphasise, no more than two statements. Multiple priorities have been eliminated.[8]

Again, an individualist approach that supports building participant capacities emerges strongly (57%) as does a process-led approach that emphasises the need to respond to group needs over a pre-determined curriculum (30%). Despite being the dominant State interpretation of the purpose of community education (as explored within Chapter 5), up-skilling for employment is not prioritised by practitioners with just 8% listing this perspective as a priority.

People are also reluctant to occupy an expert role, a reticence that equally emerges through qualitative contributions where a mutuality of learning is preferred. Describing people as "experts in their own lives", one answer offers the following description:

> I believe we learn together through sharing and communicating, and I see my group facilitation as a partnership. Where it is relevant, there may be occasions where I have more knowledge on a topic or an issue that I can share with the group, but it is their analysis of that knowledge that of ultimate importance in the group. I do not believe myself to be an expert

in any field, or to have more expertise than any person attending a group. (Survey respondent, tutor VEC/ETB)

Other community educators also tend to describe their role as a facilitative process with some respondents deliberately distancing themselves from the title "teacher". This is to ensure more individualised attention and support, and as a deliberate attempt to create an alternative environment to school settings. One survey contribution captures attitudes across a number of submissions when she shares, "most of the learners I work with have had negative educational experiences and would not attend courses if they were run by a Teacher".

MODELS OF COMMUNITY EDUCATION

These contributions are helpful in getting a sense of what community education is, as interpreted through a practitioner lens, and the equality focus discussed within the introductory chapter is clearly strong. To fully understand philosophical differences, it helps to further distil our understanding of community education. This can be done by updating work by Ian Martin (1987) where he considers community education under three broad, at times overlapping approaches. The first of these is a consensus, *universal*, or conservative model which he associates with neutral concepts of lifelong learning. Secondly, Martin describes a pluralist, model of community education referring to compensatory, or *second chance*, models for those disadvantaged. Finally, Martin's third model of practice refers to socially transformative, critical community education that sits within a conflict, *radical* or oppositional approach (Fig. 2.2).

On paper, it is easy enough to assert classifications of universal, compensatory or radical approaches. As always, context matters and in reality, community education is influenced by the sociopolitical climate, its location and the reasons why a group comes together in the first place. Categorisations can also overlap. Take for example a community development and leadership programme. Organisers most likely interpret this as radical through its challenge to hegemonic notions of leadership. At least some participants are likely to seek payment for future community activism through jobs in the community sector thereby offering them a second chance at forging a career. Recruitment for the programme may have been widespread meaning different socio-economic groups are represented in the room and some may interpret community development as more akin

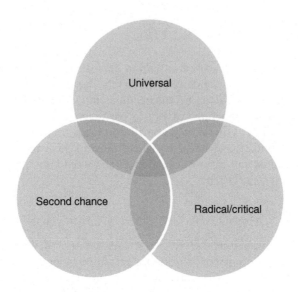

Fig. 2.2 Models of community education

to community services without believing social change is required. This would align such a programme with universal modes of practice. However, there are important differences within each approach that ultimately determine if community education sets out to comply with existing social conditions, if it tries to rebalance capitalist circumstances through equality of opportunities or if it seeks to challenge the structures that cause inequality in the first place. Each will now be explained more comprehensively.

Universal Approaches to Community Education

A universal, consensus or conservative approach is based on a homogenous view of society and a harmony of interests as all of us are assumed to share much the same uncomplicated capitalist vision for society. Martin (1987) describes this approach as epitomised by lifelong learning, integrated provision, rationalisation, volunteerism and a neutral analysis of education. Martin bases this categorisation on the growth of the Community College movement in the UK and similarities can be evoked in Ireland through mainstream education's use of community schools or community colleges when talking about technical and vocational education. Many of these community programmes relate to the functions of The Irish National Training Authority called FÁS (which was disbanded in 2013) as well as some extramural university programmes. This is where these university programmes set out to extend provision to anyone interested in accredited programmes outside of a university campus. Some education within Ireland's national network of ETBs also fall within this approach as does the work of some national organisations such as the voluntary, rural-based Macra na Feirme.[9] Some community groups in both rural and urban settings also work from universal principles depending on their mission and purpose.

One thing to observe about Martin's model, now almost 30 years old, is the way he interprets lifelong learning as a non-contentious expression that is mostly detached from other approaches to adult and community education. This reflects previous use of lifelong learning to describe recreational and hobby-based programmes (see, e.g. Rogers 2002: 9 or; Jarvis 2004: 44). One of the features of neoliberalism is its appropriation of language to extend market control (Murray 2014) and the expression lifelong learning is a good example of this appropriation. Change in meaning began with government interest in the term (Murtagh 2014: 13), especially from the 1990s onwards, as lifelong learning became an important cornerstone in European policy convergence. Many adult educators initially, though perhaps cautiously, began to use lifelong learning interchangeably with adult education in an attempt to incorporate social, democratic and economic well-being within each educational endeavour (e.g. see Field and Leister 2000; Boshier 2006; Maunsell et al. 2008; Duckworth and Timmons 2010). The difficulty is that, increasingly, anti-neoliberal commentators began to recognise how many lifelong learning policy interventions were a ruse for employability discourse and for the commercialisation of education to satisfy market demands (Johnston 2000; Borg and Mayo 2005; Brine 2006; Grummell 2008, 2014; Óhidy 2008). This colonisation, which is discussed comprehensively within Chapter 5, is important to be mindful of when we apply Martin's model today.

It is good to advocate for community spaces for broad-based learning and, at surface level, universal approaches can appear uncontroversial. The problem is the way it presents education as neutral thereby failing to challenge how dominant cultural customs can unhelpfully reinforce fixed notions about what we consider as normal and natural. To give some examples, the value of up-skilling local people so that they can get a job may appear neutral and an activity that can do no harm. Unless we also expose how important a person's social class is in determining their employment prospects (McCoy 2011) we do little more than reinforce the hegemonic idea that hard work alone ensures occupational mobility and that everyone has an equal chance to rise to the top of a particular profession. Turn this around, and the unemployed are to blame for their situation and therefore deserve the label of being lazy. Another example is the way early universal models of women's community education commonly acted as an instrument of power that enforced patriarchy and gender stereotypes. This was through the active promotion of a homemaker role with little discussion on the status of women at the time (Slowey 1979; Inglis et al. 1993). Universality can also entrench compliance with traditional views of Irishness that are blind to our contemporary ethnic, cultural and linguistic diversity (O'Connor 2010). Even where topics such as politics are studied, a universal approach would encourage seemingly impartial delivery. Take for example the Quality and Qualifications Ireland (QQI) level 5 award in politics.[10] A universal approach would encourage a descriptive approach to how national and transnational policital structures work. Less countenanced is space where adults might consider democratic deficiencies within these systems (Jerzack 2014) or problematise centralised decision-making on issues that affect local communities.

Community Education as a Second Chance

Martin's second reformist model differs from a universal approach given its premise on a pluralist society that recognises heterogeneity, diversity and inequality within. Supporters commonly agree that the school system has disproportionately benefited some over others and recognise the negative impacts schools can have on a person's well-being. They respond by creating conditions where people feel validated and valued and where they get a second chance to increase their life chances. Martin (1987: 24) links the origins of second-chance community education to certain UK neighbourhoods earmarked for priority funding. A similar historical trajectory exists in Ireland with its roots most readily linked to State-delivered VEC supports beyond secondary school. Second-chance philosophies also underpin some extramural university-accredited certificates and activities within some community groups in both rural and urban settings depending on their mission and purpose. Within Ireland's current Further Education and Training (FET) strategic plan, the Irish government emphasise the importance of second-chance education as a feature of adult education (SOLAS 2014: 20).

Ensuring equal access and participation in adult education is an important equality objective and a range of vocational and personal benefits have been measured within other studies (Denny et al. 2003; Preston and Hammond 2003; Bailey et al. 2010, 2011; Field 2011). For a community there can be increased income through falling unemployment and, where individuals progress to higher education, a normalising of this pathway which might have been otherwise considered unattainable. There are also problems with this approach. One limitation is the way perceived deficiency is located within the affected individual. This can compound the stigmatisation and self-blame of school's underachievement thereby strengthening the neoliberal internalisation of personal failure in an allegedly impartial education system. Grummell (2008) describes government promotion of second-chance education as mythical. She argues that by making people feel responsible for their own employability and life chances, the real winner is the market that benefits from a casualised workforce less inclined to call employers to account. Grummell (2008) also claims supports for second-chance education dissuades more oppositional interpretations of community education that nurture critical thinking. A second-chance model can also perpetuate continuation of the hidden curriculum. One way this is happening in community education is through increasing use of individualised evaluation tools for measuring learning that re-enforce passivity and conformism within existing social structures. This disregards more dissident ways to measure critical education such as through civil disobedience and protesting. One such evaluation I have seen measured harmonious engagement between parents and their children's school teachers as evidence of learning, but offered no analysis of the problematic power dynamics such relationships can embody.

Second-chance community education also plays an important part in directing different social classes into certain occupations. Take healthcare as an example, an educational endeavour not uncommon in community education contexts. Participants, mostly women and from communities considered disadvantaged, put significant effort into achieving professionally recognised qualifications as healthcare workers. These awards enable them to seek low-paid work either within the public healthcare system or, increasingly, within private nursing homes and home-care providers. For those who share an interest in healthcare but are from the middle and upper classes, the opportunities open to them are more likely through the university system that enables them to take up much higher paid, and higher status employment as nurses, doctors, occupational therapists and physiotherapists. This division also ensures the reproduction of class hierarchy within healthcare settings.

Radical Community Education

Ian Martin's third conflict model (Martin 1987) describes a radical/critical approach to community education that differs from second-chance and universal approaches as its primary function is to bring about structural social change. Radical community education is premised on equality of condition, described by Baker et al. (2004: 33) as "to eliminate major inequalities altogether or at least massively to reduce the current scale of inequality". As the conflict label suggests, radical community education, is overtly political, described by Crowther et al. (2005: 1–2) as a process that "unambiguously takes the side of those social interests and movements which are progressive in the sense that they are concerned to challenge inequality, exclusion and discrimination and to be part of the broader struggle for democracy and social justice". As well as believing education can never be neutral, education alone is also not the route to equality. What is required is praxis, a cyclical process of action and reflection on socially unjust systems (Freire 1972; hooks 1994, 2003) which is commonly fostered through group work (Ledwith 2007; Connolly 2008; Beck and Purcell 2010). Radical community education challenges the traditional image of education, is often non-accredited, is deeply connected to activism, is sporadic in delivery and is democratically organised so as to lateralise power between educators and participants/learners. How it translates into practice is through its root-edness in the New Social Movements (NSMs) that emerged as part of global unrest in the latter half of the twentieth century (Stammers 2009; Eschle 2001; Della Porta and Diani 2006). Archetypical uprisings included the women's movement, peace movements, green movements, gay and lesbian movements and the civil rights movement in the USA (Stammers 2009: 132). Though NSMs commonly rely on an identity-based approach to politics therefore a separation of grievances into distinct strands, they also share similar traits. These are a collective approach to politics that is under continuous review (Eschle 2001: 2), demands for political reform, conflictual relationships with the State and a shared cynicism with the singular notion of economic growth without due regard for its negative elements (Connolly and Hourigan 2006: 1; Della Porta and Diani 2006: 20). As with the UK examples (Martin 1987), the social movement community education most obviously connects to is a radical approach to community development that emerged in Ireland in the 1980s (Lee 2003; Lloyd and Lloyd-Hughes 2009).

Not all community development carries the tenets of radical/critical community education and, in truth, governmental interpretations have always been towards a self-help individualised approach (see Government of Ireland 2000) that more readily aligns with second-chance community education. There can also be misappropriation of community development by the political right. One example of this is an ideological ascendency of what is increasingly entitled "The Big Society", a UK conservative approach that, unlike Thatcherite polices before it, sets out to embrace civil society to the benefit of both market and civil society. Despite being cloaked in the language of participation, and a virtuous role for community sector organisations, Scott (2011) interprets "Big Society" thinking as a process of manipulation that seeks to marketise community rather than established quality community connections.

Where community development and radical community education merge is when each is interpreted as a bottom-up, collective process with critical education at its spine (Connolly 1996; Ledwith 2007; Beck and Purcell 2010; Fitzsimons and Dorman 2013). The resulting praxis can take many forms such as the creation of alternative spaces for dialogue, negotiation with power holders, rights-based campaigning and lobbying work and the establishment of supports that simultaneously address *and* highlight shortfalls in public provision.

Another way to radicalise community education is to bring a political dimension to subjects traditionally taught through a seemingly apolitical lens. Examples include the theorisation of personal development understood within political and structural frameworks (Ryan 2001: 65, Connolly and Hussey 2013), politicised pedagogy within modern language classes (Kane 2001: 253–256) and openly exploring relationships between vocational programmes and the global corporations that benefit from a flexible, mobile workforce (Brookfield and Holst 2011: 129). To offer another example, think about what a radical approach to teaching childcare would look like. Where universal and second-chance perspectives largely focus on the skills required for the job with varying degrees of practitioner reflexivity encouraged, a radical/critical approach would also incorporate a social analysis that asks such questions as why is there no State subsidy for child-care? Why have austerity budgets consistently reduced children's allowance? Why is childcare a low-paid, precarious, feminised occupation?

From an anti-neoliberal perspective, creating critical educational spaces such as these are to be welcomed and nurtured. However, there are difficulties with critical community education. Certification can limit radical possibilities (Torres 1993; Fitzsimons 2014) and critical questioning often fails to extend beyond the classroom walls. Kane (2010) shares concerns about the often suggested mantra of "starting where the person is at" claiming this can dissuade practitioners from explicitly addressing political questions. Kane (2010) also notes the importance of social context on practice and suggests that, in many cases, the key factor in determining the extent and direction of dialogic probing is the politics of the practitioner.

There are also difficulties with NSM approaches to community education. One problem is how much activism that is described as community development, has been incorporated into the structures of the State. Some argue that the tensions this "in and against" positioning creates are good for democracy (Paterson 1999; Chanan 2009; Crickley and McArdle 2009; Lloyd 2010). The crux of their argument is that civil society organisations can hold governments to account both by positioning themselves in power-sharing spaces of governance and by verbalising opposition to inequitable policy proposals. In truth the contradictory nature of begin funded by, yet critical of, the State raises considerable difficulties as the actions of social movements have been stymied by financial and bureaucratic interdependence on the State both nationally (O'Byrne 2012; Bissett 2015) and internationally (Steyn 2012). More recently, there are also fewer examples of community sector organisations engaging with a second wave of social movements that is moving away from identity politics through a reunified objection to neoliberalism and a class-based banner of anti-austerity (Della-Porta 2015).

IDENTIFYING MODELS OF PRACTICE

In determining the models of community education most prevalent in Ireland, one research survey question offered participants three statements, each one representing either universal, second-chance and radical approaches to community education. Participants were asked to do two things; to indicate which statement best described their own approach to community education and to identify which statement best

Table 2.3 Quantifying models of community education

		Practitioners (%)	Organisations (%)
1.	Where the emphasis is on offering a wide range of courses (vocational, personal, political) that are open to anyone who is interested regardless of where they live and what their background is. [universal]	37	26
2.	Where the emphasis is on offering a wide range of courses (vocational, personal, political) specifically targeted at those who are considered "educationally disadvantaged" thereby providing opportunities otherwise not readily available. [second chance]	35	58
3.	Where the emphasis is as a political and politicising act taking its lead from issues affecting people in communities considered disadvantaged. Its approach is collective over individual and its hope is to influence wider social change [radical/critical]	28	16

described the model adopted by the organisation where they work. The following emerges (Table 2.3).

Thirty-seven percent of community educators align themselves with a universal approach meaning over one-third of those researched favour approaches that do *not* weight practice in favour of those considered disadvantaged. This is despite identifying how most organisations positively discriminate in this way. Thirty-five percent align with second-chance approaches and 28% demonstrate a radical/critical allegiance. In total, 43% of those who answered both elements of this question are at odds with their organisation's approach. The most notable discrepancy occurs for 55% of those aligning themselves with radical approaches who work within organisations ascribing to second-chance/compensatory models.

This theme, where practitioners are working in a way that jars with the mission and purpose of their organisation, emerges within conversations at other phases of the research also. One critical community educator working within a NGO believes there is a significant gulf between what he describes as organisational rhetoric that claims to address structural inequality and the realities within his place of work. He claims individuals are attracted into the NGO because of a stated commitment to social justice but, once inside, become disillusioned by disparities between what is said and what is done. Rather than forgo critical tendencies, he talks about creating covert spaces within.

> You work on the margins basically of the organisation and the sense is that it is not only that you are working in the margins, I think of the margins in terms of a copy-book, it's in the margins that you put down notes that you really have to pay attention to. If you work in the margins where you are almost hidden, you are under the radar. (Interviewee three)

This voice is not isolated and three out of seven critical educators to participate in lengthy interviews share similar difficulties. They report a sense of isolation, a lack of support, disappointment where organisations refuse to support political demonstrations and a lack of understanding of the purpose of radically oriented practice. One woman who works within the Local and Community Development Programme (LCDP) discusses this tension at length. She talks about often having to conceal her radical philosophy to everyone except those she comes into contact with in group settings. She wishes she, and others in the same situation, could unite and encourage critical conversations within their organisations with a view to pushing community sector organisations to the left.

> It can't just be hope do you know what I mean? If the [political] right can manage to make what they do how society operates, then the [political] left can make what we do, do you know what I mean? We have to start institutionalising it. (Interviewee one)

Practitioner Discussions on Disadvantage

Table 2.4 captures survey responses to whether community education should deliberately target those experiencing social and economic disadvantage. This is measured by asking survey participants to agree or

Table 2.4   Who should community education target?

Strongly agree (%)	Agree (%)	Somewhat agree (%)	Not sure if I agree or disagree (%)	Somewhat disagree (%)	Disagree (%)	Strongly disagree (%)
13	25	31	7	13	8	3

Survey question: The target group for community education should be people who experience social and economic disadvantage.

disagree with the statement "the target group for community education should be people who experience social and economic disadvantage".

Sixty-nine percent agree community education should deliberately target those considered disadvantaged with 7% answering "not sure". Twenty-four percent disagree with this statement. In addition to this quantification, 15% of additional comments left by survey respondents related to disadvantage. Four core themes emerge. The first of these is where community educators argue against the hypothesis measured within Table 2.4. One respondent shares,

> I have strong views that community education should not necessarily be the domain of the marginalised and socio-economic disadvantaged. There is broader definition of community, particularly in rural areas, where diversity is embraced and included to bring about positive change for and within local communities. In urban areas, communities are more polarised in terms of class and geography but sometimes that just serves to further "silo" communities (Survey respondent, higher education provider)

This blurring of class distinctions in rural areas was raised on four occasions. However, the majority to argue against specific targeting within community education were working in urban settings. Some are forthright in their conviction. To give two examples:

> I have a strong belief that too many people in this country think of community education as being ONLY for socially deprived areas. True community education exists to help all communities that come together with a shared aim. (Survey respondent, Health Service Executive in a community context)

In another:

> The community is not restricted to the underprivileged, the community is everyone, the problems in the community are caused by everyone and the solutions for the community lie with everyone. (Survey respondent, tutor VEC/ETB)

These points are echoed by another community educator who "strongly disagrees" the target group for community education should be those disadvantaged arguing "education is for everyone regardless of social status" (Survey respondent, tutor VEC/ETB).

A second theme to emerge in qualitative findings is in support of targeted provision, a perspective captured below and repeated within other contributions.

> Community education . . . has a significant role for those most distant from formal education. In most cases this educational disadvantage has resulted in social and economic disadvantage also. So community education actively targets those who are marginalised or excluded and prioritises several target groups . . . recognising the particular target groups of community education and the levels of disadvantage which exists in this groups, it is vital that community education as a service and as a learner centred philosophy is maintained in a way that does not restrict or compromise this ethos. (Survey respondent, community sector)

Thirdly, there are challenges to traditional categorisations of disadvantage with both contributions below drawing out hidden disadvantage that is less acknowledged in society.

> I don't think all community education has to target educationally disadvantaged as there are other forms of disadvantage e.g. women in abusive situations or isolated because they are of a different nationality/culture etc. . . . I do believe though that inequality is a huge problem in our country and that the single most important factor in addressing it is to educate people. (Survey respondent, community sector)

The idea that disadvantage extends beyond common economic signifiers is echoed below:

> In my opinion it is extremely important that the work of community education is maintained and valued. Community education should not be about offering accredited courses and it is should not be specifically targeted i.e. social disadvantage can mean an awful lot of things it does not necessarily equate to economic disadvantage. (Survey respondent, CEF in a VEC/ETB)

A fourth recurrent theme cited by a few is that there should be deliberate class-based integration. This contribution below typifies sentiment.

> I think it is very important to target "disadvantaged" people but where appropriate it is ideal to have mixed groups. I have seen great steps towards social integration being made here from "both sides of the fence". (Survey respondent, community sector)

Table 2.5 Does community education reduce inequality?

Strongly agree (%)	Agree (%)	Somewhat agree (%)	Not sure if I agree or disagree (%)	Somewhat disagree (%)	Disagree (%)	Strongly disagree (%)
17	36	35	8	3	1	0

Survey question: Through my work as a community educator I am helping to reduce inequality in Ireland.

One final survey questions reported on in this chapter relates to whether or not participants believe their work is making a difference in addressing inequality. Eighty-eight percent agree with the statement identified in Table 2.5 with just 4% disagreeing.

What stands out is that over one-third answer "somewhat agree" (35%), with a further 8% who are "not sure if they agree or disagree". Some textual responses help us understand this ambiguity with one theme to emerge being a frustration with the bureaucratic burden of their work (which is discussed in more detail within Chapter 6). This opinion is captured below.

[my work] can be very taken up with "small" stuff, personal contacts, paperwork, etc. . . . It can be difficult to look out at the bigger picture, where the real change needs to be initiated and driven. (Survey respondent working as an adult literacy tutor)

These combined findings demonstrate a dominance of second-chance and universal approaches to community education but an equal accommodation for radical/critical philosophies. Relationships between these distinct philosophies are comprehensively explored within Chapter 4. Reluctance by community educators to interpret their role as primarily about expanding employability is equally explored in Chapter 5. The weight of support for community education as a way to address inequality is important to hold on to when we think about neoliberalism's growing rich–poor divide.

CONCLUSION

This chapter began by exploring the word community and by noting the contested nature of this expression. The purpose of education is also examined more broadly with its role in reproducing inequality exposed. Practitioner contributions legitimise an expansive meaning for community education.

However, their principle understanding is that practice supports equality and social justice. Although education to secure work can certainly be a part of this, and one that is not dismissed by practitioners, it is not the driving force but is contextualised amidst more holistic ambitions.

Accepting that models of practice determined as universal, second-chance and radical perspectives may have fallen out of favour within current debates, this chapter revives these interpretations and identifies some key criticisms along the way. The hope is that these models can help practitioners to become aware of ideological divergences so they can socially contextualise the work that they do. Through research findings, a majority leaning towards second-chance perspectives is uncovered and this theme will be returned to in more detail within Chapter 4. Before doing this, the next chapter will offer a history of community education in Ireland and will draw out contemporary examples of practice.

NOTES

1. The Gaelic Athletic Association is "a 32 county sporting and cultural organisation that has a presence on all five continents". It continues "the GAA is
   a volunteer led, community based organisation that promotes Gaelic games
   such as Hurling, Football, Handball and Rounders and works with sister
   organisations to promote Ladies Football and Camogie. It is part of the Irish
   consciousness and plays an influential role in Irish society that extends far
   beyond the basic aim of promoting Gaelic games" source www.gaa.ie/
   about-the-gaa/. Accessed 16 February 2015.
2. Fianna Fail is a centre-right conservative political party who also cite allegiance to a republican agenda
3. At primary and second level, the core intervention is the system-wide
   Delivering Equality of Opportunity in Schools (DEIS) programme introduced in 2005 and targeting specific communities.
4. The exact number of participants is unknown due to the anonymous nature
   of its survey phase as I cannot ascertain if some of those participating in
   phase one also participated in phase two.
5. Survey respondents were invited to participate in phase three if they answered
   the following question. *I will be holding group discussions around the country
   where I hope we can discuss issues raised and other thoughts people have about
   community education. Would you like further information on these with a view
   to participation? Remember that by doing this you are wavering anonymity
   relating to your survey answers. You are only revealing your identity to me and*

2 MODELS OF COMMUNITY EDUCATION 67

at no time will the answers you provided in this survey be revealed to others. Your identity will at no time be revealed in the writing up of this research.

6. Valid percentage refers to the percentage amount of 219 less those who did not answer the question. For example, when I ask how long you have worked as a community educator? Seven people failed to answer. The percentages reported on are therefore percentage values of 219 less 7, that is, 212.
7. This question has a response rate of 57% therefore n124 respondents.
8. These responses are based on a 71% overall response rate.
9. A large voluntary organisation established in 1944 and involved in the organisation of sports, travel, agricultural and community events across rural Ireland.
10. The full award is available to view at http://docs.qqi.ie/AwardsLibraryPdf/5N1837_AwardSpecifications_English.pdf. Accessed 18 December 2016.

CHAPTER 3

Community Education in Ireland

Illustration 3.1   The heterogenity of community education

© The Author(s) 2017
C. Fitzsimons, *Community Education and Neoliberalism*,
DOI 10.1007/978-3-319-45937-0_3

A key idea that I am presenting in this book is that neoliberalism is having a profound effect on community education. Quite deliberately, government-led labour market activation measures seek to co-opt a vibrant network of locally based provision as the State prioritises the needs of corporations over the needs of citizens. As outlined in the introductory chapter to this book, ongoing austerity policies legitimise budget cuts to alternative approaches, a rationalisation process that, in reality, is led by this political ideology's preference for private over State-funded practice. Later chapters will unpack these claims in more detail by examining social policies and by sharing practitioner experiences of their impacts. Before this, it seems sensible to illuminate what neoliberalism seeks to transform, to shine a light on community education, the roots of which were planted over 40 years ago. Analysing the threads of the past can help us reflect on the present. It also helps us to measure the erosion of State supports and to record the co-option of once oppositional movements.

Offering a history of community education might appear simple but it is actually quite complicated. To begin with, we should be wary of any singular narrative where complex historical and relational factors are gathered into an overriding version of events that is then presented as the truth. Rather than thinking about history as one truth, it is better to think of it as multiple truths, each of which offers a partial account of circumstances. Equally important, the documents at our disposal will have been written amidst the ideological tensions and cultural norms of a particular time. Remember those with access to resources, such as writing materials and storage repositories, will have been the ones with the power to record their interpretation of events. This means that histories carried in folklore, in songs and in lullabies may have been lost. What about the well worn, but nonetheless valid enouncement that history is written by the winners? When a class-based analysis is applied to this assertion the dominant history we learn at school can be an elitist history with the experiences of the majority population under-explored. Women's histories are also largely absent from accepted canonical knowledge with female experiences rarely centralised in records on past events.

Another complication is that sometimes attempts are made to sketch out ideological differences between a so-called community sector, whose primary concern is bottom-up collective community development work, and a separate, publically administered, *community education sector* that delivers individualised courses in disadvantaged areas. By way of example, let's take a look at companion research reports commissioned by AONTAS between 2010 and 2011. The first of these is *Community Education, More than Just a Course: Exploring the Outcomes and Impact of Department of Education and Skills Funded Community Education* (Bailey et al. 2010). As the title indicates, this document reviews publically managed community education. The second publication *Sowing the Seeds of Social Change: The Outcomes and Impact of a Social Action Model of Community Education* (Bailey et al. 2011) reviews community education where participants are drawn from the community sector. Despite the researcher's best efforts to apply ideological distinctions, this is not upheld by participating practitioners. Within *Community Education, More than Just a Course* (the report that focuses on public provision) the researchers concede this point telling us "the qualitative data shows that for the majority of case study providers, community education is part of a co-ordinated community development response to the needs of their local areas" (Bailey et al. 2010: 65). Within the second research publication, *Sowing the Seeds of Social Change*, a social action model of community education is offered that explicitly links practice to community development (Bailey et al. 2011: 83). However, many of the findings more readily align with second-chance approaches to community education with individual outcomes measured. In both reports, these researchers take a pluralist over radical/critical approach to community development and measure progress through such concepts as social cohesion and individualised over collective transformation.

In reality, public and community sector provision are deeply entwined and connections between the two have always been strong. Sectoralising practice should be avoided as it has the potential to split allies, a situation that can make co-option easier. Before considering relationships between public, community sector and other providers more deliberately, let's begin with a brief historical context for adult education more broadly and then draw out the origins of community education in Ireland.

SKETCHING A HISTORY OF ADULT AND COMMUNITY EDUCATION

It is impossible to identify an exact starting point for adult education in Ireland. One place to start is with early accounts of education for adults in within the coffee-house culture of the 1600s (Fadiman 2003).

In her colourful account of the way these coffee-houses captivated European culture Fadiman notes:

> In the days when public libraries were non-existent, and journalism was in its embryonic stages, they were a vital centre of news, gossip, and education – "penny universities" whose main business, in the words of one 1657 newspaper ad was "PUBLICK INTERCOURSE".

Two hundred years later, a time when Ireland was still under British rule, the first public library opened in 1858. This was in Dundalk, an eastern town north of Dublin and its emergence gave the general public access to books and a literary meeting point. Early adult education also includes work at the Dublin-based Museum of Irish Industry in the 1800s where non-denominational education targeted ordinary people who were traditionally excluded from elitist education structures (Cullen 2009). Skip forward into the 20th century and women's education began to emerge through the Irish Country Women's Association (ICA) (est. 1912). The ICA's stated objective was "to improve the standard of life in Ireland through Educational and Cooperative effort" (http://www.ica.ie/Breif-History.2534.1.aspx, sourced 2015). The Irish Housewives Association (IHA) (est. 1942) was another important organisation through their hosting of urban-based workshops about the status of women in Ireland including their economic rights (National Archives, 98/17, ND: 76).

There were co-educational opportunities also. Two years before the IHA was formed, the Dublin Institute of Adult Education (originally the Dublin Institute of Catholic Sociology) (est. 1940) had begun courses for women and men, again targeted at those who did not traditionally access the university system. This involvement of the Catholic Church was indicative of Ireland at the time where the Church held considerable cultural and political control. The People's College (est. 1948), founded with the support of the Irish Congress of Trade Unions and the UK Workers Education Association, were likely to offer an alternative ideological perspective. This was through the provision of "workers education" for those in jobs but who had limited education to that point (http://www.people scollege.ie/history/, sourced February, 2015). Some universities extended education outwards. University College Cork's (UCC) outreach programme (est. 1946) is documented as the first such programme to attract non-typical college attendees (Ó Fathaigh 1998; Murtagh 2014: 198) though little is recorded about the teaching methodologies employed.

When recounting a history more specific to community education, a common starting point is to begin with events in the 1970s and 1980s, a time period considered important in the modernisation of Ireland. This chapter presents this emergence along four trajectories – (1) daytime and evening adult education from within VECs and the overlying literacy movement; (2) an upsurge of women's consciousness-raising groups linked to the wider women's movement; (3) the Training for Transformation (TfT) movement influenced by liberation theology and (4) the community development/anti-poverty movement including responses to problematic drug use. The involvement of some universities will also be explored. These are somewhat forged divisions that intersect and overlap in practice and there are examples of universal, second-chance and radical approaches within each (see Chapter 2). However, each brings a different perspective to the landscape of practice and each will now be considered independently.

DAYTIME AND EVENING PROVISION THROUGH VECS AND THE LITERACY MOVEMENT

When AONTAS (The Irish National Adult Learning Association) offer a history of community education they begin by recalling night classes in vocational schools in the 1970s and 1980s (AONTAS 2004: 9). This was the first time Ireland's vocational sector was to become involved in community education through the work of its Vocational Education Committees (VECs) (est. 1930) that were scattered nationwide.[1] The adult-based evening classes of the 1970s were ad hoc and what was available mostly depended on individuals within a VEC and that particular person's interests and interactions with the communities they were located in. The audience for these programmes largely reflected the inequalities of the education system at the time; a system characterised by high exit levels after primary school and a secondary system that mostly catered for middle-class males. Because of this, community education catered for women, the working class, those with literacy difficulties, early retirees and workers whose employers supported the need to improve certain skills (Feehan 1979).

As well as VEC evening classes, a wider grass-roots literacy movement also began to emerge from the 1960s onwards (NALA 2010: 14). Often, this movement deliberately linked the ability to read and write to substandard and sometimes brutal conditions within Irish schools (Brady 2006: 41; Dorgan 2009: 13). Some of this literacy work was charitable and some was more radical. Both approaches were hugely dependent on voluntary effort as well as staff within VECs (Bassett et al. 1989: 26–28; National Adult Literacy Agency 2010: 14). Growth in the Irish literacy movement coincided with a high-profile *Right to Read* movement in the UK (Bailey 2006). Right to Read[2] had significant State support and its implementation included a series of national television programmes broadcast by the British Broadcasting Corporation (BBC). As British channels could be viewed in many Irish urban areas and in parts of Ireland that were close to its border with Northern Ireland, these programmes brought discussions about literacy into some people's living rooms. This made visible the previously invisible or certainly the unnamed. Outside of people's homes, community-based volunteer activism was growing. Many of these volunteers were women who had the support of women's organisations. To give some examples, when detailing a history of the literacy movement in Ireland, the National Adult Literacy Agency (NALA) specifically name the work of *Cherish*, a non-governmental organisation (NGO) that supports lone parents (now re-named One Family) and the *Association for Deserted and Alone Women* as particularly involved (National Adult Literacy Agency 2010: 14).[3]

Volunteers also formed AONTAS (est. 1969), although the profile of those involved was mostly male and middle class. There was State support for AONTAS from the beginning. The government Minister for Education addressed its inaugural event and announced that a task force would be established to make recommendations on future direction for adult education in Ireland (http://www.aontas.com/about/who weare/history.html, sourced Jan, 2016). The fruit of this task force's work appeared as the government commissioned *Adult Education in Ireland* (1973), or *Murphy Report*. This was the first time the State showed any real interest in adult education, and came 8 years after the OECD-led policy document *Investment in Education* (Government in Ireland 1965) which had recommended major reform of the Irish education system more broadly. On leafing through the Murphy Report, it is difficult not to be immediately struck by the partisan language throughout and how the list of committee members is all male with the exception of a female secretary. This is despite the fact that many of those accessing adult education were women. The Murphy Report describes the purpose of adult education as to ensure "adults who are no longer participants in the full time school system may learn whatever they need to learn at any period in their lives" (Committee on Adult Education 1973: 1) and offers an interesting vantage point on how the State thought about adult education. Overall, it strongly supports an equality of access perspective and positions higher education institutions as key providers. There were some positives for community education within the report. It recommended a non-statutory response to adult education through the independent management of AONTAS. From the 1980s onwards, AONTAS incorporated community education into their understanding of what adult education was and continue to advance the profile of community education in Ireland to this day. *The Murphy Report* also suggested an adult education section within the Department of Education from which Adult Education Organisers (AEOs) were appointed in each VEC in 1979. Some AEOs worked alongside volunteers and became actively involved in setting up independent community-based organisations, some of which were underpinned by a radical approach to education (Fleming 1989; Inglis et al. 1993). *The Murphy Report* was also the first time the State acknowledged some people's issues with reading and writing. However, it mostly limits this observation to rural populations therefore jarring with volunteer and VEC experiences in urban areas. Further research on literacy was suggested but no real change was offered in terms of funding or policy development (National Adult Literacy Agency 2010: 14–15). Research on literacy levels was subsequently undertaken by AONTAS and its findings ultimately led to the establishment of the National Adult Learning Agency (NALA) in the late 1970s.

A second government report followed in 1984 entitled *Lifelong Learning: Report on the Commission on Adult Education* and known as the *Kenny Report*. The *Kenny Report* (Commission on Adult Education 1984) brought further expansion by initiating Adult Education Boards and ring-fenced budgets for adult literacy and community education in each VEC. Further growth in VEC provision emerged through the Vocational Training and Opportunities Scheme (VTOS) introduced in 1988. Throughout the 1970s and the 1980s, the literacy movement continued to grow through the commitment of volunteers, paid adult literacy organisers and tutors within VECs. This work, which some other writers refer to as "basic adult education", was never properly resourced and a common subvention model was for paying participants within VECs to subsidise those unable to pay (Bassett et al. 1989). The uncertainty of this arrangement meant delivery varied from year to year.

A noteworthy injection of funding eventually came about as a result of the OECD-led *International Adult Literacy Survey Report* from which the Irish report was published by the Department of Education and Science in 1997. Twenty-five years after concerns about literacy were first muted in *The Murphy Report*, this research revealed the extent of the problem with one in four Irish adults estimated to have difficulty with simple literacy tasks. NALA (2010: 56–57) pinpoint this international study as a tipping point in evoking the political response that they had been advocating for many years claiming:

> This could not be ignored. Here was a major study from a respected international body, of adult literacy levels in sixteen countries, in which Ireland was in fifteenth place, second last to Poland. The findings were met with understandable shock on the part of Ireland's political establishment and, embarrassing as they were, also garnered a great deal of media attention. The OECD findings were later credited with prompting a dramatic increase in the new government's commitment to tackling adult literacy, reflected in both increased levels of funding and in policy developments.

Writing in 2006, therefore almost ten years after the OECD report, Bailey gives an indication of the extent of adult literacy services delivered from 135 VEC locations across each VEC. She lists 5,500 literacy tutors, 4,000 of whom were volunteers and describes their work as a combination of one-to-one supports, group work, programmes targeted at those who are unemployed, workplace literacy support, as well as programmes within prisons, community sector organisations and VEC-managed Traveller Training Centres (Bailey 2006: 26).

A key argument I am making is that, although funded by and organised through the State, the growth of VEC evening classes and literacy supports were commonly jump-started by unpaid grass-roots effort on the ground, much of which was by women, as well as through the involvement of some religious congregations (Carey 1979). As a result of these combined efforts, a number of independent community education organisations[4] emerged outside of the structures of the VECs. Some of these groups entered into specific grant-aid programmes, such as the community development programme discussed later in this chapter. Others survived on a combination of allocated tutor hours from VECs, charitable donations and once off grants including grants from the government Department of Social Welfare.

Further consolidation of VEC provision emerged as a result of *Learning for Life: White Paper on Adult Education* (DOES 2000). This policy document led to the appointment of dedicated Community Education Facilitators (CEFs) in the early 2000s and introduced the Back to Education Initiative (BTEI) in 2002. By 2003, CEFs were in place and public provision of community education appeared to be in reasonably good shape. AONTAS (2004: 11) note "a warm welcome . . . to the recognition of community education" within government policy which acknowledges its importance in reaching "participants in disadvantaged settings, in pioneering new approaches to teaching and learning in non-hierarchical, community-based settings [and] in taking the lived experiences of the participants as a starting point". Such openness to alternative approaches to education gave CEFs and others within VECs the freedom to openly adopt political approaches to community education. To share some examples, in 2009, the Kildare VEC described community education as "an approach that operates along a continuum from Personal Development to Community Development to Social Analysis and Political Participation" (Co. Kildare VEC 2009: 2). Similarly, the Waterford VEC in their publication *Building on the Strengths Community Education in Waterford City a snapshot* (which has no publication date) describes community education as a Freirean[5] process that is "revolutionary in terms of empowering the participants to develop a critical awareness of the world and power structures of the world" (p. 20). In the same document, the Waterford VEC emphasise the importance of close working relationships with allies in the community sector. You may also recall from Chapter 1 that the Community Education Facilitators Association (CEFA) also takes a critical approach to community education describing it as "rooted in the Freirean process of dialogue, reflection and action" hoping to "empower participants with the skills, knowledge and collective analysis to challenge oppression and to engage in action to bring about change" (CEFA 2011: 2). Upholding this philosophy is not always easy, with McGlynn (2012: 122–127) noting how CEFs can feel hamstrung by an ontological mismatch with their employer's individualist framework, and their own interpretation of their role as custodians of social justice models of practice.

WOMEN'S COMMUNITY EDUCATION

Separating out a history of women's community education again starts in the 1970s and 1980s, a time when women were those most likely to access the adult education courses on offer within VECs (Bassett et al. 1989: 58). Often, this was to compensate for limited school experiences. Many girls left after their primary exams whilst those to continue into secondary school received an instructional and domestically oriented education (Cullen 1987; Harford 2005). This domesticating focus often continued within early day-time VEC courses, many of which were organised by men (Slowey 1979; Bassett et al. 1989). However, during the 1980s and the 1990s, there was a growth in adult daytime programmes that were *for* women and *by* women. These programmes mostly survived on local fundraising and piece-meal grants (AONTAS 2004: 9) as women set about taking control of their own learning. Bottom-up women's community education confronted the domes-ticating nature of previous community education through its economic and patriarchal analysis in safe, supportive and self-managed environments (Tobin 1989; Connolly 2001, 2003, 2005, 2014).

Global context matters as this activism emerged amidst the second wave of feminism and the wider global civil rights movements of the 1960s and 1970s. As well as a period of civil rights activism in Ireland, this was also a period of political and sectarian conflict that included an armed violent struggle in Northern Ireland which is commonly referred to as "the troubles". The resurgent republicanism of this time included a strong feminist strand and acted as a catalyst for the republic of Ireland's women's movement and the formation of the Irish Women's Liberation Movement (Smyth 1988: 332). This radical feminist group were to have a lasting impact on the status of women in Ireland. Smyth (1988: 335) gives us an insight into their influence when she recounts their appear-ance on a popular television show in the early 1970s.

On 6 March 1971, when the controversial TV chat show, The Late Late Show, devoted an entire programme to the Women's Liberation Movement. The effect was electric. The I.W.L.M. women on the panel raised hitherto unspoken issues and taboo topics for women (indeed every-one) in Ireland on a range of social and sexual matters – unmarried mothers, working mothers, the "helpless dependency of the Irish wife," the miseducation of girls, social conditioning and so on, June Levine recounts that a "free for-all screaming match" took place. The issue of liberation had been well and truly raised and placed on the social and political agenda. Women's silence would never be quite as absolute as it had been. (Smyth 1988: 335)

Other significant milestones included the creation of *Council for the Status of Women* (CSW) in 1973. The CSW (which later changed its name to the National Women's Council of Ireland) was a voluntary organisation that was set up by a group of feminists whose goal was to gain equality for women in Ireland. The same year as the CSW emerged, the marriage bar was lifted; a stipulation that forced women who were employed by the civil service to resign on marriage. One year later, the first report from the Commission on the Status of Women (1974) was published because of pressure from a female working group within Fianna Fail, one of the country's leading political parties (Connolly 2002: 112).

Whilst the women's movement was certainly active in the 1970s, the level of visibility it gave women did not automatically extend into the lives of working-class women. Community education often acted as a bridge between the perceived middle-class nature of the Irish women's move-ment and the lives of working-class women. One research participant in this study exemplifies this perspective when she shares her experiences from the 1980s. She recalls her support for the actions of the CSW but was uncomfortable about how representative they were of her own cir-cumstances. As both a participant and organiser of women's community education, she found spaces that related more to her life and that deliber-ately set out to challenge the domesticating community education she had previously encountered.

> It was really about how women were managed in society and men as well, because there was a lot of unemployment, so it was how society valued you and where was the voice, *your* voice being heard. I would have been very critical of the Council for the Status of Women at the time because most of them spoke, okay people's pay and conditions, what-ever the issues were, but I suppose they were good, but the way they were speaking it didn't relate to my life [...] so we started to look at social studies, we started to look at health, why was women's health being ignored? (Interviewee two)

She relays a "no class without crèche" rule, a common policy within women's community education at the time, and a significant feature in expanding equality of participation. She also describes a democratic approach to education where:

> we could decide what to learn, who we wanted to have in, and it's funny because it became very political very quickly [classes were] really about learning the language and the analysis ... it was only when you start to talk to other women and analyse it you could see that it was the way society and patriarchy and [how] the system was working that you were unhappy with.

Consciousness-raising adult learning groups were not unique to Ireland as second-wave feminism took gender equality in a new direction through its epistemological challenge to mainstream knowledge (Ramazonoglu 1989; Connolly 2003). However, by the late 1980s, the women's movement in Ireland was in crisis. This was largely due to failed campaigns to legalise divorce and abortion, and a strongly negative portrayal of feminism within popular culture (Smyth 1988; Mullins 1991; Taylor 1998). Writing in 1987, Smyth (1988: 340) shares:

> It is difficult now for feminists in Ireland to avoid a sense of disillusionment and demoralisation – and therefore, a difficult period to write about with any degree of equanimity. We know now that the encounters of the 1970s over contraception, rape, equal pay were mere skirmishes, a phoney war, prior to the battles of the 1980s against the serried ranks of church and state, staunch defenders of the Faith of our Fathers and the myth of motherhood. The litany of defeats, and of victims – some known, the vast majority unnamed and nameless – is shocking.

Smyth (1988: 341) concludes her important chronology of the women's movement in Ireland on a hopeful note where "women's education and study groups-self-directed for the most part have developed with remarkable speed since 1984/5".

This growth in women's community education was, in part, resourced by the New Opportunities for Women (NOW) programme (1989), an EU initiative designed to promote equality in education and employment. In 1992, AONTAS began accessing NOW funding and offered training, support and lobbying for women's groups who were also funded by NOW. This was a change in direction for AONTAS who had previously focused much of their attention on adult and community education delivered through VECs. Indicative of the cultural backlash to feminism of the time, Brady (2003: 69) reports how "in the process [AONTAS] encountered a great deal of resistance to women's education from policy and decision makers as well as many of its own statutory members". This resistance included attempts by some members to block women's community groups from becoming members, an action that "almost split the organisation [AONTAS] in two" (Brady 2003: 69). Brady tells us this was overcome through the dynamism of the women involved who were driven by the notion of women organising and determining their own learning opportunities.

As well as NOW, other revenue streams were the National Women's Education Initiative (WEI) (1998), and the Equality for Women measure 2010–2014, a gender equality initiative part funded by the European Union (EU) social fund.[6] In 2002, the National Collective of Community-Based Women's Networks (NCCWN) was formed, a feminist organisation that describes its members as grass-roots local community development and women's groups. When reviewing the work of the NCCWN, Pillinger (2011) describes its formation as something that "consolidated many years of informal feminist networking and information sharing in the women's community sector dating back to the 1990s". The same report lists 23 network members each with their own membership of between 6 and 70 local women's groups (Pillinger 2011: 9–10).

THE SPREAD OF IDEAS THROUGH TRAINING FOR TRANSFORMATION

Another dimension of community education is through the TfT movement. This was largely initiated by members of religious congregations (again often women) who were involved in overseas development work that was influenced by liberation theology. Many subsequently resigned from religious service.[7] The Irish story starts with personal connections between members of the Irish Missionary Union and the Kenyan-based critical educators Anne Hope and Sally Timmel who authored the *Training for Transformation* series of workbooks. Originally published in 1985, these books described the work of the Delta Training Programme in Kenya which began in 1973. The Delta Project identified five influencing prongs in educational development work; Paulo Freire's approach to consciousness raising and praxis, human relations training in group work, organisational development, social analysis, and spiritual influences most notably the Christian concept of transformation (Hope and Timmel 1995: 14). As punishment for the political nature of her work, Anne Hope's South African passport was confiscated by government authorities. One of Hope's grandparents was Irish and this allowed her to apply for an Irish passport and to visit Ireland in 1978, 1981 and 2000.[8] On her second visit, Hope facilitated the first complete Irish TfT workshop. Half of the 36 participants on this TfT programme worked within education, healthcare, pastoral work and community development in Ireland, the remainder were involved in development work overseas (Naughton 2002: 10). Naughton (2002: 230) describes how this course had a profound effect on participants, introducing them to "a whole new way of working with people" that was highly participative and a translation of the theories and ideas of educationalist Paulo Freire into a working methodology. A core group Partners in Mission was formed from this initial process, its name indicative of connections with members of the Catholic Church (Naughton 2002: 231). Over the next ten years, over 400 practitioners working in community settings were to complete TfT programmes. Many TfT graduates led out their own programmes extending the influence of Hope and Timmel's approach across Ireland. Partners in Mission eventually split into two groups; Partners TfT a non-denominational organisation and Partners in Faith which retains a Catholic focus both of which remain active today. Partners TfT continue to deliver workshops nationwide and the influence of this approach has been acknowledged across the sector (Powell and Geoghegan 2004: 178).

Liberation theologians were influential elsewhere also. The Community Action Network (est. 1986) was set up with the help of funding from the Jesuit Solidarity Fund (JSF). The JSF outlined its strategic objectives as influenced by direct experience of liberation theology in Latin America claiming it "eschewed the traditional 'charity' model of community development" and instead stressed the need for an integrated approach based on "the development of individual and interpersonal relationships and transformation of the structures with which people have to engage" (Jesuits in Ireland 2012: 1).

THE WIDER COMMUNITY DEVELOPMENT/ANTI-POVERTY MOVEMENT

It is difficult to pinpoint the exact origins of a wider *community sector*, with some questioning whether a range of civil society groups can indeed constitute a sector in itself (Ó Cinnéide 1998/99: 49; Collins 2002: 96–97; Powell and Geoghegan 2004: 119). There was certainly a mushrooming of community activism following the global unrest of the 1960s and 1970s. Part-time evening courses, the literacy movement, women's community education and the TfT movement intersected with a wider foray of bottom-up community development including mobilisations in response to poor housing, anti-drugs initiatives and an active movement against unemployment (Cullen 1994: 31–37). Again context matters and historical accounts of the community development movement link it to wider European activism (Crickley and Devlin 1989) and a bottom-up politicised anti-Thatcher movement in the UK (Craig et al. 2008).

The history of community development in Ireland is sometimes linked to the actions of Muintir Na Tíre in the 1940s and 1950s, a rural enterprise with strong links to the Catholic Church (Lee 2003: 49; Lloyd and Lloyd-Hughes 2009: 29). It was not until the 1980s that politically motivated self-managed community groups emerged (including the women's groups already reported on). The core purpose of these groups was not to fill the gap of inadequate local services, but was to challenge the unequal status quo (Crickley and Devlin 1989; Kelleher and Whelan 1992; Cullen 1994). These organisations carried certain guiding principles: participation in decision-making, collective action, an agenda of social change towards equality, an anti-poverty approach and an emphasis on process as well as outcome (Motherway 2006: 2–3).

Some of these groups managed to secure funding through the EU *poverty 1* and *poverty 2* programmes of the 1980s. Although this backing enabled voluntarily run community groups to become more robust, there was also a tension between the collectivised approach of the emerging community development movement and the EU poverty programme's focus on change through a self-help philosophy (Curley 2007: 10). In the same decade, the Combat Poverty Agency Act (1986) established the Combat Poverty Agency (CPA) whose function was to offer an analysis on poverty (Office of the Attorney General 1986). Initially, the CPA was asked to oversee the Community Development Fund (est. 1991) – a domestic programme put in place to ensure continued funding for groups supported by the earlier EU poverty programmes (Lloyd 2010: 46). This second function was never really enacted and public grants were managed instead by Area Development Management (ADM) a quasi-autonomous State-established organisation that managed social inclusion budgets. The most significant public grant aid was through the Community Development Programme, the strength of which was the autonomy it gave to successful applicants. To explain, the first step in becoming a Community Development Project (CDP) was for a local group to come together and to analyse local issues. This group would then draw up a detailed work plan on how they would address these issues. This plan was submitted to the overseeing government department for approval and, if successful, funding was given to the projects themselves and were administered by local voluntary boards of management. Some direction was given as to how budgets were to be spent as each project was instructed to employ one full-time and one part-time worker. Outside of this, there was autonomy given to these boards of management and therefore to the communities themselves. Despite this freedom for communities to self-determine, the Combat Poverty Agency expressed concern that the community development programme lacked a sufficient analysis of the issues it sought to address and argued that it was unclear about the anticipated outcomes for community development (Cullen 1994: 4). This did not stop an expansion of the Community Development Programme and between 1990 and 2009 the number of CDPs incrementally grew from 15 to 185 projects.

Sometimes the work of these CDPs is presented as somewhat homogenous and as a closely connected entity. In reality, the Community Development Programme was a catch all for a range of community initiatives. Some groups did not strictly fit with programme objectives but were motivated by access to money for staff and premises (Brady 2003: 69). There were also ideological variations. These were measured by extensive research by Fred Powell and Martin Geoghegan carried out in 2004. Powell and Geoghegan (2004) uncovered a range of personal motivators for community workers including a desire to care for others, a personal involvement in politics and for religious reasons. These researchers measured a majority leaning towards individualism with a minority of practitioners influenced by radical perspectives concluding "community development appears then to be firmly rooted in liberal, humanistic values, with an emphasis on the value, capacity and worth of individuals, rather than the explicitly radical collective ones" (Powell and Geoghegan 2004: 157).

Another feature of the Community Development Programme, and one which again emphasises heterogeneity was the way these CDPs were able to leverage other EU and domestic grant aid. During the 2000s, many CDPs were administering funds that were substantially larger than their core government contribution. These funds often included return to work initiatives through FÁS community employment schemes as well as grants to develop childcare facilities in areas considered disadvantaged (Horgan 2001: 6). Some CDPs were also recipients of specialist funding for women's community education through the NOW programme.

Community Development Projects operated alongside a network of State-funded Family Resource Centres (FRCs), organisations that also ascribed to the principles of community development (Motherway 2006: ii). The FRC programme began in 1994 with 10 pilot projects. This pilot was extended and expanded and, by 2009, there were 107 FRCs across the country. Connections were not only at the grass roots

Table 3.1 Summary of project outputs in relation to participation in, and content of training and education and social awareness programmes (1996–1999) (Nexus 2002: 35)

Nature of output	Total nos. participating	Average nos. participating per year	Main target groups	Most common content
Training courses and programmes	4,321	33	Women, travellers, men, tenants	Estate management, health, community development
Social awareness programmes	2,112	23	Women, tenants	Community arts, communication, local democracy
Educational courses or programmes	1,206	15	Women, lone parents, travellers	Literacy, health and social care

as work of CDPs and FRCs was administratively combined to form the "Community Development Support Programme" whose reporting relationship was to the government Department for Social, Community and Family Affairs (DSCF). In 2002, the DSCF asked Nexus, a not-for-profit research collective with close connections to the community sector, to carry out a review of the Community Development Support Programme. This review revealed the extent to which these programmes were engaged in community education detailing how "all projects are involved, to a greater or lesser extent, in delivering training, educational or social awareness programmes within their own communities" (Nexus 2002: 33). A summary of type and participation on these programmes is provided within the evaluation report and is repeated below (Table 3.1).

More recent information on the work of FRCs again confirms that community education is a central focus. The Family Support Agency/ Family Resource Centre National Forum joint publication *Impact of Family Resource Centres in Ireland* (which has no publication date) highlights the work of FRCs during 2009 and documents "education and training" as its first activity along with counselling, information and other supports to families across the country. They quantify education and training as follows, "16,642 participants completed educational courses in FRCs in 2009, 13,710 participants completed training courses directly related to employment opportunities or gaining employment, 8,573 participants completed self-development courses".

By 2008, a rich national network of community education, community services and local activism had evolved that employed 53,098 people (Harvey 2012: 21). The introductory chapter to this book detailed a downsizing of the community sector and positioned this within a neoliberal socio-economic context. The reasons for, and implications of these mergers is the focus of much discussion within Chapter 5. For the moment it is enough to detail how this downsizing began with the forced merger of the Local Area Partnerships (LAPs) and the absorption of the Community Development Programme into these LAPs to form the Local and Community Development Project (LCDP) (est. 2013). The independence held by CDPs, however tenuous, was effectively lost at this time as many local boards of management were dissolved. A small number of CDPs managed to remain outside of this process, some of which remained autonomous. Projects working specifically with women's groups were united under the umbrella of the NCCWN, whilst CDPs working specifically with the Traveller population were united under the Traveller advocacy and support organisation Pavee Point. Further downsizing followed soon after through the competitive Social Inclusion Community Activation programme (SICAP).

Another strand of activism I have not yet captured is through grass-roots responses to problematic drug use, particularly within Dublin communities. One early example, the Youth Action Project (YAP) (est. 1981), explicitly linked its work to radical community education philosophies (McCann 1991). YAP was one of a number of community organisations that nurtured resistance to the medicalisation of addiction and rehabilitation interpreting problematic drug use as a consequence of a person's socio-economic contexts (Butler 2007; O'Brien 2007). Volunteer-led addiction support organisations continued to emerge throughout the 1980s and into the 1990s including the Ana Liffey Drugs Project (est. 1982). In 1995, a grass-roots mass meeting of activists and local representatives led to the formation of Citywide, a campaign and network organisation committed to the principles of community development (Rourke 2005: 7). One year later, there was a substantial influx of State funding through the policy document the *First Report of the Ministerial Task Force on the Measures to Reduce the Demand for Drugs* (1996), or *The Rabbitte Report*[9] as it is commonly called. Butler (2007) explains how the thinking behind this report was twofold. On the one hand, the government sought to address a growing heroin epidemic that was linked to serious crime. On the other hand, they sought to respond to growing bottom-up demands within communities to address a situation that was leading to the deaths of many young people. *The Rabbitte Report* acknowledged a structural dimension to drug use and recognised the need for complex responses. It identified 13 "black spots" where local supports were provided through newly established Local Drugs Task Forces. All of these designated areas were urban and 12 of the 13 black spots were in Dublin. This resulted in a rural/urban divide in funding opportunities despite the likelihood that addiction, especially alcohol addiction, was likely to be having devastating affects outside of these urban areas also.

Much of the funding channelled through these task forces went to CDPs, unsurprising when you think about their strong connections in these areas and the way many CDPs had already been incorporating responses to drug use into their work. Citywide entered into the Community Development Support Programme[10] in 1997 and, over the next ten years, worked with over 70 community groups encouraging them to adopt community development responses to drugs issues (Rourke 2005). Some of these projects offered Freirean-influenced community education,[11] other projects offered one-to-one and group counselling, harm reduction and other supports as determined by the needs of its target group.

THE INVOLVEMENT OF THE ACADEMY

For many years community education in Ireland has incorporated substantial involvement of individuals and departments within some universities. Three community-university partnerships in particular stand out. The first of these is the involvement of the Department of Adult and Community Education (est. 1975), at St Patricks College, Co. Kildare (now Maynooth University). Close collaborative relationships were forged between staff at Maynooth and local groups, particularly in Kildare and Dublin but also nationwide. Connolly (2014: 53) explains how these groups were already established, or were in the process of being established by women who were local to the area. Sometimes these fledgling groups were supported by Adult Education Officers (AEOs) in VECs who acted as a conduit between the groups and the university. Crucially, university staff did not occupy an academic – practitioner model where the former theorises the latter from afar. Instead academics were deeply embedded in practice recruiting for and facilitating programmes alongside volunteers and community sector staff.

In 1986, staff at Maynooth asked a Tallaght-based women's group to organise an International women's day conference at Maynooth and to invite
other women's groups who were also undertaking university-accredited
extramural certificates in women's studies. Maynooth University also offered
support to community educators within VECs and in the wider literacy
movement. This included working with CEFs in naming and shaping their
functions and maintaining close working relationships with both AONTAS
and NALA.

A second example of university-community partnerships was through
access work within University College Dublin (UCD). The Women's
Studies Community Outreach Programme at UCD was particularly congruent with the principles and practices of community education. Quilty
(2003) explains how these programmes were much more than simply
relocating the institution, but embodied an approach to education that
centralised the lived experience of participants and celebrated the knowledge and talents they bring.

It was not only Maynooth University and UCD that were pioneering in
the emergence of university-community partnerships. Educators based at
the Waterford Institution of Technology (WIT), a higher education institution in the South-East of Ireland, forged close working relationships
with women's community groups in the 1990s (D'Alton et al. 2010). In
2000, WIT entered into a partnership agreement with the Access 2000
programme which was funded by NOW. This enabled a consortium of
women's groups to develop the WIT-accredited National Certificate in
Community Education and Development. This programme was locally
delivered across the South-East and many midlands counties of Ireland.
Befitting the principles of community education, a 2004 evaluation of the
programme determined:

> Participants felt that they had benefitted considerably from the group-based
> mutual learning and shared experiences. The delivery methods also created
> an environment in which there was a reduction in the distinctions between
> the "teacher" and the "taught". Given the participatory nature of the
> learning, the emphasis was on drawing from participants' own knowledge
> and experience, which in turn had the effect of creating a shared learning
> space, considered a facilitated style of education rather than the traditional
> teacher/student relationship. (D'alton et al. 2010: 84)

In the 2000s, another Institute of Technology (IT), Carlow IT entered
into partnership with a long-standing community education organisation

called An Cosán. This now established collaboration continues to deliver higher education awards through community education for residents in West Dublin.

In summary, distinguishable yet overlapping historical trajectories can be drawn out. These are ideologically connected through their interpretation of community education as equality based. Table 3.2 synopsises historical connections between public and community providers.

Table 3.2 Connections between the community sector and public provision

Timeline	Community sector	Public provider	Overlap/relationships
Early–mid-1900s	Rural-based voluntary organisations inc. Macra Na Feirme, the Irish Housewives Association and the Irish Country Woman's association	Extramural college courses esp. from within UCC	
1960s–1980s	Literacy education initiatives influenced by the UK right to read campaign, ongoing emergence of local groups especially women's community groups	Locally based VEC centres and community schools providing programmes. Some local literacy services introduced	*Literacy movement dependent on collaboration between voluntary organisations and VEC paid tutor hours*
1975–1979	Ongoing emergence of locally based independent community organisations	Department of Adult and Community Education founded within St Patrick's College, Maynooth Adult Education Officers appointed (AEOs)	*Support from individual AEOs in establishing some community groups especially women's groups*
1980s–1990s 1988–1989	Women's groups funded through the EU NOW	Extramural women's studies certificates from Maynooth university Vocational Training and Opportunities Scheme (VTOS) FAS is formed from which Community	*Continued support from some AEOs who linked with staff at Maynooth and with groups in disadvantaged communities AONTAS acted as a bridge between VEC employees and*

(continued)

Table 3.2 (continued)

Timeline	Community sector	Public provider	Overlap/relationships
1990–2013 1992–2015 1994– present 1996– present	Community Development Projects Local Area Partnerships Family Resource Centres (FRCs) Addiction projects through Ministerial Taskforce on measures to reduce demand for Drugs	Training Workshops emerged Adult literacy scheme extended	*community groups involved with NOW Support/guidance from some academics often through strong relationships with past students and accreditation for community sector organisations Funding of tutors within CDPs and FRCs by VECs Independent practitioners operating across both provider groups*
2002– present	Nexus Evaluation revealing the extent of community education practice in the community sector	Community Education Facilitators (CEFs) BTEI	*Strong relationships between some CEFs, AOEs, ETB tutors and the Community Sector*

RESEARCH FINDINGS ON CONTEMPORARY COMMUNITY EDUCATION

To this point, a history of community education has linked practitioners through a shared understanding of practice and not their employer type. This assertion is also supported through the way community educator self-selected in this study. Survey findings also tell us more about the characteristics of community education. This begins with the types of organisations the n219 surveyed educators are working for (Table 3.3).

The account above measures how the majority of respondents (49%) work within the community sector, most prominently within the Local and Community Development Programme (LCDP). Thirty-one percent work within VECs (now merged within Education and Training Boards, or ETBs) with the highest single cohort of VEC/ETB employees describing

Table 3.3 Types of organisation participating practitioners work for

Organisational type	
Community Sector Organisations	49% (n108)
– Local and Community Development Programme	(n38)
– Family Resource Centre	(n16)
– Independent organisation with multiple funders	(n37)
– Community Development Projects not merged into the LCDP	(n7)
– Addiction related projects	(n2)
– Network organisations	(n1)
– Voluntary groups	
VECs/ETBs	31% (n67)
– As tutors	(n39)
– As community Education Facilitators	(n22)
– As adult literacy tutors	(n3)
– As Adult Education Organisers	(n2)
– Within a secondary school	(n1)
Higher Education Institutions	5% (n11)
Non-governmental Organisations	4% (n9)
Other State Providers	1% (n3)
– Health Service Executive	(n1)
– FAS	(n2)
Others (inc. private provider)	4% (n8)
Independent Practitioners	6% (n13)
Total	**100% (n219)**

themselves as tutors. Extensive connections between those working in VECs/ETBs (public provision) and those in community sector organisations are evident through 41% of VEC/ETB tutors who (through additional textual information) locate their work within community sector organisations. Similarly, over half of independent practitioners situate their work within the community sector. Through qualitative contributions others explain how they were previously employed in community sector organisations but have lost their job due to budget cuts.

Four percent identify their work as within NGOs. Although some NGOs have been involved for many years, this is often less acknowledged within historical accounts. Housing Associations, national children's charities, lone-parents advocacy groups, national Traveller organisations and organisations principally involved in overseas development work are just some examples of NGOs that incorporate locally based adult educational programmes within their activities. This latter cohort have been particularly influential in advancing what is known as *development education*, an equality-led approach to education that nurtures critical capacities so that people can evaluate their world in a way that incorporates a global perspective.

Not everyone who participates in this study is happy about the way community education is structured. One survey respondent who not only works within public provision but also has experience working in the community sector also argues:

> I would like to make the point that the structure of the VEC is not conducive to a flexible and responsive community education provision. Also, that the new "outcomes-based" approach being pushed by all funders at the moment is unrealistic and may, unfortunately, lead to the devaluing of learning which is not readily measured. (Survey respondent, tutor VEC/ETB)

As the quote below will demonstrate, her assertion is not an isolated opinion.

> State agencies are not always the natural choice of those most removed from education within their local communities. (Survey respondent, community sector)

This educator above believes that the community sector has more authentic community connections because of a strong outreach approach, a practice she perceives as absent from VECs/ETBs. This assertion fits with historical accounts of community education where extensive and slow-burning outreach built trust in communities and encouraged people to enter into community education spaces for the first time (AONTAS 2004: 23).

Network Connections Amongst Practitioners

Figure 3.1 draws out network connections between surveyed practitioners.

The first thing you will notice about the figure above is that many community educators are members of more than one network. The largest network affiliation is to the AONTAS Community Education Network (CEN) (est. 2007). This network specifically networks providers outside of ETBs therefore those within the community sector including independent community education providers and NGOs. The AONTAS CEN takes

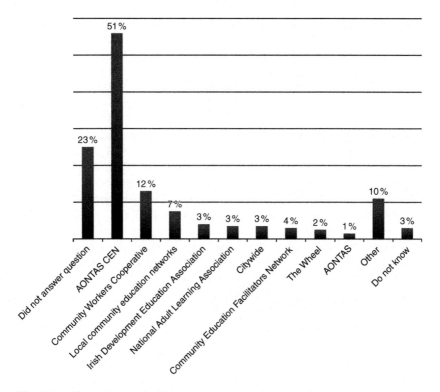

Fig. 3.1 Network membership amongst research respondents

an overtly political approach to its work through its vow to secure a distinct funding stream for community education, its dedication to raising the profile of community education and its pledge to critically evaluate practice on an ongoing basis (AONTAS CEN 2008: 2). The second most prevalent network affiliation is to the Community Workers Cooperative (CWC now called Community Work Ireland, est. 1981) a national membership organisation that supports community work as a way to address poverty, exclusion and inequality. Twenty three percent of AONTAS CEN members are also members of Community Work Ireland.

Other network organisations' include the already named Community Education Facilitators Network (which links publically employed CEFs), NALA (est. 1980), Citywide (est.1995) and the Irish Development Education Organisation (IDEA est. 2005). Eight percent of those surveyed cite membership of local community education networks, over half of whom cite the Limerick Community Education Network (LCEN) (est. 1992). "Others" represent Crosscare (a Catholic social support agency est. 1941), Partners TfT (est. 2002), the Irish Men's Shed Movement (est. 2011), trade unions, the Spectacle of Defiance and Hope (est. 2009), the National Collective of Women's Community-Based Organisations (est. 2002) and the Cork-based Social and Health Education Project (SHEP, est. 1974).

When the benefits of network membership are considered, this prevalence of network membership is not unexpected. Newer practitioners get to meet with, and learn from, those who are more experienced. There is often also free education and up-skilling (or continuous professional development) on offer, something that is particularly beneficial to those on precarious employment contracts (see Chapter 7 for more discussion). Network organisations also provide a sense of professional identity. This can be especially welcome in the absence of strong trade union presence or a legally enforced regulatory body such as the Teaching Council of Ireland for teachers or An Bord Altranais for nurses.

Conversely, there can be difficulties with network membership. These include the struggles practitioners often face in finding time to attend network meetings, something some survey respondents and focus-group members could relate to. This is captured in focus group the contribution below.

> I mean the CEN is great, but it can be so difficult to actually get out, to make that time because we are all so constrained by "we all have to do so much more with less" I think we have to really try and make that effort that we come together because we will be so much stronger if we are together. Literally we can be crying in the wilderness. (Central-Dublin, participant two)

There are other problems with networks. Large organisations can dominate membership as can those in management positions within these organisations. This can marginalise educators at the coal face who have the strongest connection to communities. Some network members can also be seen to carry more power than others given their wider cultural status. This can be said when universities are network members as they can be seen as being more important even when they are one step removed from events on the ground. Networks can also self-assume a leadership role. This role may carry esteem and credibility with policy-makers but this credibility may not be extended from the communities they purport to represent, who might not even be aware of their existence (a theme explored in Chapters 5 and 7).

Shared Examples of Practice

As well as uncovering information about community educator's place of work and their network involvement, specific examples of practice are also gathered. This was through the survey question – "Can you give an example of something you were recently involved with that best illustrates your approach to community education and the ideas underpinning it?" The response rate for this question dropped to 69% (n151 responses).

Specific population groups are named as gender-based groups; both female and male, those who are unemployed, those with drug and alcohol problems, young adults, Travellers, new migrant communities, people in poor housing, rural groups, urban groups, parents, people hoping to access higher education, people who are retired, people with intellectual disabilities and people living in disadvantaged communities. Fifty-seven percent identify their work as urban based with 33% based in both urban and rural settings. Ten per cent work exclusively in rural settings.

The types of programmes being delivered are quantified in Table 3.4. Textual examples shared have been divided into whether or not each example of practice were principally about supporting individuals, about creating critical educational spaces, about up-skilling for unemployment, about collectively acting on external events, about developing local services or about supporting educational progression.

Table 3.4 Examples of practice quantified

Support the personal needs of individuals	n76	50%
Creating critical classrooms	n32	21%
Up-skilling for employment	n13	9%
Collective actions on external circumstances	n14	9%
Support the development of local services previously unavailable	n10	7%
Educational progression	n6	4%
Totals	**n151**	**100%**

Survey question: Can you give an example of something you were recently involved with that best illustrates your approach to community education and the ideas underpinning it?

Typical examples of the courses categorised as "supporting the personal needs of an individual", are life-skills education, personal development programmes and general studies. The impacts of these programmes are captured by one account of a celebration of multiple individual achievements as part of "Adult Learners Week".

> Certificate presentations to learners, presentation of work completed and success stories reinforced that the learner is central in all this, that underpinning all community education must be enjoyment of learning and just how much a two hour a week class can change someone's life. (Survey respondent, CEF, VEC/ETB)

There are accounts of parent-support programmes some of which are about supporting the day-to-day challenges of parenting and some of which are described as about building the confidence and self-worth of parents so that they can in turn improve their capacity to engage with staff at their children's school. Another theme is women-led early parent support groups particularly ones that begin through breast-feeding support. Sometimes these groups are described as fulfilling a wider function by promoting a certain approach to parenting. Parent support work is not confined to the community sector. At the other end of the parenting spectrum, one CEF tells us about:

> Inter-agency work with a group of parents who were in difficulty with the courts because of children not attending school...the joint collaboration worked very well (Survey respondent, CEF, VEC/ETB).

There are computer classes. Sometimes these are designed to enhance communication between Irish-based parents and adult children who have emigrated and sometimes they are part of literacy supports. One FRC delivered a workshop is on cyber bullying, an example that gives us a sense of how some initiatives extend beyond the classroom walls delivering tangible outcomes for a wider cohort. The research participant explains:

> A few members of the group got together and organised a Family Communication course for parents in the school. They organised funding and got the group going in no time (Survey respondent, community sector).

There is an accredited programme for lone parents and work within an FRC that draws from public funding through the Back to Education

Initiative (BTEI) to deliver an accredited "general learning programme". There are also health and fitness classes, cookery, art, music poetry, drama and, in an FRC, work with Travellers where these participants built their own traditional wagon. One singing class that is organised by a women's network is described like this:

> I facilitate a women's singing group, where I teach songs and basic music theory. I have a very diverse group of women with varying degrees of disadvantage. Within that group there is tremendous solidarity. Friendships have been made that have changed the lives of participants. Some who have come from domestic violence situations, suffered from depression, racial discrimination etc. have found the strength and confidence to bridge that gap between isolation and personal development in the form of further education or self-employment. (Survey respondent, community sector)

In another art-based initiative the excerpt below details work within an addiction project.

> We created a book of poetry. The participants had never written poetry before but wanted to write a song (which we did as well). So we started writing poetry and then processed learning and personal development through poetry. They put it together in a book and made it freely available in the community. One of the poems was read at a national gathering. (Survey respondent, community sector)

Commonly, the tutors involved in supporting personal needs describe providing supports over and above traditional expectations. These are greater attempts to enhance cross-cultural communication, additional supports to those with learning disabilities, extra tuition time, waving fees and literacy supports.

Over one-fifth (21%) of practice has been categorised as examples of creating critical classrooms. This is where programmes overtly set out to deliver equality-based, social justice and human rights work. Examples include citizenship workshops, voter education, intercultural work and anti-discrimination work. Again, instances emerge across VECs/ETBs, the community sector, NGOs and through the involvement of higher education institutions (HEIs) as well as collaborations between organisations. One educator shares work which was funded by the VEC/ETB but delivered from within a community sector organisation. The aim of the project was "to teach old school games to children in their local primary school" and in doing so, offer an analysis on the changing nature of play. The participating group was described as parents from an urban "disadvantaged" community. The educator explains:

> they want to show the children how to play the games that they themselves used to play as children...the parents have identified many potential benefits to this project including the promotion of active play in the school yard [and], the promotion of multi-cultural play. (Survey respondent, community sector)

Another example, this time drawn from an interview conversation, is of a workshop for members of the Roma community which is described like this:

> A couple of weeks ago we ran a workshop in Dublin on the Roma community. We used development education methodologies to explore some of the issues that are confronting the Roma, using development education and participative learning, working in groups and in pairs and the world café methodology. The two trainers were people who have completed our course; they are both Romanian, very familiar with development education. (Interviewee seven, working in an NGO)

One community educator whose work is connected to the NCCWN gives us an example of global development education "where learners got the opportunity to make links locally and internationally in a positive space and encouraged discussion". Another community sector organisation also organised a series of workshops for women to come together and "evaluate their needs and strive to address these needs in a relaxed and friendly manner".

Within a VEC/ETB, we hear about close connections between community education and community development which captures collaborative learning and peer support, a negotiated curriculum and a facilitative approach to teaching. This respondent also hints at the difficulties when these principles collide with accreditation criteria, a point that is dealt with more thoroughly within Chapter 6. This tutor explains:

> I was asked to deliver a FETAC level 5 community development course to a group of learners/students from countries outside of Ireland...the first thing I did was ask them to write down what it was they wanted to learn

on the course and I then presented them with the Learning Outcomes as described in the module. I then presented them with my idea of that course would be a good way for them to learn about community development as practiced by local Irish groups. We talked over the course and decided to use a blend of the three types of learning to create a course... this was a very unusual way for them to learn, normally the "teacher" would talk to the students and students would learn. Very soon they began to see the levels of learning they could gain from each other. I took my role as the facilitator of their discussions and interacted with them to bring an "Irish" perspective to their discussions. I did struggle to fulfil the requirements of the Module but that is another story. (Survey respondent, tutor VEC/ETB)

The influence of the TfT movement also remains palpable although its prominence has somewhat diminished. Three community sector organisations continue to deliver TfT programmes. Twice, this work is specific to women's groups. Other research participants within VECs and HEIs share examples of practice that include drawing from material designed by Partners, TfT.

When the focus of education is extended towards acting on external issues affecting people's lives (9%) there are stories of anti-racism initiatives and of attempts to address inadequate and poor housing conditions. There is opposition work to cuts to the community sector and attempts to build the capacities of people in leadership roles as part of community development work. There is a theatre production "revolution" chronicling the impacts of austerity as well as a number of accounts of gathering community grievances as part of the Books of Grievances and Hope project organised by the Spectacle of Defiance and Hope. Some shared instances of organising and participating in street protests. There is a Facebook campaign against welfare cuts for lone parents, campaigns about the rights of older people and an issue-based seminar where local politicians were invited to come listen to community grievances. One VEC/ETB tutor worked on a project that brought two urban-based women's groups together explains "the group then engaged in group work to identify the role of women in the community". Participants of this process took photographs that depicted women's role in society. These were then exhibited in the city centre as well as local to where the women lived. In other examples, peer-educators are up-skilled both within the Traveller community and the drug-using population.

Nine percent of examples are vocationally oriented namely childcare for crèche workers, peer training for community workers, return-to-work programmes and entrepreneurialism. One of these vocational programmes is for people who are long-term unemployed where participants:

> Use and interpret their own life experiences to become trainers, peer educators and community workers working particularly with disadvantaged groups (Survey respondent, community sector).

Seven percent of survey examples establish local services that did not previously exist. These are a local playgroup for children, community gardens, a new community-based computer class, a women's support group for dealing with suicide, a creative writing group that is linked to local library services, a local training centre and, on a number of occasions, men's sheds, meeting places where men come together and take on a variety of mutually agreed activities that are thought to enhance or maintain men's well-being.[12] Men's sheds emerge from CDPs and FRCs, with one participant explaining the process like this:

> It began as a computer and personal development course over the space of year the guys became a fully-fledged working men's committee. They held the first [names area] Men's Health Day, produced a calendar for 2013 and have acquired two buildings in the town where they have open a Men's Shed project – Brilliant stuff. (Survey respondent, community sector)

Other work with men brings another theme to the fore, where State funding for community education is manipulated to better suit the needs of a particular group. This theme will be picked up again within Chapter 5, for the moment this example of practices gives some context.

> I have recently been asked to develop a course for men . . . there are certain conditions that are required by funder but in an initial meeting with some men . . . the response was fairly clear in that most were fed up with being forced to participate in a course that had no real outcomes. During the discussion leadership qualities were emerging and through conversation with these men we were able to manipulate the funders desires and to create a programme that would develop other skills such as networking with other men's groups, creating a dedicated website and the production of e-zines that would be used to explore and highlight issues affecting men in similar situations. (Survey respondent, community sector)

Where practice has been quantified as about access to education (4%) there is assistance offered with university applications including information on welfare entitlements, support for progression within further education and a library-based taster course for third-level studies.

CONCLUSION

The purpose of this chapter was to illuminate the work of community educators in Ireland both historically and contemporarily. Community education's inauguration through local adult education initiatives, the women's movement, anti-poverty movements including anti-drugs initiatives and the influence of liberation theology remain palpable and heterogeneity continues to flourish.

This wide ranging information about the practice of community education demonstrates how, amidst variance and political inclination, an equality perspective is shared throughout practitioner accounts. This concurs with findings presented in Chapter 2 where the dominant interpretation of the purpose of the work is not one of employability. Instead these accounts centralise both individual and community wants and needs. This is contrary to the aspirations of neoliberal policy as nowhere amidst these many examples is there any sense that practitioners centralise national economic benefits. Community education therefore remains rooted in a needs-based over outputs-based approach to education.

Although this chapter showcases the work of community education, it is limiting in that it does not capture reports from practitioners about the many pressures they experience through the increasing restraints of contract agreements with neoliberal funders. This will be drawn more deliberately to the fore within part two of this book. Before this, Chapter 4 offers a deeper philosophical understanding of education and a more in-depth account of ideological tendencies in the field.

NOTES

1. The principal function of these VECs was to provide vocational education as an alternative to secondary school. Some years later, this was expanded to include delivery of secular education at secondary school.
2. Information about the programme is available through the website of National Centre for the study and learning of literacy http://www.ncsall.net/index.html@id=520.html. Accessed 18 December 2016.

3. The Simon Community, a charity that largely works with those who are homeless is also named by NALA.

4. Independent community education organisations emerged from this historical backdrop including the Cork-based Social and Health Education Project (SHEP) established in 1974, the Kilbarrack Local Education for Adult Renewal (KLEAR) established in North Dublin in 1980, the Shanty, established in South Dublin in 1985 and the Community and Family Training Agency which opened its doors in 1987. Information pertaining to when these organisations were established has been taken from each organisation's respective website. They are examples amongst many other organisations formed at the time.

5. Referring to the philosophies of Paulo Freire which are discussed in Chapter 4.

6. Twenty-three recipient organisations include organisations within the Local and Community Development Programme, network organisations, legal advice centres and other independent Community Sector organisations. Further details are available at https://www.pobal.ie/FundingProgrammes/EqualityFor WomenMeasure/Pages/default.Aspx. Accessed 20 February 2015.

7. The influence of liberation theology was not confined to Ireland. The Paris-based Ecumenical Institute for the Development of Peoples (INODEP) which was founded by Paulo Freire and had connections with the Kenyan Delta programme influenced a team of Church groups, community workers and NGOs to bring the ideas to Britain. This was through the establishment of the UK-based Freire Institute and followed this team's participation in Parisian-based workshops (http://www.freire.org/about/history/, Accessed 27 September 2014).

8. This information was provided through a conversation with a founding member of Partners, TfT who worked alongside Anne Hope and Sally Timmel within the Kenyan-based Delta Project and was involved in organising these Irish visits.

9. Thus named after the government minister responsible for its launch Pat Rabbitte.

10. As well as community development projects, the community development fund also funded a network of support agencies whose contract with the State involved providing support to allocated CDPs in preparing their work plans and working to the vision and ethos of their projects.

11. This included within my own place of work at the time, a women's community education project for those on methadone maintenance programmes that was within a CDP.

12. For more information see www.menssheds.ie. Accessed 18 December 2016.

CHAPTER 4

Critical Education and Community Education

Illustration 4.1 The limitations of humanistic approaches

© The Author(s) 2017
C. Fitzsimons, *Community Education and Neoliberalism*,
DOI 10.1007/978-3-319-45937-0_4

103

Some readers will be immediately interested in a chapter that is principally based around the philosophies of critical community education. Others might be less keen, especially those of you who are committed to more individualised, person-centred visions of adult education which are commonly associated with humanism. As this chapter will demonstrate, most community educators in this study identify with humanistic over critical philosophical perspectives. If you are not sure what these expressions mean, another function of this chapter is to explain both humanistic and critical approaches to community education. As a start, it can be helpful to think about humanistic adult education as a person-centred approach that supports individual change. Critical (or radical) education is a more collective approach that supports social and structural change. Both of these approaches can be revolutionary when they are compared to the way many spaces that are reserved for education can be devoid of both care and criticality.

Of course all community education should be led by the experiences, insights and aspirations of its participants and some of the dualism assumed between humanistic and critical approaches should be challenged. That said, there are important differences and, I will argue, drawbacks to humanistic approaches. This is because of humanism's separation of *the self* from the socio-economic and cultural context. Theories of critical education, or critical pedagogy as it is also termed, often incorporate an interrogation of humanism. Critiquing humanism does not mean abandoning its person-centred principles rather that a person's well-being and development should be politically understood. In this chapter, I will do this by drawing from the philosophies of Paulo Freire, but also from others who have contributed to Freirean thinking and who have developed these ideas. Through critical group work I also offer a working methodology for putting Freirean ideas into practice. One place to start is to think more deliberately about *learning*, a taken for granted assumption about which there is many different opinions.

THEORIES OF LEARNING

So what is learning? One way to think about it is as something that begins at birth and continues through life as we adapt to our surroundings and negotiate our position in the world. Rogers (2002: 46) maintains much learning is unintended and happens through everyday interactions such as our dealings with media sources, our chance encounters and by accident.

There are also more condensed periods of learning such as taking a course in a particular subject, reading a book like this, or as a result of an important life event such as having a baby or starting a new job. For most adult educators, the essence of learning is when such encounters result in a change in our perspective. Believing that learning is therefore *transformative* carries the assumption that each of us has a unique way of interpreting our experiences. This *constructivist* hypothesis claims that our culturally contextualised life events are principally thought to shape our knowledge (Mezirow 1978, 2000; Tennant 2005; Illeris 2009; Cranton and Taylor 2012). Some people challenge constructivism, expressing concerns about uncritical cultural relativity (Riana 2011) and that objective, scientifically verifiable knowledge can be under-appreciated. This tells us that constructivist notions of learning are not universally agreed. They are however extremely influential within adult and community education and resonate, to a greater or lesser extent, across alternate philosophical orientations. Constructivism influences *theories of transformative learning* such as those identified by Jack Mezirow (1978, 2000, 2012). They are also prominent within critically oriented contributions such as Paulo Freire's processes of *conscientisation* and *praxis* (Freire 1972) and bell hook's *engaged pedagogy* (hooks 2003). Constructivism equally holds currency within ideas about socially contextualised *experiential learning* (Dewey 1938/1997). Cutting across these perspectives is a belief that learning is personally transformative but is also something that happens in social, cultural and political contexts.

Why Do We Need Philosophies of Education?

As adult (and community) education has grown into a distinct field of practice with an accompanying body of academic knowledge, a number of different camps of opinion have emerged on how adults learn and on how this learning can be best supported. These schools of thought are often categorised into distinct philosophies of education sometimes understood as (1) liberal, (2) progressive, (3) behaviourist, (4) radical/critical and (5) humanistic (Elias and 1995; Merriam and Brockett 1997; Tisdell and Taylor 2001). Although there are some distinctive features within each domain, there are problems with delineating ideologies in this fashion. Contexts can be under-played such as the subject matter, the sociopolitical climate and the bureaucratic structures of accreditation that shape an educational encounter. What about the pragmatism of the educator as she/he eclectically draws from more than one theoretical influence? We can also underestimate the philosophical orientation of the learner with the binary division between learners and teachers often problematised within adult education. Organising philosophy so rigidly also jars with post-structuralist insight that seeks to render such categorisations out-dated. Post-structuralists argue such divisions do not properly address how power and language shape accepted thought (Hemphill 2001) and how Western and gendered logic dominate such ideas (Shearad and Sissel 2001). Generalisations about adults are also inherent in such divisions.

Another difficulty is the way in which attempts to split theory and practice apart can interrupt the more seamless flow between the two. Sometimes, the division of theory from practice does little more than create a wedge between specialist, academically held knowledge on the one hand, and organic practice-based knowledge on the other. When this is the case, theory can become a source of privilege in its own right and something that is held by those who are powerful within the patriarchal white-supremacist structures of education systems (hooks 1994). This hierarchy often results in a situation where theories of practice are privately held within the working lives of practitioners and are therefore under-explored (Brookfield 1987: 152–153).

There are also some benefits to philosophical divisions. One such benefit again links to theory/practice relationships specifically to how a greater understanding of different approaches can put us in a better position to reflect on our own practice. If we do not understand philosophical variance, we may simply draw from our own relativist experiences of education, experiences which are commonly coloured by uncritical encounters within schools and colleges. Another reason we should understand philosophical difference is to counter a neoliberal logic of anti-intellectualism (Giroux 2011), a phenomenon that emerges in this study. Giroux (2011) explains how anti-intellectualism seeks to reduce citizenship to unquestioned pro-ducer/consumer relationships in a way that allows neoliberal ideology to fill the void of critical questioning. As chapter 1 demonstrated, this aids citizen compliance with socio-economic decisions that are often detrimental to majority well-being.

Although I am arguing against neat, hermeneutically sealed philoso-phies of education, I do think it is important to think about the values that underpin our practice and to position ourselves in conceptual spaces that enable us to take a stance. I also think it helps to have a sense of what each philosophical orientation is thought to be. Let's take liberal educa-tion as a starting point, a cornerstone in the history of educational inquiry. Its origins lie in the 19th-century separation of instrumentalist understanding and liberal knowledge (Micari 2003) and its essence is to broaden our intellectual capacities such as our ability to think critically and reflectively. Its limitations are its suspension from social and political structures (Keeney 2007) and its emphasis on objective and scientific reasoning. The notion of a strong scientific base is also shared by behaviourist philosophers. This is where learning is believed to happen only where there is measurable change. This philosophical orientation is often associated with training, a process where no intellectual activity is thought necessary (Winch and Gingell 1999: 25). Key features of the behaviourist classroom are an emphasis on uncritical reinforcement and the continual recall of set knowledge. When I think back on my own experiences in school, this is the approach that I remember most vividly as I rote learnt established facts so I could regurgitate them in State examinations. When I look at my children's experiences in secondary school some 30 years later, little seems to have changed. As neoliberalism colonises adult education spaces as an instrument to satisfy market need (Brookfield and Holst 2011; Mayo and English 2013; Murray et al. 2014), a likely impact is an increasing pull towards behaviourism.

A third philosophy of education (after liberalism and behaviourism) is progressive education, a democratic approach to education where diversity is nurtured and active citizenship is built. Progressive education offers an alternative to objectivity through a more fluid relationship between knowledge and socially contextualised experiential learning (Dewey 1997). This is through an emphasis on learning by doing, on collaboration and on self-directedness. Many educationalists consider John Dewey to be the forefather of progressive education. Not dissimilar to much thinking within community education, Dewey built his ideas on a critique of the school system, a system that represents a process of socialisation where both subject matter and standards of behaviour are generationally handed down and where "the attitude of pupils must, upon the whole, be one of docility, receptivity and obedience" (Dewey 1997/1938: 18).

Liberal, behaviourist and progressive ideas are all likely to have impacted community education, but not to the extent that humanistic and radical/critical leanings have, both in this study and in previous Irish-based research (Inglis et al. 1993; Powell and Geoghegan 2004: 175). To understand their dominance, let's delve more deeply into each perspective beginning with the former.

The Benefits and Pitfalls of Humanistic
Community Education

Humanistic philosophies education has had a significant presence across all adult education since the mid-1900s (Elias and Merriam 1995: 121; Merriam and Brockett 1997: 39; Pearson and Podescki 1999: 42; Cornelius-White 2007: 113; Rogers and Horricks 2010: 109). As well as being commonly associated with constructivist approaches to learning that are explained earlier in this chapter, humanism carries its own set of assumptions. Elisa and Merriam (1995: 116–121) summarise these assumptions as (1) that people are essentially good, (2) that each of us has the freedom to choose, (3) that we all have the potential to succeed, that the self is at the core of our being, a self that can be nurtured and can grow and (4) that we each carry personal responsibility. Heavily influenced by psychology, humanism puts each person's development centre stage and takes cues on what is to be learnt from learners themselves. By honouring the subjective and appreciating the self-directed nature of learning, humanism offers a safe, respectful haven where people can develop their intellectual capacities and find support in enhancing their own life chances. This approach can greatly differ from people's previous experience of education and it is not uncommon for adults within community education to share unhappy stories from school.

One influential theorist is Carl Rogers (1969, 1989). Rogers emphasised the importance of empathy, of unconditional positive regard, of authenticity and of reflexivity within all learning environments. The excerpt below indicates his strength of conviction in this regard.

> The individual has within himself or herself vast resources for self-understanding, for altering his or her self-concept, attitudes, and self-directed behaviour – and that these resources can be tapped if only a definable climate of facilitative psychological attitudes can be provided. (Rogers 1989: 135)

Abraham Maslow is another influential humanist through his *theory of human motivation*. Maslow proposed a five-tiered hierarchy of human needs: the physiological needs, the safety needs, the love needs, the esteem needs and the need for self-actualisation (Maslow 1943). Recognising some fluidity across these needs, Maslow (1943: 387) believed each of us are responsible for our own growth and claimed that our own social goals emerge as we satisfy each need. The concept of andragogy as developed by Malcolm Knowles is also commonly evoked within humanistic approaches. Andragogy separates learning in childhood from learning in adulthood. Adults are presented as motivated learners who are equipped with a sufficient repertoire of experiences to self-direct their own learning (Knowles 1980, 1984; Knowles et al. 2011). Although Knowles et al. (2011: 2) claim this person-centred, self-directed approach can be applied across all philosophical traditions; this is not reflected through writings on andragogy which insufficiently consider each adult's life situation. Although andragogic ideas have asserted considerable influence within adult education, these ideas have also been accompanied by consistent criticism. The very idea of adulthood has been confronted as a social construct that is open to considerable cultural variance (Rogers 2002: 40; Jarvis 2004: 45; Fenwick and Tennant 2004: 55; Boshier 2006: 59). Do children not also learn in a way that is self-directed and that draws from personal experience?

Some compelling arguments have also been put forward that incorporates a political dimension within humanism. This is including within Rogers own writings (Rogers 1989: 325–326), where personal transformation is seen as a way to strengthen democracy. The thinking behind this political perspective is that individuals can act as agents for change, a line of thinking that sits comfortably with the ideas about social agency and social capital that were discussed within Chapter 2. Weber (2014: 66) explains it like this:

Humanistic psychology's contextualism leads to participation as an intricate and delicate dance of learner, teacher, and global context, contributing to transformational kinds of learning promoting change. Such a change considers globalization's demands, people's inter connectivity, quality participation, and learning environments committed to a concern for humanity.

The educator supports each individual's development helping them to become a fully functioning person who is better equipped to take up meaningful citizenship, better able to initiate informed actions and more effective in taking positive action in their own lives. AONTAS (The Irish

National Adult Learning Organisation) appear to align itself with this approach to adult education when they comment:

> For the individual, adult learning provides a means of achieving ones full potential through developing confidence and skills essential for employability, nurturing creativity and imagination, enhancing family relationships and enabling civic participation. For society at large adult learning is essential to building a sustainable economy, promoting social change, highlighting structural inequalities and building a healthy democracy. (AONTAS 2011: 2)

In this excerpt, individualism is centre stage; a mechanism for social "participation" over transformation, whilst structural inequalities are to be "highlighted" rather than directly challenged.

At a glance, it is difficult to see downsides to person-centred humanistic approaches. After all, why would a community educator work in any other way? This approach has changed the lives of many people who access community education where second chances have enabled people to make up lost ground. However, there are problems with humanistic tendencies that make this philosophical approach incompatible with social justice ambitions. These begin with the way individualism is a largely Western notion and is therefore not culturally applicable across the globe (Merriam 2001: 5; Cranton and Taylor 2012). Humanism's promise of greater democracy through the power of individual agency becomes unstable when we question the concept of the autonomous *self*; a self that humanists claim can exercise "inner freedom" as a person realises her/his full potential (Rogers 1989: 28).

Critical pedagogy argues against the notion of the self, claiming we are "unfree and inhibit a world rife with contradictions and asymmetries of power and privilege" (McLaren 2009: 61, italics in original). As an ideology, critical pedagogy (or critical education) claims a dialectical relationship between humans and their sociocultural environments. Attempts to remove the individual from the social stratifications of gender, class, ethnicity and perceived ability that create structural inequality are futile. Connolly (2008: 33) explains this point of view well.

> Humanistic principles are very welcome, but they are fundamentally idealistic . . . [and] overlook social, gendered, and cultural causes of inequality. When individuals, acting independently, develop personally then systemic and structural issues remain unchallenged. If society is to be democratic, it needs to address social and gendered inequality.

Theoretical Foundations of Critical Education

Where humanism is concerned with how we, as individuals can be differ-ent in the world, critical pedagogy is concerned with how the world itself can be different. Critical pedagogy challenges dominant ideas such as individualism, hierarchical leadership and personal well-being through economic well-being. Commonly, a critical worldview embeds founda-tional Marxist ideology where society is thought to be largely class based (Freire 1972; Giroux 1983; McLaren 2000; Kane 2001; Allman 2001). Importantly, a critical approach claims that humanistic approaches are not neutral rather they help to infuse socially unjust, capitalist logic through-out society. A key function of critical pedagogy is to unveil the way that social structures shape our everyday lives and our everyday thinking so that people can interpret their reality through a process of *critical thinking* (Brookfield 1987).

Sometimes it can feel a bit uncomfortable rejecting individualism and arguing that individualism takes the spotlight away from systemic causes of our circumstances. Person-centredness is an important feature of adult education and is a welcome alternative to more traditional teacher-led approaches. If we separate individualism from the individuality that each of us possesses (Pearson and Podeschi 1999) it becomes easier to see the problems. Pearson and Podeschi (1999) describe three defining character-istics that hold current concepts of individualism together, (1) an ontolo-gical belief that the individual exists outside of social arrangements, (2) that the rights and attitudes of this individual take precedence over col-lective rights and attitudes and (3) that the best way to understand society is to study its individual parts. This individualism conforms to the princi-ples of free-market neoliberalism by re-enforcing the idea that we do not particularly need society as we are each responsible for our own successes and failures. Individuality is different as this can be thought of as the uniqueness that each of us hold within our social conditions (Pearson and Podeschi 1999). Individuality can thus be non-conformist and can be the space where many people resist the alienating nature of capitalism through acts of resistance (Holloway 2010).

The idea that community education and critical education are connected is not new, in fact, there is a long-standing relationship between the two. Sometimes critical community education is referred to as *popular education* (e.g. within Crowther et al. 1999; Kane 2001, 2010; Beck and Purcell 2010). This does not refer to a different ideological tendency but rather tells us about differences in how we use language in different parts of the world. In my study, some Irish practitioners felt popular education was the expression for radical/critical community education that is used in Scotland and in Latin America. Although I am suggesting critical community education/popular education can mean the same thing, there are differences with wider school of critical pedagogy. The crux of this difference is locational in that critical pedagogy grew from within the Western academy and is principally concerned with the transformation of public educational spaces such as schools and colleges (Wiggins 2011). Conversely, critical/popular community education happens outside of schools and universities, uses everyday and not academic language and is rooted in the hopes and struggles of ordinary people (Gore 1993: 17; Choules 2007; Wiggins 2011). A history of critical community education can be sketched through work with peasants and land movements within Brazil (Freire 1994; Kane 2001), through the Danish Folk High schools and within the US Highlander school in Tennessee (Westerman 2009), through community development in working-class neighbourhoods in Scotland (Kirkwood and Kirkwood 1989; Crowther et al. 1999) and Ireland (Bassett et al. 1989; Naughton 2002), within the Irish women's movement (Connolly 2003, 2005) and through Asian-Pacific community education linked to local social movements in the 1980s (Boughton 2013: 240).

The Influence of Paulo Freire

When theorising critical education, it is impossible to ignore the presence of the Brazilian educationalist Paulo Freire. Although much emphasis is placed on Freire's early writing *Pedagogy of the Oppressed* (first translated into English in 1970), Freire completed around 25 books, some in conversation with colleagues.[1] One of the things that Freire does is that he encourages each of us to think about how our own story shapes our thoughts and actions. He models this perspective within the talking book *A Pedagogy for Liberation: Dialogues on Transforming Education* (1987) with Ira Shor. Freire tells us about how, as a child, his own middle-class family experienced poverty for a time, something that opened his eyes to working-class life. He also describes the impact of material poverty at this time, especially how hunger blocked his ability to learn at school. When his family's financial and social status improved, Freire describes how it was only when he came into contact with factory workers as an adult educator, that he began "to reknow" what he had once known but had forgotten due to his own improved social circumstances. Finally, Freire talks about his exile from Brazil following the military coup of 1964. This solidified his belief that education alone cannot bring about the transformative change that is needed to create a more equal society (Shor and Freire 1987: 28–32).

It was whilst in exile that Freire principally developed his pedagogy of the oppressed, a philosophy of education for those at the receiving end of systemic injustice. Understanding Freirean philosophy begins with the belief that we can only appreciate our own existence when we historically position it within its economic, political and cultural contexts. Not dissimilar to Karl Marx's division of society into bourgeoisie and proletariat, Freire sees the world as principally divided into a privileged minority who are *the oppressor*, and an under-privileged majority who are *oppressed*. Importantly, Freire interprets this separation as bad for everyone in society claiming it "engenders violence in the oppressors, which in turn dehumanizes the oppressed" (Freire 1972: 21). Freire describes the deliberate promotion of individualism as a powerful divide and rule tactic that discourages unity and maintains "a *focalized* view of problems rather than on seeing them as dimensions of a totality" (Freire 1972: 111, italics in original). He also believes that the idea that people can move across classes, or social mobility as it is sometimes called, is not only mythical but is an act of manipulation kept alive through an illusion of partnership. This masks the oppressor's real ambition which is to maintain the status quo (Freire 1972: 116).

Along with the interconnected features of "conquest" though class privilege, "divide and rule" through individualism and "manipulation", through partnership, Freire's theory of oppression describes an accompanying *cultural invasion*. This is where the dominant cultural world view of the oppressor saturates society and dismisses alternative expressions and forms of creativity (Freire 1972: 121–122). Certain myths (or what Gramsci refers to as hegemony) hold this cultural invasion in place through the false belief that society is free and equal. Quoting Freire at length, these myths include:

the myth that this order respects human rights and is therefore worthy of esteem; the myth that anyone who is industrious can become an entrepreneur, worst yet, the myth that the street vendor is as much an entrepreneur as the owner of a large factory; the myth of the universal right of education;... the myth of the equality of all men [sic]; the myth of the heroism of the oppressor classes as defenders of 'Western Christian Civilization against 'material barbarism'; the myth of charity and generosity of the elites, when what they really do as a class is to foster selective 'good deeds'; . . . the myth of private property as fundamental to personal human development (so long as oppressors are the only true human beings); the myth of the industriousness of the oppressors and the laziness and dishonesty of the oppressed, as well as the myth of the natural inferiority of the latter and the superiority of the former. (Freire 1972: 120–121, brackets in original)

The weight of oppressor reality is presented as so strong, it convinces the oppressed of their own inferiority. This results in what Freire calls a *culture of silence* where, although not completely blind to their circumstances, the oppressed display reverence to minority oppressors as they continually seek to mirror their image. This manifests itself through an internalisation of the oppressor-led reality that *"to have is to be"* (Freire 1972: 35, italics in original) with each person's well-being determined through access to the market. Outside of Latin-American contexts (where Freire's original writings are located) this culture of silence can take the form of a *culture of sabotage* (Shor and Freire 1987: 123). An important part of Freire's theorising is therefore that oppression is more than just economic, but is an oppression of the mind and spirit also.

Where Freire's ideas can particularly resonate with people is through his fervent critique of traditional education. He details a banking approach to education which hooks (1994: 5) describes as a system that is "based on the assumption that memorizing information and regurgitating it represented gaining knowledge that could be deposited, stored and used at a later date". Freire and hooks are not trying to illuminate poor teaching, the essence of their argument is that banking approaches to education are a deliberate act in maintaining inequality. This is because of how learning environments are divided into spaces where powerful expert teachers pour dominant knowledge into disempowered passive students. The end result is the continued compliance an education system that maintains the status quo and, in doing so, suppresses our true consciousness.

Freire believes each of us hold a deep desire to become more fully human, something he calls our *ontological vocation*. As we are the creators of our own history, the challenge is to critically intervene in our reality in order to bring about social change. To do this, people must be able to interpret their lives in the context of the social structures that shape it. The task for educators is to create conditions where people can authentically name their world.

Saying that word is not the privilege of some few persons, but the right of everyone. Consequently, no one can say a true word alone-nor can he [sic] say it *for* another, in a prescriptive act which robs others of their words. (Freire 1972: 61)

This is facilitated through a problem-posing approach to education that fosters the process of *conscientisation* (or politicisation). What this looks like is classrooms (or whatever other space is being used) where people can reflect on their own life events and compare these to the life events of others. As such phenomenon as poverty, sexism, racism, social exclusion, unemployment, stress and precarity are shared, validated and analysed, each are revealed as systemically caused and not as the individual's fault. Freire brings a constructivist domain to political education as it is only by recognising and honouring the subjective, that an objective reality can be viewed.

Throughout his writings, Freire is optimistic and hopeful about people's capacity to create a more equal society, a conviction that is especially expressed in *Pedagogy of Hope* (1994). This hope is not static but is contingent on practice therefore something we must labour to create. Freire's philosophy of education is therefore different to many other writers as it encourages activism beyond the classroom walls. This involves inspiring people towards a complex of action and reflection which are "in such radical interaction that if one is sacrificed even in part – the other immediately suffers" (Freire 1972: 60). The resulting practice, or *praxis* as Freire calls it, is a continual cycle of action and reflection. Crucially, as those experiencing oppression begin to understand that their collective power is strong enough to emancipate both oppressor and oppressed (Freire 1972: 21), they are trusted to self-determine their own futures.

Whilst there is much strength in Freire's writings, there are also difficulties with his ideas. His strict division into oppressor and oppressed reduces the intricacies of our social and economic world to uncomplicated interplays between various parts. Our life experiences tell us something different with oppression better understood as often based on a series of intersecting features that include gender, ethnicity, culture, perceptions of ability and class. This explanation of oppression is often referred to as *intersectionality*. To give an example, traditional Marxism suggests binary divisions of class are determined through ownership of the means of production. This is certainly of fundamental importance but is less stable than is sometimes supposed. Neoliberalism has eroded middle-class comfort through private debt and precarious employment and global trends in migration interrupt traditional benchmarks of economic capital. As Freirean ideology grows beyond Freire's original texts, intersectionality is commonly accepted as part of its thinking (Aronowitz 1993; hooks 1994; Mayo 1999). Although Freire does not renounce class as fundamental, he is ambiguous in later writings and acknowledges other forms of oppression.

Another problem with Freirean thinking is its dependence on grand narratives. This perspective clashes with post-structuralist philosophical orientations which believe each of us are capable of seeing the world any number of ways (Lyotard 1984; Rosenau 1991; Malpas 2005) and that we should embrace contradictions in our social and cultural world. Again there has been some accommodation found with post-structuralism where the main tension relates to different ideas about the nature of reality. Critical pedagogues and post-structuralists can each be influenced by notions of social justice but often have different ideas on what it means to be critical. By way of reconciliation Jones (2012: 191) suggests that practitioners should work both "*with* and *against* certain aspects of Freire's thinking" (italics in original).

As well as the difficult balance between Freirean ideology and post-structuralism, there are other critiques of Freire's writings. Blackburn (2000: 8–9) challenges the idea that any group in society can be stuck in a powerless culture of silence citing non-cooperation with dominant norms and the maintenance of distinct minority identities as expression of power by those considered oppressed. What about Freire's over-simplification of educational settings again dichotomised as either banking or problem posing with the latter presented as the only true form of education. Others argue it is unrealistic to institute the level of change that would be required to transform current education systems into the critical, problem-posing spaces Freire inspires (Torres 1993; Fitzsimons 2014).

Questions can also be asked about the politics of Freirean practice. Are we as community educators trying to foster revolutionary struggle within the classroom as part of attempts to overthrow global capitalism? Are we supporting a reformist pathway more suited to pluralist interpretations of power? Can we do both? There is no doubt but that Freire draws influence from Latin-American revolutionary activists Che Guevara, Castro, and Cabral and it is refreshing the way he reflects on their achievements alongside the actions of ordinary people (Freire 1972). Freire does not discount a role for revolutionary political parties but is critical of how some such entities can voraciously block self-determination through their own quest for change (Freire 2005: 26). He is however ambiguous about how we should defeat capitalism and insufficiently addresses ways in which opposition can be organised. His own participation in parliamentary politics is sometimes evoked as evidence of a reformist over revolutionary approach.[2] This point, whether Freire seeks reform or revolution, is discussed through the writings of Peter McLaren particularly within *Che Guevara, Paulo Freire, and the Pedagogy of Revolution* (McLaren 2000). McLaren (2000) challenges what he sees as a domesticating turn within critical pedagogy claiming its political intentions have been depleted. One person that I interviewed as part of this study captures McLaren's concerns in an Irish context.

> It is almost like Freire has been put through a strainer, and what has been left is that the radicalism and the whole concept of society and the connection between education and society is gone…We watered it down to a large extent and we have maybe kept some aspects of the methodology. You know 'the methodology is ok', you know the active learning, the group-work, the discussion, the notion of teacher as the learner as well, all of that stuff, but what we have gotten rid of I think is the radicalism and the notion of education as a form of social transformation. (Interviewee eight, works for an non-governmental organisation (NGO))

When we think about the hegemonic weight of the psychology of individualism, this depoliticisation is to be expected and some writers encourage us to reclaim Freirean politics (McLaren 2000; Allman 2001; Moraes 2003). Both Holst (2009) and Boughton (2013) lay some blame for this depoliticisation with the academy arguing that there is insufficient acknowledgement of how revolutionary political parties often maintain critical education in the field. Another way to think about reform versus revolutionary arguments is to wonder about their helpfulness in the first place. False tensions can be created between potential allies meaning we can lose sight of the importance of uniting counter-hegemonic actions across society.

Where Freire definitely gets it wrong, even by his own admission (Freire 1994) is through an unforgivable gender-blindness, a point also raised by some community educators in this study. Within *Pedagogy of the Oppressed* Freire draws solely from a male interpretation of the world stereotyping women and subjugating their societal position (Jackson 1997). As language is constructed both by the dominant class and the dominant gender, female becomes "other" in the shadow of male and is therefore also oppressed. Though Freire amends sexist language in his later writings, he still falls short in addressing how patriarchy is largely maintained in the private realm through relationships of sexual production and the division of labour. For me, a truely feminist epistemological stance questions that which previously passed for universal knowledge viewing this as a masculine perspective where objectivity is cloaked in systemic sexism that excludes women's voices and experiences (Harding 1991; Thompson 2001: 17–18; Letherby 2003; Olesen 2005; Brooks 2006). How different would the structural inequalities identified within *Pedagogy of the Oppressed* be if a patriarchal analysis had also been included?

TOWARDS A FEMINIST PEDAGOGY

One of the most influential writers to incorporate a feminist analysis to the writings of Freire is bell hooks, a prolific and important contributor within critical education. Her *engaged pedagogy* claims to have "taken the threads of Paulo's work" (hooks 1994: 52) and woven these into a way of working that acknowledges the gendered nature of oppression where women are often denied the right to define their own realities. Context matters in all community education and we should take the lead from the generative themes that emerge from a group. This does not stop us using feminist pedagogy in all contexts regardless of the gender of participants or the issues under discussion. Feminist educators, be they male or female, should be prepared to name and problematise discrimination at both micro and macro levels. This involves challenging essentialist notions of gender that attach fixed traits through perceived biological difference with insufficient regard for gender socialisation. It also involves working in ways that ensure both female and male realities are heard. Crucially, feminist pedagogy does not just address gender-based inequality but untangles many forms of oppression. This is by encouraging us to reflect on intersectionality more broadly inviting each of us to acknowledge and reflect on a range of privileges we hold; be they related to our ethnicity, our social class, our perceived ability, our age or the institutional power we may hold.

Uncovering Philosophical Perspectives in Contemporary Practice

Community education, whether accredited or non-accredited, is a process where practitioners bring their philosophical values into the groups they work with. In determining the prevalence of different approaches amongst research participants in this study, one survey question asks "if there is a particular way of working that informs your approach (a certain belief system, theory, philosophy, etc.), can you explain or describe it" (which carried an 81% response rate). Based on responses, 56% are categorised as principally influenced by a humanistic philosophy, 35% by a radical/critical philosophy and 7% as stating no philosophical allegiance. Seventeen percent of all responses name the influence of Paulo Freire, the highest single theoretical influence named. Each of the three outlooks above – humanistic, radical/critical and where no philosophy is adopted will now be individually presented.

Examples of Humanism

Of the 56% categorised as humanistic, sometimes the expressions "humanism" and "person-centeredness" are used. Specific theorists are also mentioned namely Carl Rogers, Abraham Mazlow, Malcolm Knowles, Glasser's reality therapy, Donald Schön and Paulo Freire. The quote below gives an example of how Freirean ideology is adopted to describe a humanistic approach.

> I believe in a humanistic approach and try to cater to the needs of individuals in my group. I also would like to emulate Freire where I can in providing opportunities for individuals to become empowered and not to feel that they are not valued in society. (Survey respondent, tutor Vocational Education Committee (VEC)/Education and Training Board (ETB))

The job of a researcher using quantification is to infer meaning from contributions where recognisable categorisations and markers are not explicitly named. What this means is that many responses do not draw from theorists but have been classified as humanistic based on my interpretation of a respondent's words. To give some examples:

> [where] the individual and their need is the priority and where possible that need should be fulfilled in the locality if at all possible. (Survey respondent, community sector)

From a publically employed community educator:

> Education for me is student centred, meeting the needs of the student that reflect what is essential in their lives. My role is to facilitate self-actualisation, potential, develop self-confidence, self-esteem, and to support and encourage individuals to engage in the process. (Survey respondent, Community Education Facilitator (CEF) in a VEC/ETB)

Commonly emerging themes amidst these 56% of responses are to support personal development, to promote self-actualisation, to engender self-directedness and to instill belief and self-worth in individual capacities. Language used is of people being "empowered", having "more independence", of "gaining confidence", of "improvement in social and soft skills" and of "taking on a challenge which they would previously not have done". Many of these humanistic educators pay particular attention to creating learning environments of care. This view is captured in the contributions below.

> Because in my work programmes target those furthest away from the education system, very often there are negative associations of education to counter and so I like to work with the group to a safe learning environment for all of us together to feel supported and valued even if/when we disagree. (Survey respondent, community sector)

From another:

> That the person is in an enjoyable environment, that is giving them a skill that is improving and developing them as an individual. (Survey respondent, Health Service Executive)

This final explanation of the approach taken by a humanistic community educator demonstrates the use of many methods encouraged within adult education such as group and peer work and creative classroom methods. These are presented as important in offering an alternative to how many people experience school.

> I try to take an informal approach unlike the traditional school setting as most of my learners are early school leavers and have a fear of the traditional teaching. I use various methods of learning, interactive, group-work, discussion, role-plays etc. And their work is a continuous assessment portfolio which allows

them to achieve at the rate which is appropriate to them. Encouragement is key and when they can see that there are progression options available to them it is a great motivator. (Survey respondent, community sector)

These examples of humanism demonstrate how practitioners endeavour to provide supportive spaces for building the confidence and capacities of people, and for enriching lives through opportunities that might otherwise not have been open to their students.

Examples of Radical/Critical Philosophies

Thirty-five percent of surveyed community educators are categorised as working from a radical/critical perspective. The examples below typify broad sentiment.

Freirean approach, feminist group-work, working from community development principles . . . a belief that everyone has the potential to lead . . . leadership is about vision, about people buying in, about empowerment and most of all about producing useful change . . . the notion that a few extraordinary people at the top can provide all the leadership needed today is ridiculous, and it is a recipe for failure. (Survey respondent, community sector)

A similar analysis of leadership is echoed from another critical educator:

A belief that power needs to be decentralised to the greatest possible extent, that everyone has a right to take part in making decisions that affect them, and that they should be supported and facilitated in acting on that right – that collective action makes it much easier to indicate these rights. (Survey respondent, community sector)

There are other illustrations of the theoretical foundations that inform people's work, this time from a volunteer with a women's network.

Feminist and Critical theory: incorporating a social analysis based on critical factors of gender, class and race (and of course other exclusionary mechanisms); Freire's ideas of liberation, dialogue, domestication etc. (Survey respondent, community sector)

The quotation below again draws from Freirean ideology and emphasises its relationship with activism.

Praxis – Paulo Freire – the sense that education is not neutral and can change the context in which we live. (Survey respondent, community sector)

Paulo Freire is not the only theoretical influence named with others citing the influence of Stephen Brookfield, Margaret Wheatley, Jack Mezirow, Augusto Boal, Karl Marx, Anne Hope and Sally Timmel and bell hooks. Others disclose political affiliation. One describes herself as "socialist", another of "not believing in capitalism" and for a few, of being "feminist". Many describe their work as about addressing systemic inequality an injustice and of a power-laden system.

Examples of Anti-intellectualism

Seven percent of surveyed community educators reject affiliation to any particular philosophy. In one example the reason given is a responsibility to be led by the philosophies of the employer organisation (which is not named). A more usual reason is a deliberate distancing from theory as a useful tool in grounding practice. For example:

> I never needed other people's theories to do my job. I can read people and work on their strengths. (Survey respondent, community sector)

These combined findings uncover a dominant humanistic philosophical leaning within Irish community education practice. This holistic approach is likely to be of great comfort to many people as they grow in confidence through their interactions with a respectful philosophical approach that often embodies care. For people to truly understand the root causes of the circumstances of their lives, a key part of this chapter, and indeed this book as a whole is to nudge practitioners away from a humanistic perspective and towards a more radical way of working. A case for radical/critical education is expanded in Chapter 8, before this the remainder of this chapter discusses and describes some of the methodologies associated with the feminist pedagogies that I support.

Doing Critical Community Education

When a person walks into a community education space that is working to a feminist pedagogy, what does this look like? How *do* we create authentic, problem-posing spaces where experiences are validated so that collective responses to oppression emerge? In this research, this question was most deliberately explored within one-to-one interviews with seven selected critical community educators.³ Within one of these conversations, methodological sentiment across each discussion is particularly captured. This educator⁴ describes how, when he enters a room for the first time, he sometimes brings a suitcase filled with newspaper cuttings, knick-knacks, books and papers. These are deliberately spilt onto the floor. Group members are then invited to think about how they too are entering the same space with their own suitcase that is full of previous knowledge, life-experiences and a set of values. Where traditional education commonly stuffs more knowledge on top of an already full suitcase, critical community education is about unpacking people's suitcases and having a look inside. Through a process of dialogic learning, each person is supported to repack their suitcase in a way that is coherent, meaningful and affirming. This way of working *draws content from* rather than *presents contents to* learners.

Different critical educators I interviewed shared a similar sense of the process through descriptions of how "you facilitate the ideas out of people", you put "a lot of emphasis on people's experiences and on validating them and recognising them" and of how the work is "rooted in what people are living at the moment".

Beginning with a person's life experience is an important feature of humanistic community education also and is essential if we are to create educational communities of care. Where paths diverge is that, although critical community education begins with the events that shape a person's life, it seeks to create conditions where these events can be reflected on and understood in the context of social, economic and cultural structures. Two critical educators in this study capture this approach well, both of which are in response to me asking them to describe their work.

> Making connections to the wider world in terms of well, "what are the other influences on us", and "what are the other options that are out there for us, to try and address this issue"... you know, what is going on in the wider world that has connections to this? We look at power, culture and economics and again it's about just opening people's eyes to structures in societies and the institutions that play a role in people's lives at different levels, at local level and at nation level. (Interviewee three)

From another:

> So this is what I do, I encourage people to pool their experiences, you know, share their experiences whatever issue we might be talking about, 'what's

your view of that?' or 'what's your experience of that?'. To learn from that sharing; 'oh right that happens to you' and then to begin to unravel some of the patterns that you begin to see and use that as a way of putting the issues that people experience, that society has, up for question. (Interviewee six)

These quotes demonstrate how critical education is not simply therapeutic or self-affirming but has a historical function in humanity that is rooted in a sociological context. Shor and Freire (1987: 98) describe this process as "a moment where humans meet to reflect on their reality as they make and remake it" going on to suggest that by "reflecting together on what we know and don't know, we can act critically to transform reality". Although the critical educator is also a learner, their role is to pose problems about the events of people's lives.

Facilitation of a process of critical education is therefore not unstructured, it is not directionless and it is not something that can be taken on without a certain set of skills and expertise. Critical community education involves the use of group-work methods such as experiential socially contextualised exercises, provocative role plays, social skits and other problem-posing exercises (e.g. see Hope and Timmel 1995; Sheehy 2001; McNeill 2005; Crowley et al. 2015). Fundamentally, it is also about understanding that people are the experts in their own lives. One interviewee explains:

you recognise that people in the room have a particular knowledge and have a knowledge of life and have, they may not understand the economic system and all that but in terms of living their lives that you can survive in difficult circumstances rearing children, budgeting, managing, micro-managing their own economic system in their own family and even understand how their own community runs, that they have a huge knowledge base, that you try and tap into that, and it's more active learning in a way, it's shared learning, we facilitate it that way. (Interviewee four)

In creating the conditions for this to happen, we have to think about the physical spaces we work in and what a classroom can say about where knowledge is held. Often, this involves interrupting the set-up of a room so that we can disrupt the power-laden traditional organisation of table and chairs. Critical educators can also rotate their own position in a room so that they embody a rejection of the traditional teacher space at the front of a room.

Small group work can also be used to create conditions more palatable to those less comfortable with large group settings and, crucially, to reduce cultural dimensions of power. I have found small groups very effective in minimising both gendered and institutional power giving everyone the space to have their voice heard. Collaborative co-creation of curricula and assessments can also increase democracy in the classroom (Connolly 2008) and critical media literacy can be fostered by drawing examples from popular culture (Tisdell 2007). This can include YouTube clips, television programme and cut outs from newspapers with both facilitators and learners invited to provide such materials.

Working in highly participatory, experiential learning environments does not mean there cannot be some space for lecturing; something that can be a spoken codification within emancipatory approaches (Shor and Freire 1987: 39–40). What is important is how a lecture, or an input as I prefer to call it, is managed. Inputs should be short and should be seen as stimuli for conversation rather than a presentation of the only viable theory or set of facts. Importantly, these inputs are sometimes best delivered at the *end* of a session therefore after experiences are explored. Teacher talk is thus kept to a minimum as conditions are created for participants to name their world. At all times, we should endeavour to check our own prejudicial assumptions based on gender, socio-economic and ethnic backgrounds as well as political opinion.

When we work with a group in this way, we reveal emergent, or "generative themes" (Freire 1972: 69). To give some examples, a generative theme for young mothers might be isolation, or struggles to afford childcare. A generative theme for older people might equally be isolation or it might be bereavement, or the frustrations of physical ailments. These are only guesses and the important thing about a generative theme is that we do not guess rather we listen to the life experiences of groups. Emergent themes are a shared truth and something that can be analysed in the light of root systemic causes. This enables those affected to strategically intervene to instigate change.

Using Codes
One way for critical community educators to manage generative themes is through the use of *codes* or enactments of the ordinary circumstances of people's lives presented back to them in a provocative way. A code can take the form of a picture, a piece of literature, a dramatisation or any other portrayal of a generative theme that allows people to examine their

own circumstances in the third party. The first step in creating a code is to genuinely listen to a group or a community. This is so that we do not assume a generative theme, but allow it to emerge organically. A code should never offer a solution to an issue raised, rather it identifies a problem about which there is much feeling. One way to demonstrate the use of codes is to share the code that was used to stimulate discussion in the focus groups that form part of this study. This was designed after I actively listened to survey findings and drew out what I thought was the strongest theme I could hear. The image below was designed to capture the weight of emotion surrounding a belief amongst practitioners that the work of community educators was being controlled by powerful forces outside of the classrooms and communities where they work.

Illustration 4.2   Code used with focus groups

The period before introducing a code to a group can be nerve wracking. What if it does not work? What if it is my theme and not the theme of the group? Ann Hope and Sally Timmel (1995: 76), the co-authors of the

Training for Transformation (TfT) workbooks, give some thought to how we know if we have gotten a theme right. They believe "we recognise a generative theme has been tapped when a group suddenly comes to life". This happened when I used this code in focus groups as community educators immediately connected with the image. Reactions included "very good, very good", "wow", "that's me", and "it's like [she] is controlled by other outside forces that are much bigger". Recurring responses were an emphasis on control, the image of puppetry, and disparity in size between the person with the controls and the facilitator/ tutor in the group. At one focus group one person wonders if:

> Maybe that person at the front is not able to work from their true soul because somebody else is pulling the strings or working them. (North Dublin, participant two)

These group reactions represent the beginning of a second stage in using codes, the process of *decoding*, or what Freire (1972: 77) describes as "moving from the abstract to the concrete". Four stages have been suggested, (1) what people see in a code, (2) how this relates to their life, (3) a first analysis and related problems and, finally, (4) action planning (Hope and Timmel 1995, 77–8; Sheehy 2001: 19–20). The vast majority of focus-group participants felt their work resonated with the code presented. Concrete identities were given to those controlling the work of community education from outside the room. These are named as accrediting bodies, the Troika (see Chapter 1), funders and "policy drivers" both national and European. In South Dublin a contributor whose work is based in a community sector organisation but is funded by a VEC shares:

> The chap with the headset to me represents other people as well, for example the Troika and their influence which seems to be coming all the way down now. From my own experience, this year for example I was told that I would have to demonstrate a 50% progression rate which is completely unrealistic but I was told "take it or leave it" basically, what do you do? (South Dublin, participant two)

It is during the process of decoding that Freire describes the role of the critical educator not simply as there to listen, but as a problem poser asking why things are the way they are? Who is benefitting? Who is losing out? The purpose of this dialogic probing relates back to the fourth action planning phase of decoding where groups and communities can identify the points at which they can strategically intervene to address the oppressive circumstances within which they find themselves.

Eyebrows might be raised when one considers the momentous and complex task this process of designing and de-coding codes, facilitating discussion and supporting action planning. One research participants shares her own concerns about this when she states:

> I remember when I was training in this kind of work, training in radical education or whatever, you know we talked about all these qualities that you need to have as a facilitator, being open, being genuine, genuineness and congruence and all these sorts of things and I remember going, Jesus that's an awful lot to live up to [laughing] you know and I kind of sort of put my hand up and said "wow" that's a kind of tall order to get there. (Interviewee six)

Working to Freirean principles certainly requires facilitative teaching skills and a repertoire of experiential and participatory exercises. It also involves a philosophical understanding of the difference between dialogic, problem-posing education and what I term *participatory banking*. This is where there is an illusion of educational democracy through continual support for participants to ask questions and seek clarity on what is presented to them. Where participatory banking falls short is that these, often engaging and stimulating, discussions still revolve around established canonical knowledge and not the experiential knowledge in the room.

Freirean methods are also imperfect and different educators will approach the process in different ways. Kane (2001: 49) draws from the words of Archer and Collingham to express:

> ...the magic of 'codification' rarely works, that teachers are just ordinary (not the ideal envisioned by Freire) who often struggle to promote dialogue in groups and that Freirean efforts usually end up either concentrating on literacy skills or conscientisation but seldom achieve a balance of the two. (brackets in original)

Equally, facilitators can make incorrect assumptions about a group that assume agreement and/or mask gradient of emotion (Barbour 2007: 130). What about the politics of the facilitator and how this influences the process? Kane (2001: 48–49) argues this is a key component in how

Freirean methods are implemented as the politics of the educator determines what problems are posed and what actions a group is encouraged to take. One critical educator I spoke to shares some similar concerns and wonders if many of the methods associated with critical group work such as the experiential exercises, the role plays and the skits:

> Are just propaganda by subterfuge because you know what you want them to think, so exercises that are apparently experiential, they are actually dynamic didacticism; you are just getting the people to the same place. (interviewee five)

We also have to remember that some people within groups are not interested in politicising processes but are motivated to be present for other reasons. Groups can also tend towards consensus even where some might not agree a point.

In so much as I am encouraging a group-work approach that is influenced by critical community education and that resists participatory banking, none of us can ignore the tension that emerges when this philosophical perspective meets the demands of a set curriculum. Freire consistently presents curricular control as an example of anti-dialogic, banking approaches to education and demonstrates anathema between the two. Set formulaic curricula are interpreted as inflexible and as a practice that represents the infusion of business logic into school systems enabling the transfer of knowledge that is most appropriate in supporting elitist authority (Freire and Shor 1987: 75–76). Other critical educators continue this point (hooks 1994: 70; Beck and Purcell: 2010: 6) presenting formulaic curricula as incompatible with Freirean practice. The uncomfortable truth is that the weight of accreditation is damaging community education's critical capacities and Chapter 6 will be dedicated to this very concern.

CONCLUSION

This chapter looked at philosophies of adult and community education with particular emphasis on humanism and on critical pedagogy, the most influential approaches within community education. I have drawn from foundational theorists most notably Paulo Freire's pedagogy of the oppressed and have identified key criticisms amidst Freire's writings. This chapter also relies on findings from the field quantifying philosophical tendencies and qualifying these with textual responses. Ultimately, I support feminist, critical group work as an approach to community education. The code designed and implemented as part of this study shines a light on the concerns community educators hold. This notion of control from the outside forms the focus of the second part of this book where social policy on employability, accreditation and professionalisation discourse will each be discussed in dedicated chapters.

NOTES

1. These include *Literacy, Reading the Word and the World* (1987) with Donaldo Macedo (which includes a lengthy introduction by Henry Giroux), and *We Make the Road by Walking: Conversations on Education and Social Change* (1990) with Myles Horton.
2. Freire participated in parliamentary politics as a member of the workers party in São Paulo Aronowitz (1993:19) defends Freire's parliamentarian involvement arguing this was not an unconditional nod to parliamentary reformism as the only route to change, but as indicative of the historical circumstances of the time and the unpopularity of revolutionary movements
3. This process formed phase one of the research project and information on research design and participant recruitment are within Chapter 2.
4. Interviewee five from phase one of the research, research design in incorporated within Chapter 2.

PART II

The Neoliberalisation of Community Education

Introduction

Part I of this book explores an understanding of process-oriented, equality-based community education. This is presented amidst recognisable philosophies of adult education and through differentiation into three distinct, at times overlapping, models of practice namely universal, second-chance and radical/critical approaches to community education. A history of community education has been updated which draws out the importance of specific egalitarian social movements as well as provision through the public sector including through the involvement of higher education. The importance of volunteers is emphasised within each provider type.

Across these discussions, community education is examined through an anti-neoliberal lens, therefore one that is deeply critical of our globalised epoch of individualist, free-market economics. A key argument I am making is that the culture of wealth this socio-economic model advances conceals growing gaps in income inequality and an expanded working class. I have also disputed more recent claims of recovery as an illusionary recovery for most of us and an ideological recovery for neoliberalism through a deepening belief that the market is sacrosanct.

Part II will now focus on the neoliberal policies that shape community education. Three distinct chapters focus on employability, accreditation and professionalisation. A central claim I will make is that managerialist policies seek to redirect the function of community education to service the labour needs of the global market. The book's final chapter reasserts an anti-neoliberal argument, summarises research findings, presents practitioner suggestions for change and encourages practitioners towards a more politicised practice.

CHAPTER 5

Community Education and Employability

Illustration 5.1 Community education and employability

© The Author(s) 2017
C. Fitzsimons, *Community Education and Neoliberalism*,
DOI 10.1007/978-3-319-45937-0_5

In the last 25 years or so, the relationship between the State and the providers of community education has changed. Where community education evolved in response to community need and as part of politicisation processes, neoliberalism seeks to transform its function to one of servicing the labour market. This chapter will look at the role of social policy in directing this transition, with particular emphasis on employability discourse. Examining social policy and community education is not simply about considering the actions by far away policymakers; it also involves looking at practitioner's own involvement in policy formation. Before doing this, I will begin by explaining what I mean by social policy, so that its relationship with neoliberalism can be more purposefully examined. Key policy changes and the implications for community education are then investigated before the experiences of practitioners are presented.

WHAT IS SOCIAL POLICY?

Broadly speaking, *social policy* is the space where relationships between a State and its population are determined (Coffey 2004). Usually, policies emphasise human rights and citizen well-being and are categorised within such domains as health, housing, education, infrastructure and welfare. Policies are generally protected by law, with the foundational law of Ireland held within the *Constitution of Ireland* (1937). Notwithstanding specific constitutional limitations on citizenship, the overriding philosophy of the Irish Constitution is that all citizens are equal and that no one person is entitled to greater privilege over another. A similar equality principle is thought to underpin social policies more broadly as liberal democracies set out to safeguard citizen well-being through wide-ranging social protections (Hothersall 2012). If robustly designed, these social policies form a catch-all for the needs of each individual.

Contrary to this supposed equality function, we live in a time where many people's social needs are not safeguarded and, in many ways, community education emerged from a desire to address unmet needs. Most of this work is through a rich network of community education practice as described within Chapter 3. As well as face-to-face work, community educators have also traditionally challenged the centrality of government decision-making by actively working to shape the contents and direction of social policy. The purpose of these actions is to ensure diverse voices, and not just those traditionally heard, can contribute to public reform. Activism in the policy arena of community education has had some success. The influence of community educators and the groups they work with is palpable within some sections of the prominent policy document *Learning for Life, White Paper on Adult Education* (2000). More recently, practitioners have participated in consultation processes on the formation of the Further Education and Training Authority SOLAS (est. 2013),[1] Quality and Qualifications Ireland (QQI) (est. 2012)[2] and the government document *Community Education Programme, Operational Guidelines for Providers* (Department of Education and Skills (DOES) 2012).

Typically, though not exclusively, this work is organised through practitioner networks. We know from Chapter 3 that the most prominent contemporary networks are the AONTAS Community Education Network (CEN) and the Community Workers Cooperative (CWC, now called Community Work Ireland). Although not strongly represented in this study, the Community Education Facilitators Association (CEFA) is also important. Networks do not just coordinate collective policy submissions; they also encourage their membership to independently lobby for change. Guidebooks have been produced that explain the political system and advise on setting policy objectives. One example is *Working for Change* (Harvey 1998, 2002, 2008) a series of publications by the now disbanded Combat Poverty Agency. The AONTAS CEN has also published advocacy toolkits for legislative reform and templates for campaign letters.[3] One question worth contemplating is whether these actions make any difference or if, as one focus-group member asks, "does it slightly round sharp edges but actually do nothing to the actual shape of the object?"

One thing we can be sure of is that social policies are not neutral but are deeply connected to the prevailing socio-economic model. This can be demonstrated through an examination of domestic housing policy, a policy direction that community activism has sought to change (Dorman 2006; Bissett 2008; Pillinger 2015). A dominant trend by right-wing neoliberal governments is to look to public-private partnerships (PPPs) to address housing need. These PPPs are presented through a win-win narrative alleging benefits to the economy as well as to civic well-being. A more accurate way to think about PPPs is as part of a well-established government trend that seeks to privatise social housing thus absolving the State from responsibility for adequate housing. For many years Ireland has lived with a cultural pre-eminence of home ownership and a mantra that rent is in some way "dead money". Obsession with home ownership is commonly linked to a nationalist connection with "the land" and thus part of the cultural fabric of Ireland. The reality is that these beliefs have a context within social policy as, since the formation of the Irish republic, successive governments have pushed home ownership and undermined alternative tenure types (Considine and Dukelow 2009). Quite deliberately, these actions support capitalist models of economic growth which locate the solution to housing need within the profit generating needs of the private market. Incentives to buy are continually promoted through generous tax breaks, government grants and enticements for public tenants to purchase their homes from the State. Initially this meant that developers, landlords and estate agents all benefitted from a policy direction that fuelled the housing industry. As neoliberalism has deepened, economic growth on the back of housing need has extended to include inducements and favourable conditions for sub-prime mortgage lenders and financial speculators.

It is not just housing policy that is affected. As the State increasingly promotes liberty through the free market, its legitimacy in assuming *any* responsibility for social equality is challenged (Coffey 2004: 59). Managing social need becomes the responsibility of the market, a situation that involves radical reform of existing policies to bring them in line with business logic. Transformations like this take considerable effort and, during the current era of neoliberalism, there has been a deluge of social policies relating to equality. In Ireland alone, 25 such policy initiatives were introduced between 1996 and 1997, each of which set out to reform public welfare provision (Duggan 1999: 6–7). Adult and community education has received unprecedented policy attention in recent years, a situation that will unfold as this chapter progresses. Just why a sociopolitical model that seeks to shirk responsibility for equality should be so prolific in the social policy arena becomes clearer when we examine the nature and scope of the reforms that have been introduced. As social policy is now conceived of within the context of transnational developments (Milana 2012; Murray 2014: Murtagh 2014) the best way to investigate this assertion is to look into European Union (EU) policies of formative influence in the Irish educational sphere.

The European Lifelong Learning Agenda

As this book's introductory chapter has testified, Ireland's Celtic Tiger economic growth period of the 1990s and early 2000s was a time of unprecedented economic growth, of rapid expansion of the domestic

community sector and of growth in public provision of community education through Vocational Education Committees (VECs). The 1990s was
also a time of escalated interest in adult and community education policies, a
period when discourse on *lifelong learning* particularly emerged. The expression lifelong learning appeared within international Group of 7 (G7) communications, in Organisation for Economic and Co-operative Development
(OECD) development programmes, within United Nations Educational,
Scientific and Cultural Organisation (UNESCO) promoted adult education
work, at European Round table of Industrialists discussions and within the
European Commission (Hake 1999). In many ways, what was written about
lifelong learning mirrored ideological trends in adult education at the time.
Lifelong learning was weighted towards humanistic approaches, but was also
broad enough to accommodate more radical perspectives within (Hake
1999; Borg and Mayo 2005). Where lifelong learning had previously been
considered a branch within adult education and mostly related to education
for leisure (Jarvis 2004: 44), many educators began to adopt the expression
more broadly. This seemingly innocuous expansion of terminology allowed
educators to embrace a cradle to grave approach to learning and, outside of
the limitations of individualist tendencies, lifelong learning discourse
appeared largely unproblematic.

However, when rooted in its sociopolitical context, a more concealed
function of lifelong learning policy began to emerge that shifted its meaning
away from its humanistic tendencies. The origins of this transformation lie
with EU policy's incorporation of the concept of *human capital*, a key
component in building the so-called knowledge-economy. What the EU
meant by these expressions can be gleaned through its debut policy commitment to human capital expansion which came within the European
Commission's *White Paper on Teaching and learning: Towards the learning
society* (1995) (*Teaching and learning*). This policy called on EU members to
embrace Europe's new information society, a society where fresh avenues for
knowledge production are paramount to a country's ability to commercially
grow. *Teaching and learning* recommended "investment inputs in human
capital" and offered support in advancing this policy direction where "consultation will be initiated with Member States on promoting investment in
human resources as a fixed asset" (European Commission 1995: 55).

Hurley (2014) demonstrates how this interpretation of human capital
replicates ideas originally put forward by the neoliberal Chicago school
economist T.W. Shultz in his thesis *Investment in Human Capital* (1961).
Shultz (1961: 3) determined that by "counting individuals who can and

want to work, and treating such a count as a measure of the quantity of an economic factor" we can compare this to the way we count inanimate tools of production such as machinery. Schultz (1961: 2) notes controversy with the idea that humans can be commodified in this way sharing "the mere thought of investment in human beings is offensive to some among us" and continues, "our values and beliefs inhibit us from looking upon human beings as capital goods, except in slavery and this we abhor" (Shultz 1961: 2). However, the insatiable appetite of neoliberalism brushed the author's own concerns aside as human capital expansion was welcomed by right-wing economists in a way that has allowed this once controversial expression to have "largely gained uncritical currency" (Hurley 2014: 80).

Another influential communiqué, *a Memorandum on Lifelong Learning*, was published by the European Commission in 2000. Again the document describes lifelong learning as the pathway to a more sophisticated knowledge society where much faith is placed in expansion through technological and intellectual progress. The Commission again claims that Europe has entered a "knowledge age" (European Commission 2000: 3) continuing "lifelong learning must accompany a successful transition to a knowledge-based economy and society" (European Commission 2000: 3). Education and training systems "must adapt" to the altered economic environment. To do this, "lifelong learning is no longer just one aspect of education and training; it must become the guiding principle for provision and participation across the full continuum of learning contexts" (European Commission 2000: 3). Whilst *a Memorandum on Lifelong Learning* (2000) clearly favours employability discourse, it would be disingenuous to ignore how this policy document also claims equal billing for the development of active citizenship. The difficulty however is that active citizenship is largely couched within a person's participation in the work force, as is demonstrated within the excerpt below:

Active citizenship focuses on whether and how people participate in all spheres of social and economic life, the chances and risks they face in trying to do so, and the extent to which they therefore feel that they belong to and have a fair say in the society in which they live. For much of most people's lives, having paid work underpins independence, self-respect and well-being, and is therefore a key to people's overall quality of life. Employability – the capacity to secure and keep employment – is not only a core dimension of active citizenship, but it is equally a decisive condition for reaching full employment and for improving European competitiveness and prosperity in the "new economy". (European Commission 2000: 5)

Some of you might argue that there is little wrong with centralising citizen skills in a way that improves people's capacities to find work. Building human capital has also been described as essential in promoting individual well-being (OECD 2001) and the logic of the knowledge economy has been embraced beyond the EU (Thompson 2007; Lauder 2011). Equally, community education has always created spaces to support those wishing to take up meaningful employment. However, when employability is seen as the only real purpose of education, other possible functions such as pursuing individual interests, personal development, critical thinking and praxis are immediately marginalised (Brine 2006; Grummell 2014). Barriers instantly emerge for many people; for those who are older, for people with disabilities that render them unable to work and/or for people in a caring role. For the organisers of community education, programmes that fall outside of the parameters of employability become superfluous to policy demands making them less likely to fit the criteria for State funding.

Even if we accept the use of education for employability, there are still problems as lifelong learning policies exacerbate inequality. This is through its binary division of society into what Brine (2006) describes as those with high-knowledge skills and those with low-knowledge skills with the latter category describing those who usually access community education. This division has resulted in what Lauder (2011: 241) calls a "global auction for high-skilled work but a Dutch or reverse auction where jobs go to the lowest priced". Not only do the benefits of a mobile workforce divide unequally across social stratums, they also divide unequally across nation States. Maltone et al. (2012) measures growing numbers of working poor in newer EU Member States where there is a culture of outsourcing and depressed wages. As many Europeans are overrun with piecemeal employment contracts, low pay and difficulties maintaining a meaningful work-life balance, neoliberal rhetoric continually focuses on job quantity through private sector employment and not on job quality.

Given the managerialist ideology inherent within wider education structures (Lynch et al. 2012) publically funded education systems, including community education provided by the State, are put under constant pressure to adapt their outputs to the changing demands of the private market. Borg and Mayo (2005: 214–215) portray this use of State services as "the process of the privatization of the learner" then describe the use of public education as "a strategy that ensures the availability of an 'army of workers' that is consistently updating itself". The real winners in this situation are the needs of corporations and businesses with the needs of citizens less countenanced.

Despite such critiques of the direction EU adult education policy was taking, many practitioners within member States cautiously welcomed the sentiments within a *Memorandum on Lifelong Learning* (2000), particularly its focus on citizenship (Connolly 2006: 114). The Irish *Submission to the EU Memorandum on Lifelong Learning* (which was submitted as part of a consultation process initiated within the memorandum) praised "the breadth of the memorandum in particular its recognition of different settings for learning both formal and non-formal" (AONTAS 2001: 1). This submission also advised caution and emphasised the need to protect the idea of education beyond human resource development.

Concerns about the balance between social demands and economic demands may well have been relayed, but they do not seem to have been taken on board. The 2001 communication *Making a European Area of Lifelong Learning a Reality* (2001) reported back on the consultation process claiming a mandate that "confirms lifelong learning as a key element of the strategy...to make Europe the most competitive and dynamic knowledge-based society in the world" (European Commission 2001: 3). *Making a European Area of Lifelong Learning a Reality* (2001) centralised the self-directed individualised learner and encouraged her/him to engage with flexible, measurable, transferable knowledge in order to maximise their employment chances. Other key policy initiatives were *A Programme for Education and Training* (2002) which formed part of Lisbon goals in the lead up to the *Lisbon Treaty* of 2007, the constitution of the EU. *A Programme for Education and Training* (2002) further entrenched lifelong learning as an economic imperative and prioritised it alongside human resource development policy; a trajectory that Murtagh (2009: 165) urges adult educators to become more aware of. *A Programme for Education and Training* (2002) also asked members to measure outcomes through formal accreditation (the impacts of which are explored within the next chapter).

Relationships between adult education and employability continued through *Resolution on a Renewed European Agenda for Adult Learning* (Council of the European Union 2011). This document takes aim at those who are long-term unemployed and therefore likely to personify the multidimensional nature of unemployment. The resolution describes adult education as playing a "major role ... by enabling adults – in particular the low skilled and older workers – to improve their ability to adapt to changes in the labour-market and society" (Council of the European Union 2011: 1). Again this communication restates education, particularly Further Education (FE), or vocational education as it is sometimes called, as an instrument for servicing the demands of the global economy. *Resolution on a Renewed European Agenda for Adult Learning* dualistically stratifies learners into those suitable for Higher Education academic pathways and those suitable for FE vocational pathways (Council of the European Union 2011) and links adult education to another important influence, the *European Strategic Framework for Education and Training* (ET2020). The ET2020 set four strategic objectives for EU member States; to make lifelong learning and mobility a reality, to improve the quality and efficiency of education and training, to promote equality (of opportunity) and to ensure social cohesion and active citizenship. As should be clear by now, EU2020 continues an established trend that links citizenship to individualised policies on education and training and not more customary structures of democracy such as participation in local government.

IRELAND'S POLICY REACTION AND THE IMPLICATIONS FOR COMMUNITY EDUCATION

For the most part, public discourse in Ireland presents EU membership in positive terms and most politicians and policymakers promote Irish involvement as common sense. However, the implications of membership have not always been an easy sell. Embracing a European identity involves negotiating Ireland's cultural legacy of post-British rule where the Catholic Church held significant power throughout the twentieth century (Inglis 1998) and where there is a strong nationalist base of racial and territorial identity (Boyce 1995). Nationalism and Catholicism were deliberately inculcated through our post-colonial education system (Coolahan 1981; Inglis 1998) and became important signifiers in a still present narrow perception of Irishness (Carr and Haynes 2015). Rather than refute our problematic national identity in favour of a European mindset, Irish politicians and policymakers commonly played to national sentiments when seeking support for European-led reform (Hayward 2009: 2). Successful management of this tension has helped citizens to embrace Ireland's dual identity and there is little appetite to question the logic of Europeanisation.

A country's political relationship with the EU is however complex and the extent to which European policies are domestically incorporated depends on whether support for Europeanisation is reflected in the beha-viour of domestic political actors (Rees et al. 2010; Milana 2012). Irish policymakers have embraced *a Memorandum on Lifelong Learning* (European Commission 2000). Almost immediately, a steering committee with representatives from the Department of Education and Science (DES) and the Department of Enterprise, Trade and Employment was estab-lished. This committee "considered the Memorandum in the context of national policies and strategies for Lifelong Learning" with particular regard for "the development of common strategies for employment and the co-ordination of national policy" (DES 2001: 3). The committee described how its work followed an "unprecedented level of dialogue on the theme of lifelong learning" (DES 2001: 4) and directly referenced the *Green Paper, Adult Education in an Era of Lifelong Learning* (Government of Ireland 1998) and *Learning for Life: White Paper on Adult Education (Learning for Life)* (DES, 2000) as part of this dialogue. These two policy documents are commonly evoked as important in the development of community education in Ireland, especially the White Paper which was produced following a lengthy consultation process with civil society and public organisations. Although *Learning for Life* (2000) has a strong vocational dimension, it offers a vision for society that is built on consciousness raising, citizenship, cohesion, cultural development and community building (DES 2000: 28). *Learning for Life* (2000) also includes a chapter on what it describes as "the Community Education movement" (DES 2000: 109) offering two perspectives on community education; as an outreach arm of providers such as universities and colleges and as an ideologically led collective process linked to community development.

Despite acknowledging the importance of an inadequately funded independent community sector, government actions that followed pub-lication of the White Paper did not sufficiently support this "second-view" (DES 2000: 112) as all financial investment went to public provi-sion and not to providers within the community sector. This was mostly by appointing Community Education Facilitators (CEFs) within each

VEC. As has already been identified within earlier chapters, the CEF practitioner's position paper supports an equality focus, a standpoint that is echoed in findings from this study. However, this perspective was not determined from the top, rather grew from the capacities and expertise of these community educators themselves. Hurley (2014: 76) explains:

> While the appointment of CEFs brought a welcome dynamic to the field and led to an increase in participation because of the increased reach it conferred on VECs/ETBs, their activities are determined by Circular letter 45/02 from which any consideration of the principle of equality are absent.

As well as contradictions between the written policy and how the policy was implemented, it is equally important not to let the equality-based language within *Learning for Life* (2000) detract us from human resource policies that more deliberately set out to harmonise domestic and EU policy. The Irish policy document, *White Paper: Human Resource Development* (1997) is particularly relevant given its role in forming an Expert Group on Future Skills Needs (EGFSN). Reporting in the late 1990s, EGFSN describes a booming Celtic Tiger economy but expresses concern at its ability to meet the growing needs of the labour market (EGFSN 1998). The Irish government listened to the recommendations made by EGFSN and its commitment to human resource development was cemented. This is evident within the influential *National Development Plan* (NDP) 2000–2006 which includes a comprehensive statement on adult education and lifelong learning. Revealingly, this was enclosed within discussion on employment activation and human resource development. In a comprehensive review of Irish adult education policy, Murtagh (2009: 164–165) explains how policymakers of *Learning for Life* (2000) were acutely aware of this government emphasis on human resource development and describes how ultimately, the proposals implemented from *Learning for Life* (2000) were those that appeared within the NDP.

COMMUNITY SECTOR POLICY DEVELOPMENTS

For community education that more readily aligns with the community sector (see Chapter 3) another important policy development was the *White Paper on a Framework for Supporting Voluntary Activity and for*

Developing the Relationship between the State and the Community and Voluntary sector (*Supporting Voluntary Activity*), which was published in 2000. Long awaited by many within the community sector, this policy was again introduced following consultation with civil society organisations. *Supporting Voluntary Activity* (2000) guaranteed formal recognition for many voluntary organisations, committed to open and regular communication with the State and set out a framework for community sector representation in policymaking. *Supporting Voluntary Activity* describes funding difficulties as a "major issue" (Government of Ireland 2000: 132) and claims this would be rectified through multi-annual funding for "agreed priority services and community development activities" committing to "a major move away from the present unsatisfactory and *ad hoc* funding schemes experienced by many Community and Voluntary groups" (Government of Ireland 2000: 3, italics in original). As will be demonstrated, none of these promises were kept in the long term.

NEOLIBERALISM TAKES HOLD

On paper, policy developments in *Adult Education in an Era of Lifelong Learning* (1998), *Learning for Life* (2000) and *Supporting Voluntary Activity* (2000) should have solidified the position of community education in Ireland. Representative organisations were bringing unheard voices to the heart of policy where principles and values congruent with equality were mainstreamed in a way that should have ensured the more secure financial footing promised in *Supporting Voluntary Activity* (2000). There was also the ongoing presence of AONTAS and the National Adult Literacy Agency (NALA) as well as growing relationships with educators across the EU such as through the European Association for the Education of Adults. Practitioner-led education strategies were also emerging as community educators shaped and defined work on the ground (Ó Muircheartaigh 2004: 42). However, the 2000s was a period of uncertainty as community education struggled to assert its identity as a force for political change. Practitioners also began to report increased bureaucracy and demands for measurable outputs from government funders (Fleming 2004; Keogh 2004: 10; Ó'Muircheartaigh 2004). These changes link to sociopolitical situations as, although there were no significant policy changes at the time, neoliberal managerialist policies were filtering through to community education contexts. Changing government mentality is captured by Fleming (2004) who draws from a keynote address by the Minister for Education and Science at an AONTAS conference on community education in the early 2000s. In her speech, the minister stated:

> There needs to be accountability for that money [funding for community education] and an end result, not just a process. It is becoming increasingly obvious that, if education sectors and initiatives within them are to continue to attract and grow their funding, outcomes must be documented in terms of the objectives achieved and the concrete gains for the participants... Funding of a project cannot be solely justified on the worthiness of the client group. (De Valere, quoted in Fleming 2004: 12)

The minister injects the language of the market into community education and, in doing so, sidelines a needs-based approach in favour of an outcomes approach that is less respectful of the process-oriented nature of the work.

The Emergence of SOLAS

Because the outputs from the white paper on adult education expanded community education through public, VEC delivery and not through the community sector, this linked community education to FE, the other type of adult education the VECs take responsibility for. FE in Ireland is largely vocational, is ad hoc and is a richly diverse sector that traditionally caters for working-class students. Historically, most delivery of FE has been through a network of VEC-managed FE Colleges as well as through FÁS (The Irish National Training Authority). The neoliberal project sought to tame this diverse sector and to incorporate community education within its structures. The most significant Irish legislative change was through the creation of Seirbhísí Oideachais Leanunaigh Agus Scileanna or SOLAS, the new Further Education and Training Authority (est. 2013). SOLAS implemented wide-ranging reform. It halved the number of education committees merging 33 VECs into 16 Education and Training Boards (ETBs) and integrating FÁS into this revised structure. In 2014, SOLAS revealed its plans for Further Education and Training (FET) in the *Further Education and Training Strategy 2014–2019* (*FET Strategy*). Unlike previous adult and community education policy, the *FET Strategy* (2014) offers an extremely limiting perspective of adult education with little insight outside of a strong labour-market focus and only a cursory nod to the broader demo-cratic functions of education. The core function of community education is as a mechanism for recruiting those considered most marginalised into programmes for employability (SOLAS 2014a: 4) Support for community education as described within *Learning for Life* (2000) was therefore lost with O'Reilly (2014: 163) describing the principles of community educa-tion as "diametrically opposed to the new world of FET policy".

Community Education and Conditionaliy of Welfare

Another important EU directive thus far unnamed was demands to tighten domestic policy on *conditionality of welfare*. This is where a person's failure to attend certain training programmes can result in cuts to their weekly social welfare payments. Ireland has had the capacity to enforce conditionality of welfare for some time but this has been sporadi-cally put into practice. Murphy (2012) gives us a number of reasons for inconsistencies beginning with a culture of freedom for State employees whose job it was to implement these policies. She also believes the enfor-cement department – the Department of Social Protection (DSP) was down the governmental pecking order of priorities and that FÁS lacked policy ambition and was content instead to provide piecemeal services in local communities. Local freedoms for FÁS often benefitted community education and many FÁS-community sector collaborations supported community development and leadership initiatives, personal development programmes and a range of community employment projects.

Ireland's decision to tighten conditionality of welfare was not domes-tically conceived of but was part of wider austerity reactions to the EU and global economic downturns that are described in chapter 1 of this book. The politics of austerity that were introduced in response to global economic downturns not only sought to shore up stock-market losses, they served a hidden function where neoliberal governments opportu-nistically imposed harsh anti-welfare policies (Ladi and Tsarouhas 2014; Windebank and Whitworth 2014). Ireland began to toughen its position on social welfare in 2011 when the government appointed a senior political figure Joan Burton (the finance spokesperson for the minor coalition government partner) to oversee the DSP. That same year, the DSP created the National Employment and Entitlements Service (NEES) who set out to advance Ireland's Labour Market Activation Policy which has been conceived of a year earlier by the Department of

Enterprise and Employment. The *Project Plan for the Development and Implementation of the National Employment and Entitlements Service* (DSP 2011) explains a system of compulsory, individualised progression plans for each welfare recipient that are determined during in-depth registration processes. If a jobseeker (policy terminology) failed to comply with these personal plans their welfare benefits would be reduced or even stopped completely (DSP 2011: 4). These actions moved Ireland's welfare approach away from the passivity of processing claims and payments to a more punitive case-management style that is organised through local *Intreo* centres, newly established one-stop shops for unemployment-related welfare supports.

One way community education enters this fray is through its involvement in the Labour Market Activation Fund (LMAF). Community sector organisations as well as public and private education providers all tendered for contracts with the LMAF with concerns about an ideological mismatch possibly minimised given practitioners lengthy experience in managing disparate funding sources as is described in Chapter 3.

The Co-option of the Community Sector

Paralleling the neoliberalisation of educational policy, there were also distinct changes in relationships between the State and the community sector that dates back to 2002. This was the year the Department of Community and Family Affairs (DCFA) was dismantled, a government department that swam against the tide through its support for the idea that community development embodied participation, empowerment and social justice (Connolly 2014: 64). The newly established Department of Community Rural and Gealteacht Affairs (DCRGA) implemented much change, all of which have been detailed within the first chapter of this book. Three-year funding streams were discontinued, work plans became dependent on local government endorsement and a value for money paradigm was introduced that shifted emphasis away from previously accepted principles of capacity building and empowerment (Bassett 2007; Bissett 2015).

While there may have been an awareness of difficulties in State–civil society relationships throughout the early 2000s, nothing prepared the community sector for the changes that occurred from 2009 onwards, much of which was implemented following the government report from the *Special Group on Public Service Numbers and Expenditure Programmes*

(2009) or *McCarthy Report* as it is commonly known.[4] *The McCarthy Report* crudely analysed the work of the community sector through an outputs approach. Ultimately, the report contented there is "little evidence of positive outcomes for these [community sector] initiatives" (volume two, Government of Ireland 2009: 41). Whilst this comment caused outrage for many within the community sector, it was supported by the Fianna Fail government of the time. In an address to a parliamentary Joint Committee, the minister with responsibility for DCRGA (John Curran) commented "my Department would agree that, in general, the programmes have been lacking in demonstrable evidence of positive outcomes and that the delivery structure is not optimal".[5] Soon after, the DCRGA initiated an extensive process of downsizing. Firstly 94 Local Area Partnership (LAP) companies were reduced to 52 and, with a few exceptions, Community Development Projects (CDPs) were absorbed into this downscaled structure to form the Local and Community Development Programme (LCDP). This not only forced voluntary boards of management to disband, it effectively sequestered many assets that had been built up by community sector organisations over the previous 30 years. Some CDPs were not given the option to merge as their funding was abruptly withdrawn, a decision communicated by e-mail to the 13 projects affected.

Budget cuts were not confined to the CDP/LCDP programme but were widespread across the community sector and community services provision. One report carried out by independent researcher Brian Harvey and commissioned by the Irish Congress of Trade Unions detailed budgetary losses as follows:

> The LCDP down from €84.7m to €55.3m, down – 35%; the drugs initiative from €44.3m to €31.4m, down – 29%; the Community Services Programme (formerly the social economy programme) down – 18%; the Family Support Agency, which funds the Family Resource Centres, has fallen from €36m to €29.8m, down – 17%. Over 2008–2011, the RAPID programme in disadvantaged urban areas is down from €9.7m to €3.2m, – 67%, while the CLAR programme in disadvantaged rural areas, €24.1m at the start has been wound down. Funding for community and social inclusion has fallen from €10.2m to €2.9m (–72%) and within that, funding for community and voluntary fora has fallen from €1.4m to €587,000, down 58%. (Harvey 2012: 13)

The news of budget cuts, closures and mergers led to objection and protest from some within the community sector. Oppositional tactics included picketing the offices of certain politicians, openly objecting at information sessions and organising sectoral gatherings to propose alternatives.[6] The most prominent and united objection was through the actions of the Spectacle of Defiance and Hope, a creative resistance movement that sought to ally with trade unions, artists and other civil society and political organisations. One of the first tasks of the Spectacle was to raise public awareness as many involved felt that the ease at which the community sector could be rationalised was because the general public was unaware of its existence. In 2011, and again in 2012 and 2013, thousands of community workers, participants of community sector programmes and other supporters such as trade unionists left-wing politicians, activists and academics marched through Dublin with its key message being to "stop ripping the hearts out of community". Importantly, the Spectacle contextualised the closure of local projects amidst the government's contradictory support for financial institutions (see chapter 1 for discussion on the bank guarantee of 2008). In 2011 the Spectacle march ended at the Central Bank of Ireland (CBI) with protesters tying t-shirts, cut out hearts, ribbons and other paraphernalia to the gates of the CBI, the organisation responsible for national financial regulation. Most of the items left had been designed during community-based workshops organised in the lead up to the march.

Changes in Local Government
Another accelerant in community sector realignment was through policy changes to how local government is organised. Following the general election of 2011, the unpopular DCRGA was disbanded with responsibility for the community sector brought under the Department of Environment, Community and Local Government (DECLG, a department itself disbanded following the general election of 2016). This realignment offered no reprieve for the community sector as the *Putting People First action programme for local government* (DECLG 2012) vowed to further align local government and local development. In 2014, the *Local Government Reform Act* radically reformed local government in Ireland as City and Town Councils were merged. Local Community Development Committees (LCDCs) were also established tasked with developing and monitoring local economic and community plans including overseeing community development budgets.

These reforms, implemented from the top down and without sufficient consultation, were affective in disenfranchising many of the local activists who had been at the heart of the community sector for many years. Despite their momentous implications, many of those working within the community sector were not fully aware of the extent of change that was happening. In an attempt to address this, the practitioner network, the Community Workers Cooperative (CWC), organised a series of nationwide information sessions. Reporting back on this process, the CWC (2013: 2) note:

> The lack of information on the ground is startling, even in the frontrunner areas where it might be expected that there would be some level of awareness. This is primarily due to the lack of information (a) from the Department of Environment, Community and Local Government who have so far not undertaken any communication strategy to ensure that communities are informed of the proposed changes, and (b) from the local authorities, who, apart from some exceptions, have been very selective in their communication. Real consultation is all but absent.

Enter the Social Inclusion and Community Activation Programme
In 2015, the Social Inclusion and Community Activation Programme (SICAP) was introduced to replace the LCDP. On paper, SICAP places equality-based community education centre stage with its stated aims "to tackle poverty, social exclusion and long term unemployment through local engagement and partnerships between disadvantaged individuals, community organisations and public sector agencies" (Pobail 2015: 3). SICAP sets out three goals, (1) to support and resource disadvantaged communities and groups addressing exclusion and inequality, (2) to address educational disadvantage through life-long learning that uses community development approaches and (3) to engage with those unemployed so they can be supported into the labour market by improving their "work-readiness" and by supporting entrepreneurialism.

In reality this policy uses the rhetoric of community development but enforces an ideological shift through its sole reliance on measurable outputs. When SICAP was unveiled, some community sector employees openly objected at government information seminars claiming SICAP was a process of neoliberalism in action (Meagher 2014). Access to SICAP contracts was equally anathema to the collectivised, uniting principles of community development. This was because LCDPs were pitted against each other through a confidential, competitive public procurement process justified through the need to implement an EU directive on transparency in public contracts.[7] The newly emergent

SICAP landscape is more tightly regulated, has considerably less paid community workers and has facilitated the closure of many community supports both large and small. Take the urban suburb of Ballymun in North Dublin as a case in point. The Ballymun-Whitehall Area Partnership's failure to secure a SICAP contract resulted in its closure. Other Ballymun projects to close included Community Action Plan (CAP), the Ballymun Men's Centre, the Community and Family Training Agency (CAFTA), the Little Rascals Crèche (which was part of CAFTA) and the Ballymun Young Women's Project. Such situations are replicated in other working-class communities across Ireland.

Practitioner Perspectives on Change

Given the extent of policy change that has been described and the ensuing restructuring of community education provision, it is unsurprising that 30% (n38 of n127) of additional comments shared by survey participants relate to dissatisfaction with outcomes and employability approaches. Some comments are broad in their criticism such as the comment below.

> I think that the State is becoming increasingly hostile to community development (understandably) and seem to have little interest in community education. I think that both need to seek wholly different ways of rethinking themselves in order to reestablish their independence and to survive in any meaningful form. (Survey respondent, community sector)

Others offer a perspective that interprets policy change as detrimental to community education's equality agenda with the contributions below contextualising change within the wider austerity programme.

> The whole sector is totally constrained, even more so in these times of austerity. It is becoming increasingly difficult to challenge inequality on a societal level as we are restricted to the value for money approach of funders. (Survey respondent, community sector)

In an equally critical comment:

> Current government policies seem to be hell bent on diminishing the gains made during the boom in disadvantaged areas especially in community employment and first and second level education. (Survey respondent, community sector)

Table 5.1 Attitudinal measurement on relationships between equality and political reform

Strongly agree (%)	Agree (%)	Somewhat agree (%)	Not sure if I agree or disagree (%)	Somewhat disagree (%)	Disagree (%)	Strongly disagree (%)
33	34	7	15	8	2	1

Survey question: The only way equality and social justice can be truly achieved is through a complete overhaul of our political and economic system

By way of capturing broader opinion on the State, Table 5.1 quantifies perspectives on its ability to address inequality. Almost three-quarters of surveyed community educators (n226) believe that this can only be done through an overhaul of our political and economic system.

The manner in which labour market activation has been introduced through social policy is also emphasised by some community educators. This survey respondent who works for an independent community education organisation that receives VEC/ETB funding (see Chapter 3 for further discussion on organisational categorisations) despondently shares:

> Community Education has already changed and does not hold with the ethos it had formerly. It has been co-opted by the State into training. I have great difficulties reconciling this with my political beliefs as I don't really want to be training people so the multi-nationals will have good little workers until they decide to pull out. If the labour-market is to benefit then I would rather it was benefited by educating people so they can create worthwhile jobs for themselves and others in their community. (Survey respondent, community sector)

This quote above demonstrates support for people to get jobs, but distain for the neoliberal nature of employability discourse. Others echo dissatisfaction with labour market activation approaches across both public sector and community sector provision.

> the government pay lip-service to community education and local communities . . . the reality is this government is only interested in getting people on education and training to show they are doing something about unemployment . . . the only figure that matters is output in terms of bums on seats. (Survey respondent, tutor VEC/ETB)

> Seriously concerned about the narrowing focus on labour market related outcomes. (Survey respondent, community sector)

Arguments both for and against labour market activation emerge within focus-group conversations. One community educator supports these policy initiatives indicating how, despite "excessive paperwork" there are benefits for the participants of community education. However, this is an isolated opinion amidst many counter-arguments against a strong labour market focus. To give two typical examples:

> The big brother is the policy drive . . . the policy context is absolutely around certification and labour market activation and if you can't make direct links between your work and somebody getting a job within a very short period of time, what do you do? (Limerick, focus group)

> It's all about numbers and bums and seats and how many people get jobs and it is moving very much into enterprise and pre-enterprise and bringing people closer to the labour market. (Kildare, focus group)

In four out of eight focus groups, conversations about labour market activation also include a concern for conditionality of welfare, something that these contributors are directed impacted by. There are reports of mixed abilities in groups and of participants struggling to cover the costs of education such as transport and food. The quote below is a description of one educator's experience when she was invited to evaluate a labour market activation programme that was delivered by another facilitator/educator.

> Oh my God it was frightening. We [her and a co-facilitator] went in to do maximum an hour. We expected to be in and out in a half an hour just get their feed-back and see what they think. Two hours later there were people in tears, there was so much going on in that room it was frightening. We suggested that they collectively write a letter to the minister explaining their concerns and what the impact was, because the impact was emotionally, psychologically, on these people, and the detrimental things that were going on in their families as a result of them leaving their homes to come on a course. (Athlone, participant two)

Whilst this contribution paints a stark picture for the participants of welfare conditionality, the illustrative example below raises concerns about the impacts on the educators involved.

> They are up-skilling people who are long term unemployed and disadvantaged groups in our communities are now being forced to engage in

154 COMMUNITY EDUCATION AND NEOLIBERALISM

training to get their social welfare payment. So it is kind of a contradiction, in one sense the tutor doesn't really have as much control as the students coming into the room because if the student is not happy and doesn't engage, it would affect everything, it would affect your reputation, your ability to bring that learner through, it would affect your figures, pro rata payments, and really what has happened in the last few years is the total commodification of unemployed people. They have become a commodity for the education awards. (Central Dublin, participant one)

Negative accounts of welfare conditionality are not isolated to this study. On examining similar programmes in the UK, O'Grady (2008) concludes compulsory attendance is not only unlikely to improve educational capacities but can amplify previously held negative experiences of education.

Reports of difficulties with labour market activation also contrast with claims within a recent review of the LMAF by the Irish government where the involvement of the community sector was praised.

The inclusion of providers outside the mainstream delivery agencies (e.g. from the private or community and voluntary sectors) was found to be a key attribute of the LMAF . . . there were certainly notable successes arising from the inclusion of such providers as they often brought a new approach and way of thinking to the table. There is, therefore, a rationale for continuing to allow such open competition for activation funding on the basis of outcomes. (DOES 2011: iv)

Another theme to emerge from research is that many make reference to increased accountability demands, a hallmark of new public management approaches (Lynch et al. 2012) and a theme further explored in Chapter 6. One community educator shares a useful image of an inverted triangle where, more and more, bureaucratic procedures that have been put in place support less and less work on the ground. He describes a managerialist fixation with paperwork compliance that is often considered more important than the work itself explaining:

It doesn't matter about the outcomes at all . . . it's about covering your arse, being able to say that you did the thing, as long as you can show on paper that you did it, that you did what you were supposed to do, that's all that matters (Interviewee five, community sector and HEI).

Another example also captures the burdensome nature of outputs approaches as follows:

> So it is all these boxes, we have to fit into, these particular box systems and then there is loads of recording, now I don't mind recording and detailing but it's all, it's taking a huge amount of time and it is taking you further and further from the people on the ground. (Interviewee four, community sector)

Community Sector Co-option

Respondent's views on co-option largely support many of the arguments put forward in literature. Table 5.2 measures 62% in agreement with the notion that the Irish community sector has been co-opted with 23% disagreeing.[8]

Across each research phase, Just n2 comments are in support of reform of the community sector both of which are shared within one-to-one interviews. Both of these participants work in large non-governmental organisations (NGOs). One interviewee believes the community sector "probably needed a big shake-up", the other cautiously welcomes change believing there was "too much duplication". All other qualitative comments gathered are against the restructuring of the community sector.

Sometimes community educators locate the roots of co-option in the managerialist polices of the early 2000s. One research participant who cites over 30 years working in the community sector, describes the State as "so anti-community development" continuing:

> I think the social change bit in what happened even before the financial crash, the suppression of dissent, the cutbacks in The Equality Authority,

Table 5.2 Attitudes on community sector cooption

Strongly agree (%)	Agree (%)	Somewhat agree (%)	Not sure if I agree or disagree (%)	Somewhat disagree (%)	Disagree (%)	Strongly disagree (%)
8	18	36	15	12	9	2

Survey question: The Irish Community Sector has been co-opted by the State and is not a force for influencing change

> Combat Poverty being put into social welfare, all of those things for us
> really said where the State was coming from...they wanted community
> development to be service delivery whereas all of the work that had been
> going on since 1988 and the bottom-up approach and the social change
> agenda, I mean just look at the way that has been picked off, bit-by-bit.
> (Waterford, participant two)

This is not an isolated opinion. Another research participant with almost
20 years working as a community educator explains:

> ...when crisis hit in 2008 and since then, it has become really obvious how
> quickly that [support] could be withdrawn, even the good parts and the
> genuine gains that people had made, they could just be withdrawn and be
> undermined – in four years, how stuff has been simply undermined so
> quickly. And I think what that suggests is, you know, that we didn't have
> the power that we thought we had. (Interviewee six, community sector)

Others solely focus their criticisms on the period after 2009 and the downsizing of the community sector. This first example is shared by a woman
who works in an independent community education organisation that was
previously funded as a Community Development Support Programme. In
2008, contracts between these support programmes and the State were not
renewed. She explains this action as follows:

> It was the flick of a pen. He [the Minister for DCRGA] could just decide that the
> whole programme was down by two million you know, or that it just wasn't
> value for money. That is soul destroying. (Interviewee two, community sector)

The project this research participant works within has managed to stay open
on a combination of self-generating incomes and philanthropic donations.

Similar language is used by another person, this time with reference to
the closure of CDPs some four years later. When I ask her about the
reasons for policy change she answers:

> Well there could be a number of reasons, number one they don't understand
> it, two they don't like the fact that people are able to think for themselves and
> they don't like the fact that people are getting together. They are getting an
> awareness through coming into groups and they feel threatened by that,
> maybe... I think that it is extremely worrying the way the community sector
> is going, and I think a lot of it is being dictated by government and by the fact
> that McCarthy and his "wisdom" [sarcastically] just put a pen through

community projects and it is shocking and it is unjust you know [...] more and more as you get sucked into the centre, you find less and less freedom to challenge the State and what it doesn't do. The shotgun is with the State so they have you under a barrel really. (Interviewee four, community sector)

This idea, that downscaling and co-option was an attempt to silence opposition, concurs with arguments put forward by O'Byrne (2012) and Bissett (2015). In this current study, not all of the blame for co-option is levelled at the State as some community educators are critical of action within the community sector itself. Some challenge the presumption that the community sector as a whole was in fact ever a political force for change, a situation that made it easy to co-opt. This point is raised in two one-to-one interviews and within two focus groups. The first chosen contribution draws out some of the philosophical differences amongst providers as discussed at length in Chapter 4. This community educator, influenced by a racial ideology, is unhappy with policy negotiators who adopt pluralist perspectives when they act on behalf of communities in attempts to negotiate power-sharing.

> ... there is a kind of complacency and a satisfaction of "job done" ... For the past 25 years, all of the institutions from the unions down have pushed the pluralist model that there is something in it for everyone, but there wasn't something in it for everybody, we know that, and what is really happening is that people in the lower tiers and the echelons of the system are paying absolutely enormous prices for the bigger questions. (South Dublin, participant three)

This challenge to a self-appointed community sector leadership is captured elsewhere through further discussion about policy negotiators. The first excerpt draws out a class-based disconnection.

> I think that there is a great lack of understanding of where people are coming from, I mean most of the policies, it is a class issue as far as I am concerned most of the policies etc. are drawn up by middle-class people who just simply don't understand where people are coming from (Central Dublin, participant two)

This second example relates more to how the isolation of a recognisable leadership can aid co-option through compliance.

> ... a real grassroots community development project would continue to focus on the issues at hand, and it didn't take place that way because it is much

easier for them if they [the State] can get one person into a room...and then they get bought off effectively, that is the way co-option works...(Tele-interviewee six working for a Traveller-specific project)

Both of these themes, the role of leadership; and class-based divisions amongst practitioners, are teased out more comprehensively within Chapter 7. This final insight gives voice to a survival mentality within the community sector (Crowley 2013) as follows:

The kind of context that we are operating in...you have the wider, gloomy economic picture so, it's very tricky right now and I think at the moment it is about trying to get through this period, this period of austerity and policy change and funding reductions and hope that we emerge from it strong enough as a sector whereby we can rebuild. (Interviewee seven, NGO with an emphasis on development education)

One way that participants in this study are strategically managing relationships with the administrators of government policy is through their approach to the use of public funding. Instead of uncritical compliance with funding regulations, many community educators stretch the parameters of government intentions so that they can more appropriately address community need. One response captures broader sentiment well as follows:

you would be watching what funding is coming in and you are trying to match, and you are looking at, "can that bit fit here", and "can I make that bit fit that", something like that, or, "if we twist it this way it could match" (Waterford, participant three).

This is not an isolated example but is echoed by another contributor.

Now that I am a tutor and also a funding applicant I can say whatever is necessary to get that money and I will teach whatever the group want in that classroom, but I am a complete fake, you know what I mean? I will falsify everything to make that happen. (Central Dublin, participant one)

Although evidence of some malleability in government funding, this excerpt demonstrates the lengths that this community educator feels she as to go to in order to effectively respond to the needs of the participants of community education.

STRATEGISING RELATIONSHIPS WITH POLICYMAKERS

When I ask focus-group members why more is not being done to address problematic relationships with the State, there is a sense of powerlessness in acting for change. Specific reasons for inaction shared are the perceived co-option of the trade union movement, a sense of sectoral apathy, the forced closure of the CDP programme and concerns about job insecurity (a point examined more deliberately in Chapter 7). Not all engagement with policy-makers is described negatively as one example emerges where efforts to shape policy are successful. In different focus-group settings, two CEFs tell us about a recent position paper on community education that was circulated by the DOES. One focus-group participant[9] speaks of being "kind of flabbergasted" when proposals outlined by the Community Education Facilitators Association were accepted into government policy continuing, "We thought 'my God, they listened to us'. So it is the value of having something written down that you can come back to, that is supportive".

Although this is an isolated comment, this surprise is understandable when it is contextualised amidst the sheer volume of non-negotiated change that was instigated without consultation. Participation in the policy arena can be demoralising. O'Reilly (2014: 166), a key negotiator with AONTAS, captures the difficulties with this work when she describes her own "internal conflict between one's perception of being a 'sell-out', or dedicating your life work to fighting a losing battle". One way forward is to consider a framework offered by Crowther and Shaw (2014) which helps us both reflect on and strategise our relationship with the State. Acknowledging how participation is commonly encouraged in order to *advance* and not *change* established government agendas, Crowther and Shaw (2014) encourage us to renegotiate the terms of engagement through a model of "strategic participation" and "strategic non-participation" when dealing with policymakers. Strategic participation is encouraged when to participate enhances democratic efficacy and expands the pool of involvement beyond the few. On the other hand, strategic non-participation reminds us of the importance of creating democratic spaces outside of traditional governance structures. This approach is broadly summarised in Table 5.3.

Crowther and Shaw's conflation of the desire to participate in policy spaces and the historical purpose of democratic community education, does not dismiss the many constrains practitioners face. These include limiting contracts of employment, cultural contexts of partnership and the wider political climate. What strategic participation/non-participation does do, is

Table **5.3**   Strategic participation/non-participation

Strategic participation	*Strategic non-participation*
Where intervention can make structures more democratic and effective	The creation of convivial, democratic educational spaces
Where politicians and institutions can be held to account	Strengthened democratic spaces outside of traditional governance arrangements
Where democratic processes have grass-roots support and not just a "consultative elite"	Support the autonomous development of local groups by emphasising distinctions between policy priorities and group ambitions
Where there can be challenges brought to tokenism and manipulation	Challenging the framing of democracy through policy instead of practice; making demands on government that reinforce its democratic capacities
Where the limits of democracy can be tested through democratic engagement	Emphasising the destructive implications of neoliberalism

Source: Adapted from Crowther and Shaw 2014: 402–404.

to help us differentiate between useful points of intervention and exercises in co-option that are to the detriment of grass-roots relationships. Rather than the occasionally paralysing perspective of having to choose to wholly engage or wholly disengage, this approach accommodates both possibilities freeing us up to act in response to likelihood of enhancing democracy.

CONCLUSION

A key ambition of neoliberalisation is to co-opt civil society organisations so that their day-to-day actions can support the neoliberal ambition of continued economic growth to the detriment of all else. For community education, European lifelong learning policies have altered domestic policies which now encapsulate a human capital, employability outlook. This pulls practice away from its previous capacity to support equality through a range of approaches. In this study, research findings expose a gulf between practitioner perspectives of how best to address inequality and policy discourse which often limits equality to the pursuit of low-paid employment. This gulf between policy perspectives and the perspectives of adult educators is somewhat unsurprising given the diminished quality of participation in recent policy reform.

Given our cultural preference for consultation, be this real or perceived, in the lead up to policy agreements, opportunities to engage with policymakers will continue to emerge. If we adopt a model of strategic participation/non-participation (Crowther and Shaw 2014) we can deliberately and purposefully contemplate whether the seductive nature of these negotiations is unhelpfully detracting us from building democracy from the ground up or if it is providing genuine opportunities to influence change. Perhaps it is possible to do both. Discussions about the future direction of community education re-emerge in more detail within Chapter 8. Before this, the next chapter examines the impacts of accreditation, another policy trajectory that has had a profound effect on community education.

Notes

1. AONTAS invited considerable dialogue with its members before submitting its submission "the voice of the adult learner" to the SOLAS consultative process. It can be viewed at http://www.aontas.com/download/pdf/aontas_submission_on_solas_consultation_process.pdf. Accessed 31 July 2014.
2. All submissions made to QQI during their consultation process can be viewed at http://www.qqi.ie/Consultation/Pages/default.aspx. Accessed 20 July 2014. Furthermore, at an AONTAS CEN meeting in March, 2015, the CEN membership reported making over 20 written submissions to QQI since its establishment.
3. These advocacy packs and specifically targeted policy work including submissions can be viewed at www.aontas.com. Accessed 20 July 2014.
4. This is because the chairperson of the special group on public service numbers and expenditure programme was the economist Colm McCarthy.
5. Address by John Curran TD Minister of State at the department of Community, Rural and Gaeltecht affairs to an 27 January 2010 retrieved from www.changingireland.ie. Accessed 20 April 2016.
6. These actions are reported within editorial and news accounts within Spring/Summer editions of the Community Sector magazine *Changing Ireland* An independent national magazine for community development who produce a quarterly print magazine which is sold across Ireland.
7. Directive 2014/24/EU in public procurement called for the awarding of public contracts by or on behalf of members States to comply with certain principles, most specifically non-discrimination, proportionality and transparency in the awarding of contracts (European Parliament 2014).
8. When these figures are broken down in terms of employment type, 77% of independent community educators, those not directly employed by a community sector or State provider outside of casual employment contracts agreed with this statement. Twenty–eight percent of those working within the community sector disagree and 60% agree. Sixty–six percent in

VECs and 55% in NGOs all agree with the statement. *The Irish Community Sector has been co-opted by the State and is not a force for influencing change.*

9. I am deliberately not sharing which focus group this comment was relayed within as to do so would compromise the anonymity of this CEF.

CHAPTER 6

Community Education and Accreditation

Illustration 6.1   The impact of accreditation

© The Author(s) 2017
C. Fitzsimons, *Community Education and Neoliberalism*,
DOI 10.1007/978-3-319-45937-0_6

A strange thing happened to me a few years ago when I was working as a community educator in a large Dublin-based non-governmental organisation (NGO). Twelve adults had enrolled for a six-week *Certificate in Housing* which was designed to explore current trends and issues in housing. The group was made up of people who worked in the community and non-governmental organisation (NGO) sectors as well as State-run housing authorities. There were also some tenants of social housing who were involved in the management of their own estates.

My job was to facilitate discussion on topics such as public provision of housing, tenant's rights, rent arrears, problem behaviour on estates and community development responses. I also introduced students to existing research on housing policy and practice and offered established theories to help them make sense of current situations. Throughout the process, I endeavoured to take my lead from the themes that emerged from the group, whilst at the same time keeping an eye on the prescribed *programme descriptor*. I remember feeling encouraged by energetic discussions within the group and, in response, designed assignments that would match the interests and concerns being expressed. In the end, participants were asked to select any housing-related issue they had come across (e.g. poor maintenance of social housing) and to analyse its personal, community, economic and political factors. The resulting social analysis spiral[1] allowed people to identify the points where a community could strategically intervene if they wanted to try and bring about change. I hoped this task would open up possibilities for action beyond the classroom.

I also wanted to model *assessment for learning*, where an assignment becomes a continuation of learning as directed by the knowledge and interests of the students. This is instead of the more traditional *assessment of learning*, a process where students are tested on their ability to ingest certain knowledge and relay it back through an essay or other form of project work.

The essays people submitted were insightful, at times profound, and always informative. They were also presented within the literacy and linguistic standard I believed was right for the qualification level which, in this case, was at the lower end of the national qualifications framework.

What was strange was what happened when these essays were presented to the accrediting body for external authentication. Rather than marvel at the student's work as I had done, the outside adjudicator admonished my supervision informing me that, at this level, these adults were *not allowed* to analyse. She preferred a more descriptive, skills-based assignment believing this would produce a more uniform response. That way, learning could be more easily benchmarked against the accrediting body's marking criteria and each person's future vertical progression could be more effortlessly measured. Technically she was correct. This was because she was the one interpreting national frameworks verbatim, a matrix where such human capacities as analysis and synthesis are reserved for programmes thought to be more advanced. These students would be awarded their certificates, but my future instructions were to make changes before any repeat delivery of the programme.

I had reservations about writing a separate chapter on accreditation. These reservations dissipated when I realised that I was not the only one struggling with aspects of contemporary accreditation models. In the survey element of this study, accreditation is the most frequently cited theme to emerge and although there is majority support, there is also much ambivalence. This chapter draws out a deficit between common models of accreditation, and attempts by educators to make these models work. It examines terminology, policies and practices relevant to accreditation, all of which contribute to the anecdote above. The role of national qualifications frameworks, learning outcomes approaches and quality assurance procedures will each be discussed. Before doing this, a good starting point is to consider what accreditation is and where it first came from.

THE ORIGINS OF ACCREDITATION

Accreditation is a word used to describe systems of quality assessment that approve an educational institution, an education programme, or both (Kohler 2003; Harvey 2004; Saarinen and Ala-Va¨ha¨la¨ 2007). What is assessed includes the learning environment and learner supports such as adequate resources and appropriate teaching staff. Curriculum design and course contents are also evaluated along with safeguards for the fair and consistent assessment of learning, programme accessibility and progression, and good governance. When the relevant accrediting body (e.g. Quality and Qualifications Ireland (QQI)) determines these conditions are met, providers are authorised to recruit participants, to deliver programmes and to give credits. These credits build into certificates, diplomas, degrees, masters and doctoral awards.

It is not uncommon for people to associate the origins of accreditation with policy convergence measures that were introduced as part of the European lifelong learning policies of the 1990s (discussed in Chapter 5). The *Bologna Declaration* (1999) and the lesser known *Declaration of the European Ministers of Vocational Education and Training*, and the European Commission, or *Copenhagen Declaration* (2002) stand out as do the Education and Training policies within *The Lisbon Treaty*, signed in 2007. These policies certainly shape contemporary practices, and each are discussed in more detail in due course. However, the practice of awarding certificates for learning actually predates State interest and has emerged from educators themselves. The bachelor's degrees awarded by universities are as old as the university system itself, dating back to medieval times. Other recognisable tenets of contemporary accreditation to come from universities include voluntarily initiated peer-review processes across institutions, which began in the 1800s (Harvey 2004; Brittingham 2009) and peer-evaluations designed to assure quality, which were made popular in the 1900s (Anderson 2006; Elassey 2015). Learning outcomes approaches were similarly introduced by the university sector offering a welcome release from the teacher-centred approaches that preceded them (Hadril 1995; Beno 2004).

Accreditation within schools also has a long history. In Ireland, *The Intermediate Education Act* of 1878 introduced public examinations (Coolahan 1981:53). Although some reforms have been introduced since then, terminal exams have pretty much shaped the school system ever since. Certified learning in vocational education was more ad hoc and there was variety across providers as to what constituted an appropriate programme of education (Coolahan 1981: 87–88; Clancy 1999: 95). As vocational education was often thought of as a bridge between work and school, exit standards mostly depended on the practical skills required to do a particular job. From the 1930s onwards, technical exams emerged including the national *Group Certificate* in 1947 and apprenticeships certificates in 1960 (Coolahan 1981: 100–101). In 1985, the European Social Fund enabled the Department of Education (DOE) to develop the *Vocational Preparation and Training Programme* which is often called the Post-Leaving Certificate (PLC) programme. Initially these PLCs were under the auspices of the secondary school system and accreditation was through certificates of attendance that were issued by the DOE. Most of these PLCs were delivered by Further Education (FE) providers and inevitably, public vocational awards were used such as the National Council for Vocational Awards (NCVA, est. 1991).

Historically, the process-oriented, equality-based community education that emerged from the 1970s onwards (see Chapter 3) was mostly non-accredited. This meant that learning was not formally recognised outside of the classrooms and communities that were directly involved. Many organisations issued certificates of attendance and, when doing so, often replicated the ceremony of conferrals where friends and family were invited to share in a person's achievements. Some organisations did award formal certifications. Early supports for women's community education included extramural certification through St Patrick's College in Maynooth (Connolly 2014: 53–54). Access outreach programmes were also accrediting community education through University College Dublin (Quilty 2003) and through the Waterford Institute of Technology (D'Alton et al. 2010). Public vocational awards such as those of the NCVA and FÁS (the now disbanded National Training Authority) were equally made use of during the late 1980s and early 1990s. City and Guilds, a UK-based private vocational accreditor, was also popular while other community educators prepared people for Intermediate and Leaving Certificate exams that were more usually found in schools (Kelly 1994: xxi–xxiv). Accreditation was however sporadic and the chances of a person's learning being formally recognised usually depended on the impetus of the individual provider.

Given community education's rootedness in an equality agenda, it is not surprising that access to accreditation became an important issue for those involved in community education. The most comprehensive account of bottom-up demands is captured through research called *Can you Credit it* (1994) undertaken by community-based practitioner Mary Kelly and jointly commissioned by the Combat Poverty Agency and AONTAS. Kelly's mixed-methods study captured much interest in accreditation with support for certification measured at 79% of learners and 74% of providers. Kelly (1994: xix) gives three reasons for such high demand:

1. The right of adults in disadvantaged communities to have options for securing credit for competency, developed at local level, on the basis of merit.
2. The need for accreditation options, to improve access of disadvantaged groups and individuals to paid work, and to strengthen the argument for more paid jobs in the Community Sector itself.
3. The need for accreditation to improve the current inequitable access, of those with no or low levels of qualification, to places on continuing education and advanced training courses.

Although the majority were in support of accreditation, over one quarter of practitioners were against the idea. Early apprehension focused on the potential for accreditation to individualise and liberalise grass-roots practice and to promote education as a way out of a community, rather than as a way to challenge the structural causes of inequality in the first place (Kelly 1994: 6). Kelly (1994) also highlighted emerging EU policies she believed lacked clarity on the relationship between accreditation and organically conceived non-vocational community courses such as some of those described within Chapter 3.

THE EUROPEANISATION OF ACCREDITATION

Irish interest in expanding accreditation was not happening in isolation. The late 1980s and 1990s was a period of intense European focus on uniting the many different national systems of accreditation. Where the advent of accreditation was once with educators, by the 1990s government ministers with responsibility for national education policy were taking an active role in discussions (European Universities Association 2014: 6–7). Negotiations between educators and politicians culminated in the signing of the well-known *Bologna Declaration* in 1999. This document bookended a process where agreements were reached that would significantly alter the educational landscape across 29 European countries, many of whom had previously resisted convergence measures (Van Der Wende 2000: 305; Saarinen and Ala-Va¨ha¨la 2007: 33; Croché 2009).

Signatories of Bologna approved the development of easily transferable degrees at undergraduate and graduate levels. They also agreed to cooperate through comparable, formal, quality assurance mechanisms and to standardise curricular developments. This was as well as interinstitutional collaborations through integrated programmes, greater staff and student mobility and cross-country access and training for teachers and researchers (European Higher Education Area 1999). Three years later, *The Declaration of the European Ministers of Vocational Education and Training, and the European Commission*, or *The Copenhagen Declaration* (European Commission 2002) extended convergence into vocational education (or Further Education as it mostly called in Ireland). These agreements had a ripple effect beyond participating nations as many neighbouring countries voluntarily adopted these measures (Harvey 2004: 200; Young 2007).

The Development of National Qualifications Frameworks

One of the main features of convergence was that each participating nation created a tiered *national qualifications framework* (NQF). These frameworks are hierarchical, linear and measurable in their approach to learning. Crucially, NQFs describe the relationship between different qualifications, each of which is pitched at a different numeric level. Each country can award credits at each level which, in turn, can be mapped to a broader European Credit Transfer System (ECTS). Since the Bologna Declaration (1999) was agreed, NQFs have become an omnipresent feature of the global education and training landscape.

The Irish NFQ, which was introduced in 2003, carries all the hallmarks of international NQFs as it structures individualised learning across a 10-level *grid of indicators*. At each level, learning is neatly measured across categories of "knowledge", "skills" and "competencies" (KSC). As a person moves up the framework, greater KSC complexity is demanded. The Irish NFQ also divides the advantages of education as either for learners or for employers. Learner benefits are listed as to enable career progression, to allow comparisons between qualifications, to assist informed decision-making and to offer a more coherent progression route "thereby avoiding education and training cul-de-sacs" (NFQ 2003b: 6). For employers, there is promise of an easier way to measure the standards of potential employees, and thereby, easier identification of "the most appropriate fit" for a particular position (NFQ 2003b: 7). National frameworks promise transparency, simplicity, quality, flexibility and transferability for both learners and employers (NFQ 2003a: 11; Hanf and Hipach-Schneider 2005).

There are a number of difficulties with the ideas that support the NFQ, most centrally the presumption that all learning can be objectively measured. Close reading of the NFQ grid of indicators demonstrates its own dependence on a level of subjectivity that contradicts its claim of uniformity. To demonstrate: when educators are asked to calculate a student's "competence insight" – one of the competencies assigned at each level – each learner (policy terminology) at level 4 is expected to "assume partial responsibility for consistency of self-understanding and behaviour"; at level 7, the anticipated "competence insight" is to "express an internalised, personal world view, manifesting solidarity with others" (NFQ 2003c: 3). One can imagine the challenges in assigning numeric value to such elusive and slippery statements. Entwistle (2005) equally points out difficulties with the assumption that similar benchmarks at each level can be used to measure learning across different disciplines. Can we really benchmark activism against the same criteria as arithmetic?

Another difficulty arises when we think about how these frameworks divide learning into either high-capacity or low-capacity learning. The Irish NFQ strictly allocates levels 1–6 to FE awards with levels 7–10 preserved for Higher Education (HE) awards. The logic behind this is that, as learners continue to learn, they become more adept at high-knowledge skills and thus vertically progress up the framework. The language of national frameworks reveal a lot as, at levels 1–6 learners are commonly instructed to "define", "describe", "list" and understand existing knowledge. It is not until they progress to the upper rungs of the framework that they can begin to "analyse", "critique" and "evaluate" (thus explaining the anecdote that opens this chapter). For me this delineation encourages a behaviourist-oriented, banking approach to education at the lower rungs. As discussed within Chapter 4, behaviourism fails to acknowledge the constructivist nature of knowledge as it seeks to transfer fixed canonical knowledge into largely passive learners. Immediately a power-dimension emerges as those learning at levels 7–10 are the ones believed to be capable of high-level analytical thinking and of generating new knowledge. Conversely, FE becomes a space where learners ingest the knowledge that is created by others, usually people whose socio-economic contexts differ greatly from their own (West 2006).

Ultimately, the controller of the curriculum controls whose version of events count (Giroux, in Freire and Macedo 1987: 18–19; Freire and Shor 1987; 75–76). Over the years, many community educators have interpreted this curricular control as an opportunity to create conditions where learning is not dictated by subject specialisms but is more congruent with the lived experience of its participants. Where community educators must follow preset contents, this is at best problematic and at worst incompatible with the aspirations of community education, particularly critical community education. Take a course in healthcare as an example. A critical approach would begin by inviting members of a group to reflect on their own health and the health of their community. Through conversations, the social determinants of health such as inadequate housing, poor working conditions, the cost of healthcare and limited access to a healthy diet would invariably emerge. Community educators can then introduce theories and information on health many of which are likely to match standard curricular expectations, but which explore these from the vantage point of the group. Health is thus explored from the personal to the political allowing people to analyse the dominance of the medial model and to appreciate the relevance of socio-economic contexts. When forced to work within the confines of a set curriculum, this process is more difficult to implement. As professional regulatory bodies within certain professions increasingly determine curricular contents (Harvey 2004) the probability is that uncritical accounts of the medical model with prevail. This is also likely to be what students are tested on in order to pass a programme. As community education is more and more interpreted as an instrument for employability (see Chapter 5 for more discussion), healthcare is narrowed even further as it is reduced to the technical skills required to find work as a healthcare worker. The critical educator has to squeeze in spaces for a bottom-up dialogic approach as she/he contends with the demands of covering set contents.

Another problem with the NQF's laddered approach is the way adults can be assigned to particular courses based on their literacy and numeracy capacities. This process of dividing people into different classes based on their perceived intellectual capacities can reinforce negative school associations. Many people's futures were (and still are) determined by streaming practices in Irish schools, a practice that fails to consider how each of us have different capacities in different contexts as well as within the same educational space.

Learning Outcomes Approaches
On paper, the shortfalls identified above – the subjective nature of measuring learning, the binary division of high-capacity and low-capacity learning and the lateral stratification of learning are addressed by asking each learner to prove that they have reached a set of specific *learning outcomes* at each level. Learning outcomes are not unique to adult education as they are widely used within primary and secondary schools. They are also not universally applied across all national frameworks and are less embedded within the university system. However, the rate at which the language of learning outcomes has become ubiquitous within educational discourse is worth emphasising. Routinely contents, methods of assessment and even teaching methodology are shaped around a set of pre-determined outcomes, therefore, outcomes decided upon before a learning group even comes together. As accreditation becomes more bureaucrised, these outcomes are usually written by people

with no connection to the students or the communities involved in an educational encounter. Certainly educators should communicate with groups about what is to be covered in particular session(s) and there is no harm in setting expectations about what might be achieved. Those in favour of pre-determined learning outcomes also argue that professional status and standards are maintained (Harvey 2004) and that uniformity of educational outputs are ensured. However, the way learning outcomes are interpreted is deeply problematic and their centrality within education has become onerous. The very idea that the outcomes of an educational encounter can be agreed so definitively fails to capture the complexity of learning, ignores self-directed, self-determined, delayed or unanticipated outcomes and greatly under-appreciates the knowledge and experience a person brings to any learning experience. This approach leaves little scope to capture other dimensions of education or significant moments amidst an educational process. Increasingly, educators take on the arduous and bureaucratic task of matching anticipated outcomes to measurable outputs. This is largely because it is what they are expected to do, and not because they believe it is the best approach to education (Hussey and Smith 2002: 224). To quote Hussey and Smith more broadly (2002: 222):

> Learning outcomes have value when properly conceived and used in ways that respect their limitations and exploit their virtues, but they are damaging to education if seen as precise prescriptions that must be spelled out in detail before teaching can begin and which are objective and measurable devices suitable for monitoring educational practices.

Another problem with learning outcomes is the way in which they help to commodify learning. Listing anticipated learning outcomes has become the formative way to promote a programme. This misappropriates learning outcomes into little more than a marketing tool that again reduces the richness of education to its end result. Allias (2007: 69) believes this emphasis on the end product is of particular benefit to the neoliberal market as it dismisses contexts and processes and leads to a situation where public funds are awarded to whoever delivers on a set of prescribed outcomes at the lowest cost.

If these are not reasons enough to reconsider the use of learning outcomes, their adoption strongly favours the static summative assessment *of* learning I referred to in the introductory paragraph. This is to the detriment of constructivist, problem-posing, assessment *for* learning where the richness of learner insight is deliberately explored. There are also emotional dimensions to having your learning assessed by another person (Boud 1995: 43; Fitzsimons and Dorman 2013: 52). This can get lost amidst a bureaucracy of box ticking and form filling that increasingly accompanies the submission and correction of a student's work. These are not the only problems with the formal assessment of learning. Anyone familiar with correcting essays, projects and other types of assignments can appreciate the enigmatic nature of this task; a power-laden exercise where different educators often interpret the same work differently (Orr 2007; Boyd and Bloxham 2014). Educators can also have diverse opinions about how much attention should be paid to factors such as presentation and style of writing and can disagree on what an appropriate national standard should be.

Quality Assurance Frameworks
To make sure practitioners comply with the rules of accreditation, each provider is asked to draw up a set of *quality assurance* (QA) procedures which must be approved by the accrediting body. In the past, it was common enough for a range of local QA models to co-exist across many provider types. These were designed by educators and were contextualised amidst their particular student group and circumstances. Detailed reflective evaluations are also a mainstay in community education and regular reviews of practice are well established. The AONTAS publication *Flower Power* is a good example of practitioner-conceived quality assurance within community education. *Flower Power* (AONTAS 2009) offers a quality assurance framework for women's community education that is positioned within the struggle for women's equality. Its ambition is to support both individual educators and organisations to critically reflect on their practice thus ensuring it is appropriate and to a high standard.

More recent approaches to quality assurance are very different to *Flower Power* as they set out to standardise procedures with a central focus on *external* monitoring. Outsider perspectives can certainly bring benefits through fresh eyes, a less entrenched perspective and experiences from other locations. However, there are also difficulties. Firstly, the word *quality* means different things to different people so there may not be agreement between internal and external perspectives. Quality assurance requirements are also time consuming and the richness of

educator evaluations can be lost amidst the increasing use of quantification to measure quality (Scheele 2004; Anderson 2006; Elassey 2015).
Crucially, there is often a gap between managerialist objectives on quality
which are principally concerned with minimum standards and accountability (Newton 2000; Harvey 2004: 209) and the more reflective tendencies of educator conceived quality assurance. Demonstrating the
strength of educator mistrust in systems of QA, research by Anderson
(2006: 171) goes so far as to suggest that the most effective way to
ensure quality is to resist the formal QA models that are increasingly
imposed on educators.

THE IMPLEMENTATION OF QUALIFICATIONS FRAMEWORKS

To this point, I have analysed key concepts that support accreditation
frameworks and have problematised the often uncontested nature of the
language of accreditation. Whilst all systems of accreditation share many of
the same contentious characteristics, it is also worth emphasising differences in the way these systems were implemented across participants of the
Bologna (1999) and Copenhagen (2002) declarations. Sometimes, qualifications frameworks were hastily introduced under pressure from the
European Commission (EC) who was worried they would not meet the
education and training demands within the Lisbon Strategy. The 2004
communiqué *Success of Lisbon strategy hinges on urgent reforms* (European
Commission 2004) named this concern and asked for immediate action
from participating countries. One thing we learn from this document is
how, when the EC had its back to the wall, it starkly clarified its rationale
for NQFs; not to improve standards in education or to encourage reflective practice, but to benefit the economy. The Communiqué reminds
educators that action is needed so that the EU complies with an earlier
agreement by heads of State "to become the most competitive and
dynamic knowledge-based economy in the world, capable of sustainable
economic growth with more and better jobs and greater social cohesion"
(European Commission 2004: 1).

Implementation in Ireland had begun before this. The *Qualifications
(education and training) Act*, which was brought into law in 1999,
created the public Further Education and Training Council (FETAC)
which merged all previous FE accreditors. The act also created the
Higher Education and Training Council (HETAC)[2] to oversee
HE awards in Technical Colleges and private third-level colleges.

Importantly, these initiatives coincided with a time when social partnership was a well-established feature of the Irish political landscape. There were shortfalls in Irish social partnership models and, as I have outlined in chapter 1, critics interpret this governance structure as a ruse for neoliberalisation. Whatever the shortfalls, partnership did establish a culture of consensus meaning much responsibility for advancing accreditation was delegated to existing education providers (Killeavy 2005).

Growth in community-based Accreditation

Community education greatly benefitted from this devolved approach as the vocational intentions of the NFQ were stretched to incorporate wider purposes of education. Firstly, FETAC allowed any organisation that could successfully meet their quality assurance criteria to become a registered centre at a much lower cost than the registration fees demanded by universities. Many community sector organisations availed of this opportunity and, by 2012, over 200 "Community and Voluntary Sector" organisation were FETAC-registered centres. This figure represented 24% of all FETAC providers at the time.[3] Public providers also opted for public vocational accreditation as each Vocational Education Committee (VEC) became FETAC approved.

Once registered, community education providers were able to access a variety of FETAC awards and could deliver them in a way that best suited the contexts they were working within. These included vocational awards in childcare, healthcare and computers as many local people were up-skilled to take up jobs both within the community sector and further afield. Another key feature of FETAC was that registered centres could themselves design programmes and submit them for FETAC approval. This opened up exciting possibilities for community educators who created programmes where the aims, objectives and anticipated learning outcomes suited the contexts and purposes of community education. Certificates in leadership, community development, interculturalism, social studies, social analysis and group work were all designed by community educators and became a permanent feature of the wider suite of FETAC programmes from which all registered centres could draw from.

Whilst opportunities for accreditation certainly opened up, these were not uncritically welcomed. In research with VEC tutors, Keyes (2004) shares how some tutors felt a sense of inadequacy around subject specialisms and were worried about learner autonomy. As the quote below captures, she observed a pull towards behaviourist, banking approaches to education that jarred with the constructivist, dialogic principles carried by many community educators.

> The primary tension that existed for our tutors was that of a perceived conflict between a student/learner led curriculum and a subject led one; they perceived accreditation as taking the major focus away from the student to the subject, something which they saw as in direct conflict with their ideological position on adult education. Whereas they would have worked from a "curriculum" previously, it was one that was negotiable and very much driven by the learner's needs. (Keyes 2004: 71)

In a cooperative inquiry that I helped to facilitate (Fitzsimons and Dorman 2013), a paradoxical relationship with accreditation was equally captured. Certification was thought to build confidence, give credibility to community research, develop critical capacities, document practice and enhance the status of community education. There was also a sense that accreditation on a subject relevant to life struggle can lay a foundation in personal confidence and that formulating arguments in writing for the purpose of assessment can sharpen people's thinking. However, equal levels of dissatisfaction were evident namely concerns about how the prescribed nature of curricula can both stifle self-determination and can position the educator as expert. Other concerns were about standardisation, excessive bureaucracy, meritocracy and the reality that some awards carry much more cultural and economic capital than others (Fitzsimons and Dorman 2013).

Changes to Accreditation Policy Since 2012

A key argument that I make within Chapter 5 is that social policies are not neutral but are closely connected to the political context they emerge from. Although Ireland's culture of consensus allowed significant room for manoeuvre, the ideological driving force of EU convergence measures was to advance labour market activation (Van de Wende 2000; Hussey and Smith; 2002, 2008; Harvey 2004; Scheele 2004; Lock and Lorenzo 2007; Young 2007; Allias 2007; Bennett and Brady 2014). From 2012 onwards, the year that the *Quality Assurance and Qualifications (Education and Training) Act* was brought into law, much autonomy was lost. This legislation established QQI a merger of HETAC, FETAC and aspects of the Irish Universities Quality Board (IUQB). QQI was to manage the NFQ and to oversee all Irish qualifications (with universities and the Institute of Technology sector entrusted to give their own awards). Amidst much reform, QQI introduced two key changes that particularly impacted accreditation within community education.

First of all, QQI reorganised all awards at levels 1–6 which up to now had incorporated different design models depending on each award's legacy provider.[4] One *Common Awards System* (CAS) was created which standardised all FE awards. Rather than simply slot existing FE awards into this new system, QQI used this opportunity to introduce significant change. Some minor awards were withdrawn by QQI without negotiation even where organisations were actively delivering these modules (Fitzsimons 2014: 159). For those to survive, each FE provider was instructed to undertake a lengthy application process to *migrate* each award they wished to deliver into CAS. This migration process involved submitting a detailed outline of the reason for delivering each programme, the anticipated progression for learners and the expected contact hours and self-directed study time. Each application also involved preparing lengthy suggested (or indicative) contents to satisfy pre-determined learning outcome and preset methods of assessment. This labour-intensive migration process, which was introduced without consultation, put enormous strain on community education providers who, up to now, could deliver any FETAC programme once their quality assurance policies were approved by the accrediting body. The redesign of FE awards into CAS also greatly strengthened QQIs power over FE providers by transferring much control into the hands of administrators.

As well as tightening control over FE awards through CAS, a second action by QQI was to publish a set of consultative green papers to inform policy development in areas such as access, progression, protection for learners, recognition of prior learning and provider fees. The opening paper *Green Paper on the Comprehensive Implementation of the Functions of Quality and Qualifications Ireland* (QQI 2013a) gives us a flavour of QQI's managerialist approach when it describes the QQI-provider relationships as follows:

> As a result of public sector cutbacks staff numbers have fallen by approximately 25% since the amalgamation was announced in 2008 and no new staff members have been recruited. Our operational budget has been

reduced and we have also incurred costs in relocating and restructuring. The close and supportive nature of the relationships between the predecessor bodies and providers will be difficult to sustain in these circumstances. Moreover the nature of these relationships will need to be examined in the context of emergent QQI strategy. (QQI 2013a: 3–4)

This severance of a "close and supportive" relationship between QQI (formally FETAC) and registered providers marked a new direction for Ireland's public accreditation body as it overtly took on an authoritarian, directional and monitoring role. Its decision to introduce fees for providers to bolster its diminished financial stability was another blow for community educators, already overstretched and operating on shoe-string budgets (AONTAS CEN 2014: 2).

As well as changes within QQI, the *Further Education and Training Strategy 2014–2020 (FET Strategy)* which was published in 2014 by SOLAS (the National Further Education and Training board) is also important. Congruent with the FET strategy's reductionist and instrumentalist approach to community education (see Chapter 5), the document sees the only purpose of accreditation as to up-skill the Irish workforce. The strategy describes the NFQ as "a key tool that the FET sector . . . intends to build-on" (SOLAS 2014a: 53) and draws from previous targets in the *National Skills Strategy*, stating that 50,000 of the workforce will "need to progress by at least one NFQ level, 170,000 to Levels 6 to 10, 260,000 to Levels 4 & 5, 70,000 to Level 3" (SOLAS 2014a: 60). Within this discussion the "not-for-profit" sector is singled out as a site where greater numbers of accredited awards can be conferred.

QUALITY ASSURANCE AS A PROCESS OF SURVEILLANCE

Earlier in this chapter, I have linked quality assurance with managerialist tools that monitor compliance with outcomes approaches (Newton 2000; Anderson 2006). As QA procedures evolve in the field, a process of surveillance has emerged with a significant power dimension. By way of example, let's again look at the Irish QA systems for FE, the awards most commonly applied in community education contexts. When approving the quality of each student's work, QQI-led QA imposes three tiers of assessment. Firstly, a learner's work is commonly organised into individual folders[5] which are corrected by the educator who delivers the programme. Corrected work is then put forward for *Internal Verification* (IV) where a designated person in the same organisation reviews the standards and transparency of the first corrector's work including the appropriateness of assignments and the rigor of marking. This precedes a third phase of External Authentication (EA) where an individual or team approved by QQI oversees each previous tier. QQI describe the functions of external authentication as to review minimum intended learning outcomes and other objectives, to verify learner attainment using information agreed with the education provider and to check learners have satisfied the relevant awards standard. They must also validate assessment procedures, approve the standards and strategies of assessment and report findings with recommendations to the provider (QQI 2015: 1–2).

On the surface this can all seem like a sensible approach. It is not dissimilar to approaches in other education settings such as school and colleges and it can be argued it is an approach that guarantees fairness and transparency for each learner. But what about the message it sends to community educators? The terminology of "verification" and "authentication", have become normative in accreditation discourse, expression that communicate that the only way that knowledge can be thought reliable, is if it is approved by outsiders in superior roles and with no connection to the programme under examination. Increasingly, this system of *hierarchical observation* (Bourke et al. 2013: 86) is controlling educator performance. Repeatedly qualified and experienced adult educators share stories of student's work being prevented from progressing through the channels of QA. In my own experience I know of at least four occasions where groups of learners were delayed in receiving awards because either internal or external evaluators queried marking schemes, assessment methods or methods of evidencing learning that were implemented by experienced and qualified adult educators. In each situation educators could offer clear pedagogic rationale for the decisions they made, but were prevented from exercising these decisions where they were thought to breach bureaucratic requirements. These stories, of which there are likely to be more, leave learners disadvantaged and adult educators demoralised.

This culture of surveillance, that micro-manages qualified and experienced educators, commonly stems from internal and external verifier's *interpretation* of quality assurance. As policies relating to internal and external verification grow, the requirements of an accreditor become consumed by a wider, and often unnecessary, scaffolding of policy directives that are built around QQI's original structure. One reason for this is the constant search for higher standards a discourse that is based on the assumption that things can always get better, can always be more transparent and can always demonstrate even more rigor. Wearily adult educators accept any number of checks, balances and quality assurance policies as the substance of an educational endeavour gets lost in a sea of form filling and bureaucracy and the original purpose of quality assurance gets drowned out.

To give an example, there is a growing refusal by many Irish authenticators (internal and external) to accept *tutor verification* as sufficient guarantee that a student has accomplished a particular skill, even where this represents as little as 5% of an overall mark. This is despite this method of assessment having a long history in assessment in both FE and HE contexts and, most importantly, sometimes being the most pedagogically appropriate way to assess learning. Increasingly, educators are asked to video record every action a student does, such as washing their hands on a healthcare course, having group conversations as part of team working or deleting a file from a desktop on a computer course. The justification given is that there must be verifiable *evidence* of each task. Where educators object to the need for substantive proof outside of their own supervision, one rationale offered is the possibility of a learner formally challenging their grade up to and including litigation.[6] Were a learner to evoke this right, the argument is that yet another layer of external examination would transparently deal with any appeal. An alternative approach would be to support the educator in the first place so that she/he can defend the mark she/he gave. The more important impact of this practice is that a message is sent to the educator involved that their word is not to be trusted. Much energy must now be spent on video-recording skills demonstrations regardless of whether or not a learner wishes to be filmed or whether the group's time could be better spent. This search for verifiable proof has a detrimental and power-laden impact on learners too, as any possibility of self-assessment and/or peer assessment is simply not considered.

This phenomenon can be interpreted as a process of *self-regulation* where the structures of education are imposing rules and regulations that are above the actual demands of the accrediting body. Instead of laying all the blame with internal and external verifiers and the facilitators/tutors of community education, another vantage points it to draw from Foucauldian logic on the nature of power. Foucault, a prominent French philosopher, explains a processes self-regulation, or self-policing, through ideas he originally conceived of through a genealogy of prison architecture and its use of panoptical observation (Foucault 1977). Believing that power is manifold and thus present at the extremities of society, the crux of Foucauldian thinking relevant to this situation is that the possibility of surveillance alone is sufficiently powerful for those under surveillance to internalise and amplify the demands of the regulator. For Foucault, this theory only holds substance where society is individualised thus where experiences are not shared with and validated by others.

PRACTITIONER THOUGHTS AND EXPERIENCES ON ACCREDITATION

Chapter 3 offers a lengthy history of community education which demonstrates the largely non-accredited nature of its emergence. This is no longer the case as this research reveals how 83% of those surveyed deliver accredited education and training. Table 6.1

One thing this table reveals is that although 83% work with accreditation, only 11% answer that this is all of the time, the most popular answer being "sometimes on some courses". Of those that do confer certificates, 74% use Irish FE awards, 10% work with both FE and HE awards and 12% use Irish HE awards alone. Four percent access UK-based accreditation. Table 6.2 measures 60% support for accreditation. However, it also measures ambiguity with 29% "somewhat agreeing" accreditation is good for community education and a further 13% not sure if they agree or disagree.

Accreditation was the single biggest theme to emerge through additional survey comments with 31% of remarks related to the topic. Just one of these n39 comments (below) is wholly positive.

Table 6.1 Quantifying accreditation

Never (%)	Sometimes on some courses (%)	Most of the time (%)	Always (%)
17	44	28	11

Survey question: Do the courses you are involved with offer accreditation?

Table 6.2 Attitudinal measurements on the benefit of accreditation

Strongly agree (%)	Agree (%)	Some what agree (%)	Not sure if I agree or disagree (%)	Somewhat disagree (%)	Disagree (%)	Strongly disagree (%)
18	13	29	13	17	7	3

Survey question: The fact that most courses are now accredited is a good thing for community education

The accreditation of community education and development courses is important particularly when participants are seeking employment and competing with graduates for limited job prospects. (Survey respondent, working for a HEI)

This response encapsulates policy interpretation of the need for accreditation and there is no doubt but that some participants of community education have benefitted from professional qualifications. In other responses, ambiguity emerges. Some comments are not overtly negative rather they are cautious about the relevance of accreditation in community education contexts. To give some examples:

Accreditation is not always the ideal route for community education. Some people have disengaged from education for reasons other than social disadvantage such as being unable to cope academically with the learning by rote methods used in the past. We need to discover new ways of measuring the soft outcomes that non-accredited courses can achieve. (Survey respondent, working as an independent practitioner)

In another example accreditation is linked to standards but tempered with the impacts its introduction can have on the participants of community education.

Accreditation is important to maintain standards [but] I have a real concern that it will discourage those in the community who may be intimidated by the process involved. (Survey respondent, tutor VEC/Education and Training Board (ETB))

This next comment echoes the same concern:

Accreditation is good however it is putting pressure on our learners again. Sometimes I fear we are putting them back into a system that has already failed them. We must be careful this does not happen. (Survey respondent, independent community education organisation)

In another response:

My strongest thought here is that courses should not only be valued (funded) if they include assessment and certification. Especially in the area of personal development that is often inappropriate, but also introductory

Table 6.3 Attitudes on the suitability of FETAC (now QQI)

Strongly agree (%)	Agree (%)	Somewhat agree (%)	Not sure if I agree or disagree (%)	Somewhat disagree (%)	Disagree (%)	Strongly disagree (%)
6	21	26	26	8	7	6

Survey question: FETAC is the most suitable awarding body for community education

courses in other subjects. Certification can be seen as intimidating and off putting to many who have had bad experiences of education. (Survey respondent, tutor VEC/ETB)

The possibility of certified learning exacerbating negativity towards education that began in school concurs with the opinions of other contributors to the accreditation debate (Quilty 2003; Cullinane 2003: 82).

The next issue I will turn to is use of FE awards in community contexts. Within Table 6.3 there is mixed opinion about whether FETAC (the accreditor of FE awards at the time of the survey) is the most suitable way to certify community education with 53% in agreement of whom half "somewhat agree". Twenty-six percent are equally unsure.

Again qualitative comments help to contextualise the uncertainty uncovered through attitudinal responses. One survey contributor shares:

FETAC offers an excellent model of accreditation however it is poorly resourced which makes it vulnerable therefore its providers are too. (Survey respondent, community sector)

Another survey respondent is initially sceptical of the dominance of FETAC describing it as "the only show in town" but asserts the importance of educator ingenuity believing "it is possible to be creative with a syllabus". Some criticisms are more specific. The quote below reveals one person's sense of incongruence between process-oriented community education and the use of FE awards.

Although I see the value of FETAC accreditation . . . I am concerned about the constant and growing requirement for alignment of standards and the restrictions this puts on tutors to respond to the diverse needs of the groups involved in training. FETAC was originally envisaged as a community response to educational disadvantage. (Survey respondent, community sector)

Noteworthy about this excerpt it how it captures paradoxical opinion. As well as these broad-based concerns, there are specific issues relating to changes since 2012. Some relate to CAS, others to anxiety about an organisation's capacity to continue to independently offer accreditation. At focus groups in Limerick, Cork, North Dublin and Central Dublin there are concerns about impending fees structure. In Limerick, there is also concern about capacity within QQI, given their internal budgetary constraints. One conversation makes reference to the impossibility of some providers finding the time to migrate awards.

> FETAC are pretty much throwing small providers out the door by saying to a provider that anything you have done previously, for credits to be transferable you have to put it into your common awards system. Small providers can't do that so it is a kick in the face for access, transfer and progression as far as I am concerned. (Waterford, participant two).

Even when CAS is available to providers, there are concerns it is individualist, inflexible and overprescribed. Programmes are thought to be too long and, repeatedly people complain of excessive numbers of learning outcomes. One survey respondent explains difficulties in putting learning outcomes models into practice.

> Accreditation has become so popular mainly because it is an easily measured outcome e.g. 150 people achieved a certificate in communication skills at level 3. Are these 150 people more able to reflect on issues concerning them or their community? Are they any more aware of the role they can play in making their community/country a better place to live? No. But they can write a formal letter and understand non-verbal communications, probably not very relevant to their lives at the moment and not the skills they will use at this stage . . . there is currently no reporting mechanism to the department for outcomes other than certification and number of people unemployed etc which is the main reason it has become so popular. (Survey respondent, CEF in a VEC/ETB)

This is not the first time I have been involved in research which reveals discontent about the volume of learning outcomes, particularly at levels 1–6 (Fitzsimons and Dorman 2013). A number of community educators are also unhappy with the weight of assessment and the pressure this puts learners under. Some make comparisons with university accredited programmes.

I feel that the pressure that is put on participants from the onset and the amount of outcomes that students must meet in order to gain any kind of accreditation, it is enormous. And if you put it beside a certificate course or your first or second year in college, there is no comparison. (Athlone, participant two).

The quote below also illustrates a similar comparison and comes from a community educator working with both FE and HE awards.

FETAC is very difficult to be honest . . . it is very assessment heavy for one module. I know there are people who don't feel that, but I would feel that you could nearly get a first year of a degree for what you would get of one module, for what you have to do. (Tele-interviewee three, working for an NGO).

Another educator, who again works with both FE and HE awards, equally attests:

My experience with FETAC, just with the workload and what is expected, the time frame that it is expected in as well, it just doesn't work at all . . . so much of the emphasis is on the assignment and getting an assignment completed. Whereas with [names university], so much of it was about reflecting on the experiences in the room and being, having time to take it in and not having a constant burden of assignments over their heads, so it wasn't preoccupying people at all. So [on a university programme] people could be in the space when you are doing group activities and group exercises, groups are breaking up and they are staying focused where, I think, with FETAC after a certain time you would walk around and people are talking about their assignments. (Interviewee three, working for an NGO)

As well as these specific concerns, several comments relate to connections between accreditation and wider labour market activation models.

The activation agenda has taken over policy in terms of education and training. Governments pay lip service to community education and to empowering local communities. The reality is that this government is only interested in getting people on programmes to show they are appearing to do something about the unemployment figures . . . the only figures that matter is outputs in terms of bums on seats and formal accreditation . . . Jobs, jobs, jobs are all that matter now. How long community education can survive in this climate is open to debate. (Survey respondent, community sector)

The social expectations placed on each person to progress from a programme of education to paid employment, whatever the quality of that job may be, is also captured in the quote below where we get a sense of how curricula are shaped by this expectation. This comment is shared following some paired conversation between two focus-group participants.

> There is definitely manipulation going on and both of us [referring to participant one] identified with…where we are on a very short leash and you basically have to get them [learners] through the learning outcomes, all the FETAC courses are very vocational and focus on, like when they get up to level 3, level 4 they all have a work experience module, they are all designed for employability. (South Dublin, participant two)

Repeatedly, surveyed community educators also complain about unnecessary paperwork, both for themselves and for those completing certificate programmes. Survey responses that convey this issue are a desire to "dump most of the paperwork" and that accreditation is "weighted down with paperwork, evidence etc." Others relay that "FETAC should be overhauled and examined" and that "if 50% of your day is spent filling forms and ticking boxes then that only leaves 50% for the action work, the form-filling is just a joke". This comment below captures recurrent paradoxical opinion where the benefits of an award can be out weighted by the detriments of bureaucracy.

> Accreditation driven education does not suit everyone and can hinder the work of the tutor, weighting us down with paperwork, evidence etc. In some cases it is used as justification for funding and may just be another piece of paper meaning nothing to the recipient. For others it is a genuine achievement and sets a person on the road to higher education. There needs to be a balance. (Survey respondent, tutor VEC/ETB)

One community educator links growing bureaucracy with an influx of educators from traditional education contexts.

> External evaluators who come from mainstream education facilities are placing increasing requirements of form filling and standardisation of training on providers. (Survey respondent, community sector)

Although this connection between traditional school practices and the rise in bureaucracy is an isolated opinion, it does lead into discussions that verify a culture of excessive self-regulation and surveillance that is greater than the demands of the accrediting body. Supporting evidence emerges in this research from two interviewees both of who are employed as tutors within VECs/ETBs. In the first instance, this educator compares her work across two VECs/ETBs drawing out stark differences in the instructions she is given. In one setting she reports significant loss of power as she must deliver a pre-designed programme verbatim explaining:

> I am handed all of the assessment briefs, you know – these are the ones to deliver – now to some degree, they are actually, whoever designed them is very coped on, they are actually very good. But that is very inflexible, extremely inflexible. They do a generic approach so that it should fit most groups but you know, and there is no option in that system to do something else other than the brief that you have got so that doesn't work very well. (Tele-interviewee four, tutor VEC/ETB)

In another setting, she describes a very different set-up where, "we develop our own [assignment] brief which is great, we can develop them to suit the group that we have". Immediately she tempers this latter comment with reference to the workload involved continuing "but you know that's tons of extra work, tons of it that we are literally not paid for". In the second example shared, this VEC/ETB tutor takes on some additional work as an independent practitioner to subsidise her part-time income. This allows her to make comparisons between a VEC/ETB and a NGO both delivering the same award. What is noteworthy about this contribution is that, at one stage, the educator blames QQI thinking that they are at fault for what she interprets as poor programme design. She begins by complaining about a lack of tutor autonomy where she is "bound by the VEC module descriptors" instructed not to stray from the preset contents. She elaborates:

> I delivered this module; it was terrible, it was so badly written it was so broad, it was all over the place, and I just thought, "Okay that is FETAC [QQI] and FETAC have given this terrible module, they have written this terrible module. (Tele-interviewee two, tutor VEC/ETB)

When she is asked to develop the same award for migration within another NGO, her perspective shifts.

> I realised, actually FETAC, their direction was fine ... it was whoever had taken that on for the VEC and who had written it, they just did not

understand the subject and they just did not understand how FETAC works or how any assessment process works. The content did not match what the assessment was and everything was overcomplicated and when I actually got to write it for myself I realised how badly written they were, and I thought it was FETAC and it wasn't, it was the VEC and I realised that actually the FETAC guidelines, they were quite good.

These two accounts offer concrete examples of different rules being implemented by different providers.

Given the restrictive nature of qualifications frameworks, be these real or perceived, it should come as no surprise that some findings detail attempts by practitioners to stretch the confines of accreditation. Before sharing some qualitative context, Table 6.4 reveals how a slim majority (53%) believe that accreditation interferes with how they would ideally like to work.[7]

Some examples of working adaptively with QQI awards emerges where survey respondents detail responses to group needs that are outside of curricular limitations. There is sex education introduced to a group of young adults, suicide awareness and prevention in response to the support needs of a women's group and map-reading in response to a participant's uncertainly about the physical geography of Ireland. Two survey participants and one interviewee share stories of basic English programmes that are funded to offer vocational supports but are delivered in a way that better matches group need. Here is one typical example.

[the class] did not just involve teaching English – many of the students had good English. They need to learn about the Irish system of education and health care. They needed to know how the tax system worked, that

Table 6.4 Attitudes on whether accreditation interferes with practice

Strongly agree (%)	Agree (%)	Somewhat agree (%)	Not sure if I agree or disagree (%)	Somewhat disagree (%)	Disagree (%)	Strongly disagree (%)
8	20	25	18	11	11	7

Survey question: When I am delivering accredited courses, my experience is that this interferes with the way that I would ideally like to be as a tutor their husband could use their tax credits if they were not working, that they could claim child benefit and FIS [Family Income Support]. They asked about car tax, car insurance, how to get a PPS [social insurance] number – lots of basic questions that they needed help with. Those who had good English translated the questions and the answers for the others. (Survey respondent, tutor VEC/ETB)

Making Space for Non-accreditation

Within one focus-group conversation about the day-to-day limitations of working with accreditation, one community educator shares:

People have a lot of passion for it [community education] and I feel people in the sector who are tutoring – are activists, they are critical educators and they are trying to do that and at the same time to conform to the strangling process that is involved with FETAC and that is the only way I can describe it. (Athlone, participant two)

This contribution captures a sense of the passion that is expressed when contributors talk about the importance of preserving space for non-accredited community education. In this study, 27% are against accreditation and of those who work within FE and university certification mechanisms, 44% only sometimes offer credits for the programmes they deliver. Anti-accreditation comments emerge from community sector and public sector provision alike. To demonstrate, "accreditation is not a core objective of community education" (from a CEF) and "community education should not be about offering accredited courses" (community sector). Accreditation is described by one person I interviewed as a "major issue" with this point extended as follows:

I think it is extremely divisive, I think it really re-enforces that whole thing, that whole idea of you are measured in life and someone has the power to tick that box. What you are actually doing is reinforcing that system of rewarding measured ability, so there is no recognition of prior learning, you can't get "well there is your accreditation for living, for actually having reared two kids and fighting poverty and dealing with an alcoholic husband, there is your accreditation" . . . It is like the whole thing of symbolic violence, who defines it? These are my issues with it. (Interviewee one, community sector)

As well as those who are against accreditation, a more common position was for educators to strongly express an opinion that accreditation should remain optional.

> In community education the rise in accredited courses I believe is to be welcomed. It gives students an accessible way to climb the educational ladder and become more successful in their lives. However I strongly believe that it is the entrance courses i.e. personal development, parenting that breaks through isolation and builds confidence in people. There should be a high value put on these courses as I believe this is where the real personal growth starts to happen for people. (Survey respondent, community sector)

This desire for both accredited and non-accredited education to be valued is echoed in the example below where the contributor also shares concern that non-accredited education is being squeezed out:

> While I promote the idea of accreditation I strongly feel that it should not be to the exclusion of the personal and social aspect of training. Unfortunately this is happening more and more within community education since the introduction of FETAC and with the current changes in FAS and the upcoming amalgamation with the VECs. Personally I foresee a situation where personal and social development will disappear, certainly in the area which I work in (Survey respondent, community sector)

Research my McGlynn (2014:56) would support this perspective where he claims that Irish policymakers are behind their European counterparts in recognising the value of non-accredited learning.

There are other concerns raised that have not been reported to this point. There is disquiet about how some learners have gathered a number of accredited modules which, when combined, do not add up to a measurable qualification. A suggestion is also made that practitioner networks should do more to advance systems for the recognition of prior learning.

Can we Accredit Our Own Programmes?
One concrete suggestion made during each research phase is that community educators should try to seek alternatives by developing their own models of accreditation. One survey response captures this perspective as follows:

Communities should set the standards of accreditation and be the accrediting bodies (ownership) it cannot and should not be the preserve of the universities or government bodies (Survey respondent, independent practitioner, brackets in original).

This proposal is fleshed out within one focus group where the suggestion is that groups should come together and design their own model of accreditation. The proposer argues that this would better match the ambitions of critical community education explaining:

People go to university; first there is the cost, secondly they tend to go as individuals so they are not part of a group anymore and they are, unless they are at the very highest levels of the academic ladder they are not following their own generative themes. So to actually try to reclaim that space, by community educators reclaiming that space so that they can do that stuff so the kind of educational processes that go on at masters level can go on in our local communities for residents living in that community around the generative issues that are in their community so that is what we thought we can do. (South Dublin, participant eight)

Another in the group immediately adds:

Can community educators get together and get accreditation in a holistic way for the kind of stuff? That is really important for community development ... it is possible in the university level why can't it be accredited at the lower level and I think that for me this is huge and there is a huge resources issue. (South Dublin, participant seven)

The idea that community educators develop their own systems of accreditation has been suggested before (Kelly 1994: 123; Fitzsimons and Dorman 2013) and alternative models for measuring the effectiveness of practice have been advanced (AONTAS 2012b; Neville et al. 2014). Although this can seem like an obvious and attractive option, the trouble is these alternative models lack social and economic capital, a key driving force in early demands for accreditation (Kelly 1994: xix).

One way forward is to think about the different elements that influence an educational encounter which I am simplifying as threefold; (1) the group, or learners (to use accreditation terminology), (2) the philosophy of the educator/s, be that humanistic, radical, progressive, etc. and (3) the certificate/module being completed (Fig. 6.1)

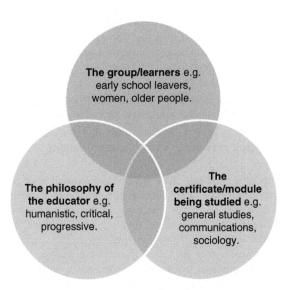

Fig. 6.1   Three dimensions of accredited learning

At the moment, this third element, *the certificate/module* is disproportionately influencing community education to the detriment of the
group and the underlying philosophy. The task for community educators
is to ensure that each of these three dimensions are attended to where
curricular requirements are approached in a way that is meaningful in the
context of the life experiences of the group and congruent with the
philosophies being drawn from.

Conclusion

Accreditation is both beneficial and problematic for community education. Recognisable qualifications can build confidence, improve job
prospects, open pathways to higher education and build capacities in
literacy, numeracy and critical thinking. On the other hand accreditation
accelerates employability and pro-business agendas to the detriment of
other functions of community education. This is by reducing the end
game of education to the achievement of a measurable, marketable
award. By dividing education into low-capacity and high-capacity
awards, contemporary accreditation deepens educational inequality and

encourages non-critical, behaviourist, banking methodologies. This illuminates contradictions between the aspirations of egalitarian educators and the EU labour market activation agenda.

The bureaucracy involved in accreditation is eroding educator autonomy, an ironic turn of events given neoliberalism's open disdain for the bureaucratic nature of leftist models of liberal democracy. Although community educators are to this point managing to create spaces for non-accredited learning, one message from some research participants is that these spaces are becoming increasingly difficult to find.

NOTES

1. This exercise was designed by Banulacht, an independent development education organisation disbanded in 2009 in part due to the severance of State funding.
2. HETAC replaced the National Council for educational Awards (NCEA) which had conferred Institute of Technology (IT)-based qualifications to that point. The IT sector was particularly responsible for applied studies, vocational awards and technical advancement.
3. A full list of registered centres can be viewed at (www.fetac.ie, Accessed 10 April 2014).
4. Prior to the establishment of FETAC, Irish FE awards were conferred by FÁS, a Bord Iascaigh Mhara (The Irish fishery board), Teagasc (the agriculture and food development authority), Fáilte Ireland (the National Tourism Development Authority), small training centres, VECs, schools and FE colleges as well as by private colleges and professional bodies.
5. Although there is nothing to my knowledge within QQI documentation that instructs work to be presented in folders, there is a near obsession with the use of folders in the field. In my own experience I once had work submitted by my students removed from the folders they had used and rebound into standard black folders before being presented to the external authenticator. I do not know who did this only that it was another member of staff at the ETB in question. The only difference between these folders and the folders the students used was that the original folders were in different colours.
6. This has certainly been my experience as it was a reason given to me to justify why all learners had to be photographed washing their hands as part of a skills demonstration on a healthcare course.
7. Based on a response rate of (n193) therefore a 12% drop in participation.

CHAPTER 7

Insiders, Outsiders and the Professionalisation of Community Education

Illustration 7.1   The Professionalisation of community education

© The Author(s) 2017   195
C. Fitzsimons, *Community Education and Neoliberalism*,
DOI 10.1007/978-3-319-45937-0_7

196 COMMUNITY EDUCATION AND NEOLIBERALISM

A chapter about professionalism and professionalisation gives me an opportunity to share my own journey into community education and this is where this chapter starts. In 1997, while working as a general nurse with a university qualification in addiction studies, I applied for a job as a "Project Leader" that I saw advertised on a hospital notice board. Given my previous lack of experience working in community contexts, I was surprised but delighted to be offered the job and left behind a career as a nurse to take up work in the growing community sector. I went to work for a Community Development Project (CDP) that operated out of vacant public housing units across three high-rise blocks of flats. This was in a North Dublin suburb often described as socio-economically disadvantaged and a very different world from the suburban affluence of my youth where neighbourhoods such as these were considered no-go areas.

As was typical of these CDPs, most of the positions on the voluntary board of directors were held by local people. There were also people from outside of the community. These were some members of a religious congregation, a volunteer from a middle-class neighbourhood and a paid community worker also from a more advantaged social background who was working in other organisations. From time to time some experts volunteered to help. I remember the organisation being approached by an accountant and a human resource expert, both of whom joined the board for a set period.

Most of the CDP's work was educational and was particularly informed by the philosophies of Brazilian educationalist Paulo Freire as well as an Irish influx of the Training for Transformation (TfT) movement. Staff and board members were united in one ambition; to work in a participatory, hands-on way that was deeply respectful of the local people they encountered. As a project leader, I was responsible for a programme that was designed to meet the needs of women with a history of problematic drug use; a label that greatly undersold their many abilities and insights. These women were directly involved in determining the mission and ethos of the project, in designing the curriculum and, when possible, in participating in consultation processes on local and national policy.[1] I did not work alone but was paired with a local "unqualified" community educator who had crafted her trade on the job. She brought an authenticity to the work that continually compensated for my unfamiliarity with many cultures and experiences strong within the group. Together we traversed such topics as local history, women's health, politics, social analysis, computers and creative writing. We also organised work experience for the women involved, something resisted by certain employers but supported by others. The project also forged relationships with some academics at Maynooth University who were interested in supporting women's community education.

We smoked cigarettes, drank tea, laughed, cried, discussed, debated and, where we could, collectively extended our energies towards tangible community outcomes. At one stage a service-users forum was set up so that clients of addiction services could give feedback on the quality of the care they received. Women from the project also participated in demonstrations against the closure of a local swimming pool as well as against a government-led downscaling of community employment. This CDP has since closed, a casualty of the community sector realignment discussed in earlier chapters. The recovery-based education project I helped to set up has survived, but is funded through the healthcare system so no longer managed by an independent board of directors.

The account above captures many of the themes that are important to the professionalisation of community education namely the reliability of qualifications as a determinant of credibility, the relationships between the field and the academy, the importance of volunteers and the precarious nature of employment. My own narrative encapsulates a particularly important theme, the blurring of boundaries between *professional* (in other words qualified), and *lay* (in other words unqualified) practitioners. Often, this latter cohort includes past participants of community education who are local to the communities in question. The purpose of this chapter is to explore debates about professionalism and professionalisation. As this book claims community education is evident amidst public provision, the community sector and other non-governmental organisations (NGOs) and through the actions of some universities (see part one), professionalist discourse has to be considered along two, at times overlapping lines of inquiry. These are the professionalisation of community development (or community work as it is increasingly called) and professionalisation through adult education.

What's in a Word – Explaining Professionalism and Professionalisation

A bit like the word community, the notion of the professional is mostly seen as a good thing and as something that is beneficial for everyone. It is good for the skilled expert who gets better pay and conditions and greater occupational support. It also benefits the clients, in this case a community, who is guaranteed higher standards from well-trained professionals as well as protections from rogue traders or unsafe practitioners.

Use of the word professional is also changing. Where it was once reserved for certain specialist occupations, we can now get our gardens professionally tended, our houses professionally painted and our nails professionally manicured. More and more, there are calls to dress professionally – usually meaning to wear business attire regardless of our occupation. When the term professional is used in this way, it indicates that a task or behaviour is being carried out to a certain standard. Although there may seem little wrong with using the term in this way, it inadvertently takes our attention away from the power-dimensions inherent in the term professional when it is used in relation to certain occupations. In this context, to be *professional*, or to display *professionalism*, describes what is required of, and expected from members of a particular closed profession (Evans 2008: 25). *Professionalisation* is something else as this describes the process an occupation must go through to become a closed profession.

In the past, common logic decreed that only certain jobs (such as being a doctor) could be considered a profession, a differentiation that was based on the presence of its scientific base (Flexnor 1915/2001). This thinking was reversed in the latter half of the twentieth century when arguments were put forward that any occupation could transition to professional status so long as certain recognisable touchstones were achieved. Cyril Houle (1980) was one of the people to advance this idea arguing that, to professionalise, each occupation must agree prerequisite attributes, determine certain standards of practice and approve particular education and training programmes, including Continuous Professional Development. Professionalisation also typically included the establishment of a regulatory body to oversee membership (Houle 1980; Cevero 1988; MacDonald 1995; Evans 2008). These features of professionalisation are as relevant today as when they were first muted nearly 40 years ago. The idea that professional knowledge needs scientific verification has not been lost but has been expanded to include the social sciences as each professional field of practice depends on an accompanying body of specialist knowledge that is validated through universities (Larson 1977; Houle 1980; Cervero 1988; MacDonald 1995). As well as cooperation with universities, cooperation with the State is also paramount. This is because of the State's role in legislatively empowering regulatory bodies to enforce qualifications and standards for practitioners (Houle 1980; Cervero 1988; MacDonald 1995; Evans 2008). Examples of such regulatory bodies are *the Teaching Council of Ireland* who manage a registry of qualified teachers and *the Royal Institute of Architects Ireland* who regulate the architectural profession.

Problematising Professionalism

Professionalism is however a problematic concept as its socially constructed meaning is in constant flux. Acceptable standards often change. Think about how psychiatry has supported people with a diagnosis of clinical depression. In the 1950s and 1960s electric shock treatment (ECT) was the appropriate professional response; today ECT is surrounded by controversy and is rarely used. Approved standards do not only change over time, rather, differences can exist at the same time. Take the case of home births. Advocates oppose the medicalisation of childbirth and emphasise a women's right to choose. Those in support of home births also cite higher levels of patient safety and fewer medical interventions (Noble 2015). On the other hand, those against home births challenge the midwives involved presenting their practice as unethical and unprofessional through claims of unnecessary patient risk (Licqurish and Evans 2016).

Differences of opinion on professional practice also exist within community education where one practitioner's idea of good practice can be dismissed by another as unprofessional. In my own experience I have been in conversations where my refusal to use Microsoft PowerPoint in every class, my casual attire, my choice to put chairs in a circle and my reluctance to endorse a particular textbook have all been thought unprofessional by someone else. Displays of emotion can also be dismissed as unprofessional and an indication of poor boundaries. I do not agree with this analysis and, in my years as a community educator, I have hugged many students, I have cried, shown sadness and expressed frustration as people share their, often painful, life experiences.

Differences of opinion on professional standards are also illustrated through the experience of a community educator I interview who talks about a disjuncture between his way of working, and how others where he works perceive his approach.

I hear "soft" or "those games, you are doing, all those games" or "all the fun kind of things" ... It's, I suppose that it's people who don't really have experience of it are trying to find an appropriate language but yet in not finding the right words to describe the work we do, they are undermining it to an extent in calling it all these things, games and you know "he's just having a bit of crack in there, it's all just chairs around in a circle and things like that" and even gags about flip-charts and stuff. (Interviewee three, working in an NGO)

No matter how much I, or the educator quoted above, can justify our pedagogic position, the power to determine acceptable parameters of professional practice ultimately rest with each profession's regulatory body (Harvey 2004).

But what happens if we question the validity of professional discourse in the first place as some sociologists have done? Larson (1977, 2014) is one noteworthy contributor who wonders about altruistic assumptions thought to underpin professionalisation. She interprets an occupation's transition to a profession as a process of socialisation that is principally about prestige, where the real winner is the professional who benefits from significant cultural and economic capital. For the client, their experience is often to be locked into a power-dynamic where it can be difficult to assert an authoritative voice. One survey respondent, who has been working in community education for just two years, gives voice to this perspective through the following comment:

Answering question 26 [the directional hypothesis *"through my work as a community worker I am helping to reduce inequality in Ireland"*] made me think about what I do and who benefits. At the moment I think that the people organising these community based courses benefit more than the individuals taking part in them. It seems to be jobs for the boys as such and I can't help feeling a little disheartened by it. I also feel complicit. (Survey respondent, tutor Vocational Education Committee (VEC)/Education and Training Board (ETB))

This power that is exercised *by* professionals over their clients is not the only issue. There is also significant power *over* a professional that is exercised by each regulatory body. The significance of this power relationship becomes important when we interrogate how these regulatory bodies emerge in the first place. Usually, this is through the actions of a self-appointed elite in each fledgling profession, an elite that are instrumental in determining acceptable standards and, crucially, in agreeing the parameters of a profession with the State (MacDonald 1995: 7–8; Goodson 2003).

The Professionalisation of Community Development

Claims that community development could professionalise can be identified in North American literature in the 1940s (Hawley 1969: 124) and in British discourse in the 1960s (Smith 2006). In Ireland, interest in professionalisation emerged in the late 1980s and 1990s. Ó Cinnéide and Walsh (1990) were one of the first to put forward a case for professionalisation. This is by presenting community work as a specialist activity therefore something that required paid employees and significantly, was dependent on State funding.

> If community development was something that happens automatically or that could be done by amateurs on a part time basis then there would be no need for funds. Funds are needed, by common consent, because full time workers are needed; full time workers require appropriate community development skills or qualifications. (Ó Cinnéide and Walsh 1990: 334)

Two years before Ó Cinnéide and Walsh's contribution, a working group in the network organisation the Community Workers Cooperative (CWC) had published an alternative position paper that was against professionalisation. Although this paper acknowledges the need for paid workers, it describes professionalisation as "anathema" to the principles of community development claiming:

> The process of professionalisation is about gaining status. It is a search for power, money and control over the practice of community work. It is a process whereby a small group decides on the rules of entry and works to have them accepted and so build up a membership. The profession resulting from this process would be:-exclusive with restricted right of entry; – self-regulating and as such, not answerable to the community. (in Whelan 1989: 154)

The CWC were not alone in their criticisms as two camps of opinion emerged on the appropriateness of the professionalisation of community development (Powell and Geoghegan 2004: 130–133). In one camp, arguments were advanced that suggested the community sector is only viable if people are both paid for their labour and were supported to develop certain skills and knowledge. In the other camp, those less convinced highlighted the risks associated with professionalism through its potential to depoliticise practice and distance grassroots activism.

A central aspect of these latter concerns centred on an analysis of relationships between what Whelan (1989) refers to as *outsider* and *insider* community workers, a classification that is equally applicable today. "Outsider community workers" are deeply concerned with social inequality and are keen to influence change but live outside of the working-class communities where bottom-up politicised community development is practiced. In the past, these outsiders often held qualifications in other fields of practice such as nursing, teaching, social work and general degree qualifications in the social sciences. "Insider community workers" are also deeply concerned with social inequality but have first-hand experience of poverty and exclusion given that they live in the very communities under discussion. In many cases, insiders, many of whom were women, lacked the formal qualifications their outsider counterparts often held. Some had left school early and many were not in a position to take up education as adults both because they could not afford it and because of care responsibilities (D'Alton et al. 2010: 78). Whelan (1989) argues that, when grand aid for community development enabled people to be paid for what was, up to that point a voluntary activity, tensions between outsiders and insiders were inevitable. She explains, "when people from these different backgrounds sit down to talk about training and professionalisation in community development work, issues of class, status and privilege are there before the discussion even begins" (Whelan 1989: 152). This state of affairs is starkly illustrated by D'Alton et al. (2010: 79) when they note:

> This situation came to a head in the early 1990s as development funding for anti-poverty work became available to disadvantaged communities. The activists who organised groups and submitted funding applications were then rejected for the paid community work jobs that were created, because the jobs went to applicants with academically-recognised qualifications. To add insult to injury, these same voluntary workers were expected to train the newly employed graduates.

Professionalisation Gathers Pace

Despite their earlier reservations in the 1980s, the CWC were to become a central figure in attempts to professionalise Irish community development work. This was by opening conversations with selected community workers and academics to fashion a shared professional identify. This consultation process culminated in the publication of *Towards Standards for Quality Community Work (Towards Standards)*, an outline of the values, principles and working standards of quality community work (CWC 2008). Despite assertions from those at the helm that the process "should avoid professional self-interest as a main defining character" (Crickley and McArdle 2009: 20), it is unclear how this was to be prevented as the document follows all the usual touchstones of professionalisation that are outlined earlier in this chapter. Should a person wish to become a professional community worker, *Towards Standards* describes prerequisite attributes, suggests acceptable standards of practice and endorses certain educational programmes (CWC 2008). *Towards Standards* also seeks backing from the State and commits to "networking, solidarity and engagement with all of the stakeholders, including central government and local authorities" (CWC 2008: 13). This comment reveals the pluralist persuasion of the negotiating elite, a situation likely to alienate radically oriented practitioners.

A second publication was produced by the same ad hoc group in 2010. *Community Work/Development Education and Training in Ireland* (2010) offered a database of all Ireland Education and Training and mapped progression routes for potential professionals. That same year, the CWC established the All Ireland Endorsement Body (AIEB). Governed by selected members, the AIEB took over the work of the Towards Standards ad hoc group (Community Work Ireland 2016: 4) and took on to co-ordinate what it describes as a pilot endorsement process of what it determined as suitable professional programmes in community work/development. In 2016, the AEIB published *All Ireland Standards for Community Work* which details the standards required to satisfy their endorsement process (Community Work Ireland 2016). This publication documents the knowledge, skills and qualities required by professional community workers across five core values. These are: (1) collectivity, (2) community empowerment, (3) social justice and sustainable development, (4) human rights and (5) participation. Although this comprehensive account of core values are useful in defending an equality-based focus for community development, the self-initiated endorsement process of the AEIB again carried the hallmarks of an emergent elite that is seeking State approval to become a professional regulatory body. Nowhere in *All Ireland*

Standards for Community Work (2016) is there reference to the forced closures and mergers that transferred much power away from the communities from which practice emerged (see Chapter 5) or the employment precarity experienced by many community workers which will be uncovered later in this chapter.

The Professionalisation of Community Education Through Adult Education

In the case of professionalisation through adult education, one early influence was a dedicated chapter within the Green Paper, *Adult Education in an Era of Lifelong Learning* (1998). This chapter made three core recommendations on professionalism: that an inter-agency group be established to make recommendations on the recognition of adult education qualifications, that a practitioner forum of adult and community educators be established and that mechanisms for in-service training and career progression be developed (Government of Ireland 1998: 112–113). Two years later, the succession document *Learning for Life; White Paper on Adult Education* (2000) supported these recommendations and called for the establishment of an inter-agency working group "to progress the issue of formal recognition of qualifications in adult education" (DOES 2000: 151). This working group was given four key tasks: to represent the range of agencies in the field, to identify practitioner training needs, to explore the development of flexible approaches to third-level education for adult and community educators and to make recommendations on the recognition of qualifications "in the Adult Education sector" (DOES 2000: 151). Both Green and White papers (which are discussed within Chapter 5) suggest that any process of professionalisation should recognise the diversity of adult educator backgrounds and the expertise held by those with no previous qualifications. As has already been pointed out, many recommendations within *Learning for Life; White Paper on Adult Education* (2000) were not advanced and, although an inter-agency group did meet, this was suspended soon after its inception and there were no real outcomes from the process.

Although adult educators have been making a case for professionalisation since the 1990s, there was no emergent elite with an interest in regulating practice within the university ranks of adult and community education. Professionalisation was however accelerated through the actions of *the Teaching Council of Ireland* (the council) the professional regulatory body for secondary and primary school teachers whose remit was legislatively extended to incorporate Further Education and Training (FET) in 2009.[2] Because of community education's reliance on FET-accredited awards (see Chapter 6) this impending council review of standards and practices in FET had implications beyond traditional FET providers. One of the first changes proposed was that all publically employed FET educators must be registered with the Teaching Council meaning prospective approved educators required a primary degree as well as a council-endorsed post-graduate programme.

This legislation caught many adult educators off guard and concerns arose about a misunderstanding between the principles that underpin adult education and the principles more readily associated with traditional schooling. In 2010, the adult education representative organisation AONTAS formally responded to the council asking them to broaden its consultation to include adult and community educators based in the academy who were already delivering specialist adult education programmes (AONTAS 2010). The following year, the council invited universities and other higher education providers to seek to have their programmes endorsed. Ten programmes were approved[3] including those AONTAS (2010) had identified as the most fit for purpose. This endorsement did guarantee the preservation of an adult education ethos; however the Teaching Council forced providers to adapt their programmes in a way that centralised technical over critical skills and that underplayed adult and community education's rootedness in an analysis of inequality (Grummell 2014). This is likely to have forced universities to tone down their political edge thus compromising spaces where practitioners could cultivate their critical capacities alongside improving technical skills.

The Teaching Council of Ireland was not the only external imposer of so-called professional standards. In Chapter 5, I explain how the *Further Education and Training (FET) Strategy* (SOLAS 2014a) is the State-endorsed strategy for publically delivered community education. Section nine, just two pages of a 158 page document, is dedicated to "Qualifications and Professional Development for Staff involved in FET". Principally SOLAS outline a process of data gathering where the qualifications of public employees delivering FET awards are to be captured so that a comprehensive "Continuous Professional Development Strategy" can be implemented (SOLAS 2014a: 110–112). Overseen by a national project advisory group, this data gathering began in 2015,[4] was completed in 2016 and, at the time of writing, is under review. Where the Teaching Council of Ireland has no adult education representation at council level, this advisory board is made up of representatives from ETBs as well as from SOLAS.

Key Debates Within Professionist Discourse

A central theme within debates about professionalisation is that, whilst the benefits of practitioner education cannot be dismissed, compulsory qualifications for community educators can undermine the also valid lived experience of a practitioner in determining a person's suitability to practice. Critics argue that dependency on qualifications distances local, grass-roots activism and labels practice that falls outside of a regulator's parameters as "unprofessional" (Collins 1993; Wilson 1995: 167; McVeigh 2002; Henderson and Glen 2006: 282). In other research I carried out (Fitzsimons and Dorman 2013), I seek to unpack the complexities of these relationships by drawing from an analysis of power that differentiates *credibility* from *credentials* framed through a model of three sources of authority:[5]

> Authority from above – conferred by a role we occupy or designation from a higher authority, – authority from below or around – conferred from those we work with in the respect or recognition they have for us, and authority from within – that which we give ourselves through self-confidence in the validity of our position. (Fitzsimons and Dorman 2013: 53)

The problem with professionalisation is that it gives greater esteem to *authority from above* over other authority sources. This is compounded by inequalities in higher education where upper- and middle-class population are more likely to gain entry to college courses (O'Connell et al. 2006; McCoy et al. 2014) therefore more likely to obtain relevant qualifications.

Another important part of the professionalisation debate is how some outsiders can underestimate the significance of their lack of lived experience. This creates tensions when they take up representative roles on behalf of communities, often with little consultation with the people they purported to represent (Ikeotunoye 2002; Meade and O'Donovan 2002). Where outsiders also legitimise policy directives and suppress dissent without sufficient permission to do so, they at times became an unsuspecting vanguard that unwittingly deepens neoliberalism (Shaw 2009; Powell and Geoghegan 2009; Meade 2012). This is because, inadvertently, outsiders can create what Freire (1972) calls a *cultural invasion* where the dominant ideas of the privileged class permeate throughout society (see Chapter 4).

As outsider practitioner's act out of their middle-class cultural norms, this extends the societal "othering" of the working class (Lawlor 2005) into to the very heart of working-class communities.

One way to understand insider/outsider relationships is to draw from the ideas of the Italian Marxist Antonio Gramsci. Gramsci (1971) believes each of us is capable of intelligent thinking, but also argues that each social stratum, bourgeoisie and proletariat, has its own intellectual base. Gramsci divides intellectuals into organic intellectuals and traditional intellectuals. Organic intellectuals are present within both social stratifications and are distinguishable, not by their profession, but by their organising function in promoting the cultural norms and objectives of their class. Traditional intellectuals are those "whose position in the interstices of society has a certain inter-class aura about it but derives ultimately from past and present class relations" (Gramsci 1971: 3). Apply this thinking to community education and organic intellectuals within the outsider class are those that advance a hegemonic worldview that business logic benefits us all, that capitalism is inevitable and that there will always be inequality. On the other hand, insider organic intellectuals who occupy critical community educator roles can cultivate counter-hegemony, or an alternative vision of society. This is through the problem-posing education described in Chapter 4, where people's lived experiences are validated and theorised and where praxis is nurtured. If we accept this Gramscian analysis, outsider community educators who also seek to also cultivate counter-hegemony can think of themselves as traditional intellectuals therefore separated from their original class identity. Their role becomes one of *ally* to the insider organic intellectual where their responsibilities include naming their privilege and recognising their outsider limitations.

PRECARITY AND PROFESSIONALISM – A CONTRADICTION?

Another unnamed but equally important part of the professionalisation debate is neoliberalism's growing employment precarity. As we move away from a rights-based society there has been an erosion of job security and expectations on employee flexibility, both of which are hegemonically framed as just another feature of our global economy (Kalleberg 2009; Lorenz 2012; Spillane 2015). Precarious employment takes its toll on those affected not just through increased debt (Kalleberg 2009: 2) but through the stress of uncertainty. Job contracts are often temporary or short term and although a person's hourly rate of pay might seem acceptable, half-time or part-time contracts can add up to an insufficient living wage. Insecure working conditions for adult and community educators are not new rather they were identified as a problem in the 1990s within Green Paper *Adult Education in an Era of Lifelong Learning* (1998). Accepting a certain reductionism in assuming a strict dualism between neoliberal managers and emancipatory educators (O'Neill 2014: 151), especially within smaller organisations, there are particular difficulties when precarity meets the managerialist policies of neoliberalism. Lorenz (2012) claims this meeting of phenomena marks a process of de-professionalisation where the logic of managerialism gives managers increased power not only to determine terms of employment but to decide what appropriate practice should look like. Employees working on uncertain contracts, and fearful for their own employment, can do little else but accept direction from above thus enforcing conformity with externally determined occupational outputs.

Another factor in the expansion of precarity relates to the impact of growing numbers of women entering the workforce. Our so-called third wave of feminism has given essentialism a new lease of life diminishing previous gains that emphasised the social contractedness of gender (Klinger 1998; Thompson 2001; Heilmann 2011). The ongoing societal denigration of emotional and care work into the family sphere, and there by as a core function of women, also shapes how to think about work (Lynch et al. 2012: 79–80). As essentialism extends into the workplace, women cluster in care-based occupations including in education (Ridell and Tett 2010). Couple this with how feminist demands for flexibility and part-time work met neoliberalism's distain for trade unionism and its culture of outsourcing and a situation emerges where women are the ones most affected by low and unequal pay and unstable working conditions (Fraser 2009; O'Sullivan 2012).

PRACTITIONER PERSPECTIVES ON PROFESSIONALISM AND PRECARITY

Many of the debates about professionalism that appear within literature are also uncovered through the experiences of practitioners in this study. To begin, the externally imposed nature of much professionlist change enable tensions to be recorded that relate to the involvement of the Teaching Council of Ireland (the council), a council with a long-standing relationship with the secondary school system. One focus-group participant suggests incompatibility between traditional education and the principles of adult education, a perspective that is draw from her qualifications in both spheres.

> ... I am trained as a [school] teacher as well and then I had to re-train to do adult education, and I think people who teach adult education, it is much better if they are not, if they don't have a H. Dip [for school teaching] because you learn a certain habit and a way of teaching on a H. Dip and it does not work. I mean that is the way that most of them [participants of community education] were put off education, by that person coming to the front and the minute you do that they nearly switch off and you don't remember anything. (North Dublin, participant one)

A sense of incongruence between community education and the values of secondary school are also relayed in the contribution below.

> I feel that by expecting tutors to have a third level qualification to deliver accredited FETAC courses now is not the right thing to do. I feel that a lot of extremely skilled tutors will be left out of the net. I also feel that this will encourage teachers into the community education sector and this I feel would be detrimental to the clients who avail of these courses as some of them have had particularly bad times in school to begin with. (Survey respondent, community sector who is herself a mature student)

What this survey response also relays is a strongly recurrent theme that community educators who do not hold professionally endorsed qualification will be marginalised within their own profession. Here are some examples of this perspective.

> The whole thing of having to register with the Teaching Council, that was another block and I was the only one qualified within [names organisation] to do that, and that put a lot of pressure on me, and it meant that other people can't tutor and they don't have the piece of paper qualification. They might have 20 years experience and be absolutely fantastic but they don't have the piece of paper. (North Dublin, participant three)

What is interesting about the quote above is that, in this community sector organisation (a CDP that did not merge into the Local and Community

Development Project (LCDP), see Chapter 5) there is already a presumption that council regulations will be extended into community education spaces. Other comments are more broad based but appear to communicate the same theme.

> Insisting tutors have degrees is both elitist in impact and disregards the ability to engage well with a group. (Survey respondent, community sector)

From another, this time drawn from a focus-group exchange:

> I think they took a shot-gun to people's lives, you know there is a lot of people out there who, as you say have years of experience but have no qualifications. (Focus-group participant who is connected to a university outreach access programme)

From another:

> The "professionalisation" of the Community Sector has played a role in that as people can be hired as educators/community workers on the grounds that they have a degree, rather than their capacities to work with others to bring about changes which are supposed to be implicit to community education and development. (Survey respondent, community sector)

In this next contribution, the respondent is less specific about the cause of their discontent.

> The new regulations that all tutors in Further Ed. have to have a degree and higher diploma will have a very negative impact on community education in my opinion. (Survey respondent, tutor VEC/ETB)

In the final excerpt in this section of the chapter, there is an echoing of dissatisfaction with externally imposed minimum standards and an alternative suggestion that power is retained by the education provider in deciding a person's suitability to teach.

> As long as the umbrella organisation is satisfied that the trainers/facilitators are sufficiently trained, and have a proven record of providing satisfactory education (and all that this entails) then very successful community education can result (brackets in original). (Survey respondent, community sector)

Table 7.1   Attitudes on the need for formal qualifications

Strongly agree (%)	Agree (%)	Somewhat Agree (%)	Not sure if I agree or disagree (%)	Somewhat disagree (%)	Disagree (%)	Strongly disagree (%)
11	19	25	12	11	15	7

Survey question: The need for all those delivering FETAC-accredited courses to have formal qualifications at degree level is desirable so we can ensure high standards.

Qualifications Levels of Survey Respondents

Many surveyed community educators are not against practitioners holding qualifications, in fact Table 7.1 demonstrates majority support (55%) for the suggestion those delivering accreted programmes should be educated to degree level. Ambiguity is however strong with 25% answering "somewhat agree", 12% "not sure" and 11% somewhat disagreeing.

Information about the qualifications levels of community educators is gathered in this research. Over half of those surveyed (58%) hold a post-graduate degree with a further 18% qualified to degree level meaning over three quarters (76%) of all participating community educators are educated to at least degree standard. Twenty-one percent hold a lower form of qualification and just 3% list having no qualifications.

A second survey question asks practitioners where they first entered post-secondary education.

One of the things Fig. 7.2 tells us is that 41% of those surveyed progressed to higher education straight after school. Forty-six percent returned to education as mature students. As just 8% of all full-time college goers are mature students (Irish Universities Board 2016) this figure is significantly higher than the national average.

Insider and Outsider Experiences

This research also captures the numbers of insider and outsider practitioners amidst survey participants. This is through the closed question "The Combat Poverty Agency describe 'educational disadvantage' as something that especially impacts 'individuals from poorer socio-economic backgrounds and communities' is your own background typically described in this way?" There are conceptual problems with this question as some of the words used can mean different things to different people depending on

Table 7.2   Measurements of 'insider' and 'outsider' practitioners

	Yes (%)	No (%)	Do not know (%)
The Combat Poverty Agency describe "educational disadvantage" as something that especially impacts "individuals from poorer socio-economic backgrounds and communities" is your own background typically described in this way?	33	61	6

factors such as age, culture and locality (De Vaus 2002: 98). Community is also a contested concept and the expression "disadvantage" is highly subjective. To demonstrate – disadvantaged when compared to whom? (see Chapter 2 for further discussion on these points). Results are recorded in Table 7.2.

If these findings about socio-economic background are set against the information gathered in Fig. 7.1 about the levels of qualifications practitioners hold, there is no discernible difference meaning outsider and insider practitioners are equally likely to hold qualifications. If compared with the findings in Fig. 7.2 that uncovers when practitioners first access Higher Education (HE) awards, a difference emerges as 71% of those who describe their socio-economic background as disadvantaged (insider community educators) return to college as mature students. This compares to

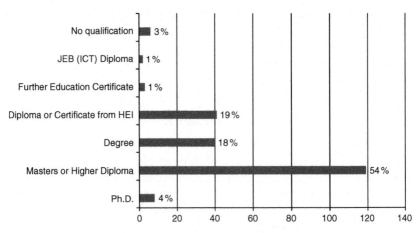

Fig. 7.1   Highest qualifications held by researched community educators

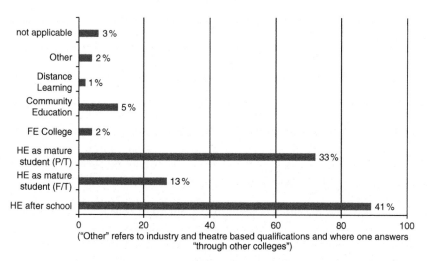

Fig. 7.2 How community educators gained their initial qualification. (Where did you gain your initial qualification?)

44% of those with a more privileged upbringing (outsider community educators) who more often go to college straight after school.

Spontaneously, some insider practitioners share experiences from higher education. In four out of eight focus groups there is discussion about the cost of going to college as the greatest obstacle. This is not surprising as, other research (Cullinane et al. 2013) demonstrates how government grants to support access to higher education are insufficient and that current eligibility criterion leaves many falling outside of rigidly imposed parameters. It is not only money that prevents access to higher education. One multilayered, gendered experience reveals very practical difficulties for a woman who is in a caring role. It also illuminates essentialist notions of womanhood which commonly lock woman into the bulk of the world's childcare. The women quoted below tells us what it was like for her when she returned to college to do a specialist postgraduate course.

I remember being asked at the time "would you not mind your own children instead of pursuing this education?" It just really wasn't expected that I pursued my third level education. So I had to struggle with that with my family, my peers, my husband and I understand that struggle. But if you are not brave enough, if you don't say "you don't want to mind my kids, okay" and move on, if you are not brave enough to do that. Sometimes

> I had to go to [names university] and let them play tennis on the grounds while I was in the room getting my class or else it wouldn't have happened. It is not a given for people and it has to be fought for. (Central Dublin, participant one)

Another insider gives voice to what he describes as an "imposter syndrome" (Kildare, participant one) where he is unable to shake the feeling that university life is the preserve of another social strata. Although this is again an isolated experience, it gives us an example of what Murphy and Fleming (2000) describe as a *college knowledge* deficit where inequality is not only about access, but continues after a student arrives in unfamiliar, middle-class surroundings.

As well as some insiders telling us about their college experience, nine research participants I interviewed describe their insider backgrounds as an important influence in becoming a community educator. I have chosen two examples to demonstrate this beginning with an example spontaneously shared.

> I sit at my desk and I look out the window and I look out at people hanging around at a bench, they could have addiction problems, and I grew up with those people, we have the same knowledge, all that separates me from them is a glass window. I always think back to those people, "there's whoever, and we grew up on the same street". That motivates me to continue what I am doing because if these people can come in, whether it is the parenting course . . . they don't really think that they are doing a good job and they don't really believe they are, and it is just fantastic when you can say to somebody, "you are a good enough parent and you have a lovely child" . . . when a penny drops and they realise something and believe they can do something else, even if they have left school at 12 [years old] . . . Everyone's life is important, what everyone went through is important. (North Dublin, participant three)

The second example comes from a man working in an organisation that supports migrants, refugees and asylum seekers who believes his own migrant status and ethnicity makes him more authentic. This allows him to adopt a role where:

> You are a counsellor, you are a manager, you are able to bring the enthusiasm that you need to meet the outcomes, those things can really get redirected with all the outside interference. (Central Dublin, participant four)

Table 7.3   Attitudes on 'insider' versus 'outsider' suitability

Strongly agree (%)	Agree (%)	Somewhat Agree (%)	Not sure if I agree or disagree (%)	Somewhat disagree (%)	Disagree (%)	Strongly disagree (%)
7	9	25	20	16	18	5

Survey question: Those who have themselves experienced social and economic disadvantage are best suited to work with local community education groups.

I also hear about being an outsider community educator, but only once. This is through his reflection on a sense of activism in his community of employment, but in-activism where he lives.

> I drop into a community and I deliver a course and meet lovely people, and they think I am lovely too, but I am always drawn to the fact that I don't do anything where I live and I am not used as a resource. (Cork, participant three)

I ask him why this is the case and he adds:

> Something about wanting my own privacy stops me but I am probably getting to a point where there is so much lacking in my own community, this stuff needs to be there too.

As well as qualitative experiences, this research also quantifies opinion on whether those who have themselves experienced socio-economic disadvantage are most suited to community education with the results recorded in Table 7.3.

Forty-one percent agree and 29% disagree. If we isolate responses from insider/outsider practitioners who answer this question, a majority of 55% insiders agree and 33% of outsiders agree. This cross-tabulation is explained in detail in Table 7.4.

This is not the first study to draw out some of the complexities in relationships between insider and outsider practitioners. In one UK study by Henderson and Glen (2006), the benefits of outsider perspectives are drawn out where community workers from more advantaged backgrounds are said to bring certain expertise, a fresh perspective and a beneficial distance that helps them to analysis events from a less entrenched position. However, the same study also reports how qualification levels and the middle-class

Table 7.4 Cross-tabulation of socio-economic background and suitability community education work

| | | Is your own background typically described in this way? | | | Total |
		Yes	No	Do not know	
Those who have themselves experienced social and economic disadvantage are best suited to work with local community education groups	Strongly agree	11	4	1	16
	Agree	11	7	1	19
	Somewhat agree	18	30	4	52
	Not sure if I agree/ disagree	12	25	4	41
	Somewhat disagree	11	20	2	33
	Disagree	7	31	0	38
	Strongly disagree	2	7	1	10
Total		72	124	13	209[a]

[a]5% non-response rate when cross-tabulated.

attributes of outsiders are often held in higher esteem and that some paid workers simply did not register the role and importance of insider volunteers. In Ireland, the National Adult Learning Agency (NALA) have also pinpointed tensions where some volunteers have felt marginalised in favour of paid, qualified workers (NALA 2010: 46). Fitzsimons and Dorman (2013) also uncover a belief from community educators with grass-roots experiences that greater esteem was often given to more "qualified" outsiders.

Relationships with the Academy

An anti-professional stance is not an anti-standards stance and it is not one that is against creating spaces where practitioners can come together to develop technical skills, name their own world, reflect on their practice and strategise future actions. The university is an important space for creating these conditions and for holding the theories and traditions that discourage anti-intellectualism. In this study, five out of eight critically oriented educators that I interviewed, spontaneously spoke about a process of radicalisation that resulted from participation in higher education postgraduate programmes. In the first of two typical comments, the interviewee refers to her experience on a specialist equality studies postgraduate programme:

> I wouldn't have been as feminist as I am now only through a process of meeting other women in a forum where there were feminists ... it doesn't just happen naturally; you don't just wake up and read Paulo Freire's *Pedagogy of the Oppressed*. (Interviewee one, community sector)

This second comment relates to postgraduate studies in adult and community education:

> That course really radicalised me I would say, and then I kept on radicalising if you like, but that course really radicalised me. That course introduced me to critical theory, Adorno and Marcuse, people like that and Freire and so on and I kind of went from critical theory to Marxism and at the same time, very much at the same time, maybe a year after, half way through that course I got politically active. (Interviewee five, community sector)

However, others report a sense of disconnection from the academy. At one focus group, a sense of detachment is described where universities are interpreted as less open to bottom-up theorising than they were when the community sector first emerged in the 1980s and 1990s:

> ... that theory is in there [gesturing with her arms to the university] and not being generated by us (Waterford, participant two).

This contribution reminds us that many people practicing from rich theoretical spaces may never have conceived of these ideas through associated academic terms and how intellectual privilege can exacerbate inequality (hooks 1994). The contribution below, from an insider practitioner who ascribes to radical philosophies, also illuminates tensions between practitioners and the academy this time drawing out diverse ideological perspectives.

The whole of the academic sphere of the community sector is negotiating with the State about the lesser of evils if you like . . . so much so that five years ago the biggest community work conference that was held in this country for a long time was "*From the margins to the mainstream*" and completely missed the fact that within six months everything had just gone belly-up . . . all of the institutions from the unions down have pushed the pluralist model that there is something in it for everyone, but there wasn't something in it for everybody, we know that, and what is really happening is that people in the lower tiers and the echelons of the system are paying absolutely enormous prices for the bigger questions. (South Dublin, participant three)

A gulf between circumstances at the coal face and perceptions within universities is echoed by another community educator:

The fact that you are working with people who are actually living on an estate and working on an estate, you are getting a variety of different perspectives where as if you are going to university to learn about community development, the majority of people who are learning it have either never worked in it . . . or they have no practical experience of it [. . .]I think there are many within [names a university] who haven't a clue what is going on, the changes that there are now, they are starting to make it more and more difficult for community education to actually happen and I think that is a very negative thing. (Tele-interviewee three, working in an NGO)

More disharmonies are shared in Limerick where a complainant tells others about an invitation to academics to visit civil-society organisations so that relationships between the two could be strengthened. This contributor, herself paid by a university but based in the community, describes a missed opportunity as many academics seemed principally interested in two things – sourcing work placements for their students, and advancing their own research agendas for academic kudos. This story sparks interest from another group member who expands discussion to universities and their relationship with policy. She begins as:

Not to pillory the universities but there has to be a discussion about that [community-university relationships] . . . I mean we can chip away . . . but we need to be trying to make a shift at policy level . . . you can see in industry – the role of universities, in science – the role of universities. In the social sciences who is doing it? I actually think the universities have not engaged enough at policy in terms of influencing what has come down and the gap between academy and practice and policy is huge in terms of adult education ... a lot of community education going back, it was very much the bottom up approach where as you know, now it is policy driven and there is nobody influencing that policy outside of possibly AONTAS, NALA. I don't see the universities doing it. (Limerick, participant one)

Again this is not an isolated opinion. Another community educator I spoke to also wishes academics were more proactive around policy describing them as allies:

To give us the language, to say what it is that we are doing because we [practitioners and academics] don't speak to each other enough. (Tele-interviewer one, community sector)

A gap has clearly developed between practitioners and academics (like me) and work needs to be done to strengthen relationships. Practitioners are however unlikely to be aware of the impacts of neoliberalism within universities such as the marginalisation of social sciences in a system that is principally interpreted by the State as about growing the knowledge economy (see Chapter 5). The neoliberal managerialist policies outlined in earlier chapters have profoundly affected universities (Ball 2012; Lorenz 2012). Lorenz (2012) explains four key impacts for universities, increased teaching loads for academic staff through worsening student-to-academic ratios, a disconnection between teaching and research with the latter increasingly outsourced, higher college fees for students resulting in greater student debt and greater precarity for university staff.

The Precariousness of Practice

One of the arguments raised in this chapter is that there is an incompatibility between the professional concepts of protection and status for practitioners and the neoliberal precarity of working conditions. In this study, over half of those surveyed, 80% of who are women, work part-time (52%). Just n4 out of n39 tutors employed through the public sector work full-time with some taking on additional work as independent practitioners to subsidise their public income. This leaves them without the protections associated with employer–employee relationships. Other evidence of precarity are uncovered through redundancies, less hours, pay cuts, poor hourly rates, lack of resources for planning and preparation, little or no support for practitioner-led research and a sense of disparity between other teaching opportunities and community education. This final finding is captured below as:

> Working conditions (from a tutor's perspective). Become a secondary school teacher if you want to be a teacher as there do not appear to be any "proper jobs" in the adult education sector. (Survey respondent, tutor VEC/ETB)

Another research participant, this time working in the community sector, gives us a sense of how the project she works with has been affected by cuts and how this has been passed on to employees:

> The cuts that have been happening since 2011 is having a huge effect on the CDP [name] women's group. Staff have taken a 21% cut in salaries since 2011 which has meant shorter hours even though the workload has doubled. (Survey respondent, community sector)

The comments above, and indeed all comments in this book to this point, have been gathered during an active phase of field research in 2011–2013. This means they were gathered before the merger of VECs into ETBs that is described both within Chapters 1 and 5. In 2015, I sought to capture an experience from a community educator who was detrimentally affected by these mergers.[6] She tells me how "out of the blue" she received a letter from the newly formed ETB announcing that her services were no longer required. This was despite the fact that, in the previous three years, she had worked with 11 different groups across four centres. She shares her feelings about the experience like this:

> One of the most hurtful aspects for me in all of it was that my managers all knew this was coming. After I was let go I still had to spend a week correcting 20 portfolios which I handed over in August, can you believe it! I have never felt so exploited in a work situation before, but this is exactly what I felt like with [names ETB]. I feel my work ethic was exploited, my dedication to the learners and especially to the group I coordinated.

Anecdotally, this educator explains how she learnt from other tutors that up to 30 people received letters like this, all from this one ETB. Some people successfully sought redundancy but this was based in each person individually perusing the ETB rather than being offered redundancy as a matter of course.

Where Chapter 5 identifies a survival mentality within the community sector where projects deliberately tone down political activism for fear of losing State funding (Crowley 2013), the findings reported below reveal the stress the resultant precarity creates. One survey participant who works within the LCDP evidences this when he comments:

> The community sector is in a lot of flux at the moment. Funding is almost non-existent. There is no job security. There is a fear of becoming "yellow pack workers" so within that framework some of the questions [in the survey] I am uneasy answering and I certainly wouldn't give my name. (Survey respondent, community sector)

The impact of uncertainty starkly emerges when community educators at two focus groups (Limerick and Kildare) were directly asked "If you were to work in complete harmony with your philosophies, what would happen".[7] At the Limerick focus-group people share, "I'd lose my job", "you wouldn't be employed", "it would be very stressful" and "just stress". Similarity in Kildare, participants share:

> I know if I was to try to work in a way that I feel I should work, I am relatively new to this; I reckon I would be out the door in the morning, seriously. (Community sector employee)

> Well I'd just have to leave my job [laughing], but that is just not practical so the trade-off is the piece about, you know, we don't live in a utopia, that is the balance, the trade-off. (Public sector employee)

A Culture of Volunteerism

In 2004, research by Powell and Geoghegan describe how the community sector bucks national trends in volunteering where, despite the influx of paid professionals that began in the 1990s, there were still high levels of active

Table 7.5 Number of community educators working outside of paid hours

	Yes (%)	No (%)	Sometimes (%)
It is usual for me to work more hours than I am paid for	69	9	22

volunteers. In this study, 11% identify themselves as volunteers with a further 10% working in both a paid and voluntary capacity. However, this dichotomisation of workers into either volunteers or paid employees often fails to capture an unhelpful culture of volunteerism where practitioners are expected to work for many more hours than what they are paid for. In an attempt to learn more about this phenomenon, I asked community educators about their own levels of up-paid work. Discounting volunteers, Table 7.5 identifies how 91% of surveyed community educators report working more hours than they are paid for.

Qualitative findings provide invaluable context. Demonstrating organisational precarity, this person who is quoted below works for an organisation that is part funded by the department of social protection and part funded through philanthropic donations.

> In my experience, I feel the people who work in community education do so because they believe that everyone deserves a chance to better their own situation through education. People who work in community education often put in many more hours than is per their job description. (Survey respondent, community sector)

Other response reveals pressure to work without pay:

> I'm not against volunteering or anything, many people give their time, but a notion that somehow you should be doing that and that people aren't worth paying for, that their skills and dedication and commitment aren't worth paying for and then it is sort of used against them that "they are taking the food out of the starving child's mouth" sort of thing, which I think is an abusive sort of thing you know. (Interviewee six, community sector)

Within public provision, one ETB employee describes the demoralising impact this situation can have. She tells us about being asked to take on significant extra work as part of a Quality and Qualifications (QQI) review of accredited modules commenting:

> That kind of pissed me off because that wasn't named, nobody said – thanks for everything, you have written everything and we need to acknowledge what you are doing. (Tele-interviewee two, tutor VEC/ETB)

What stands out strongly from these narratives is the uncertainty many community educators are working with on a daily basis. O'Neill (2014: 153) eloquently turns these circumstances back on educators as follows:

> As educators we sometimes miss the irony that what we advocate for the good of our students' development as learners, we rarely call for in our own development as educators. Most of us would, in some way or another, believe in and practice a form of pedagogy that has a social and dialogic element. In trying to achieve this, we work hard to create appropriate and safe spaces for such learning to occur. But do we fight as hard to create similarly appropriate spaces, temporal and physical, for our own development as educators?

CONCLUSION

As I wrap up this chapter, I am struck by my own paradoxical feelings about professional discourse, a paradox shared by many research participants. I see the risks to grass-roots political activism but also see the benefits of creating university spaces to problematise practice and nurture practitioner's critical capacities. The tension is between maintaining spaces such as these, and the pressures from regulatory bodies to centralise technical skills at the expense of radicalism. In negotiating its own survival mentality, the academy must make sure newfound involvement with the Teaching Council does not lead to a pronounced redirection of energies towards developing critical capacities within the FE sector. This could result in the academy turning its back on more historical connections with community educators, weakening its own potential for praxis. Concerning professionalisation through the All Ireland Endorsement Body for Community Work Education and Training (AIEB), the tension is between holding the importance of critical education and not doing so to the exclusion of grass-roots activism.

Another key feature of this chapter has been debates about relationships between insider and outsiders. Insiders and outsiders learn from each other and enhance opportunities to influence change. Having said that, there is an onus on outsider practitioners to name their privilege and embody their understanding of this. Whatever our opinion on professionalisation, the extent of precarity at the heart of practice greatly undermines the feasibility and sincerity of professionalist actions. As managerialism shapes professional identity, practitioners are removed from the decisions that shape their field of practice. In the final chapter of this book, I hope to recalibrate this in some small way by giving voice to practitioner suggestions for change.

Notes

1. The women attending the programme in the late 1990s prepared a submission for the Department of Education as part of the consultation process leading up to publication of the White Paper Learning for Life.
2. This was through the Teaching Council [registration] regulations, 2009. A directive introduced on foot of section 38 of the legislative *Teaching Council Act* 2001. Section 38 'review of standards required for entry into teaching profession, (a) review and accredit the programmes of teacher education and training provided by institutions of higher education and training in the State, (b) review the standards of education and training appropriate to a person entering a programme of teacher education and training and (c) review the standards of knowledge, skill and competence required for the practice of teaching, and shall advise the minister and, as it considers appropriate, the institutions concerned'.
3. Recognised programmes are offered at NUI Galway, Mary Immaculate College, Limerick (two programmes), National College of Ireland, Dublin, Waterford Institute of Technology (two programmes) NUI Maynooth, Co. Kildare, Marino Institute of Education, Dublin, Dublin City University and the National College of Art and Design, Dublin.
4. Data are being collected about qualifications, length of service, training, confidence in skills areas and staff opinions on future education and training supports There is extensive information about the Skills profile for the FET workforce on the ETBI website at this address http://www.etbi.ie/etbi-services/education-resources/further-education/fet-skills-profile/ Accessed 28 May 2016.

5. This was built from ideas originally conceived of within work of the Community Action Network and Partners TfT.

6. I spoke to this person in person and also by e-mail, full and informed consent was given before inclusion of this comment.

7. This question is asked on a personal reflection sheet which is circulated within the first two focus groups.

CHAPTER 8

Rekindling Community Education in Neoliberal Times

The levels of exploitation, corruption and inequality are simply unacceptable and the levels of suffering that people are experiencing are also unacceptable. We need to change this and community education is one of the key tools that we have for doing this. Let's continue the journey!

(Research participant, focus group)

This first major study of community education in Ireland is presented from an anti-neoliberal perspective. Sometimes this positioning is dismissed as reductionist; where the complex and complicated interplays of capitalism are unrealistically explained through the actions of a tiny elite. Claims of growing income inequality (Allen 2003; OECD 2011, 2014; Oxfam 2014; O'Connor and Staunton 2015) are also discredited by counter-statistics that allege an overall increase in global well-being, measured through decreases in numbers of people living below the commonly referenced poverty line. The *World Bank* is possibly the most high-profile organisation to calculate this sort of decline. Their 2016 world development indicators estimate that the number of people living in extreme poverty has fallen to less than one billion for the first time in over 30 years. If we take a more in-depth look at these statistics, the fallibility of quantitative research is revealed as the researchers responsible for producing this report doubt its own reliability. They do this by citing unreliable variances in national reporting systems and country-to-country inconsistencies in data collection (Beegle et al. 2016: 21).

© The Author(s) 2017   227
C. Fitzsimons, *Community Education and Neoliberalism*,
DOI 10.1007/978-3-319-45937-0_8

In reality, estimates on the extent of poverty, inequality and other forms of oppression are problematic. The chief benefit to statistical measurements is how they help reveal the structural nature of inequality. Its pitfall is that the quantification of social phenomenon focuses our attention on the metrics of global inequality and not on the human stories behind these figures. These stories include accounts of terrorism and war that may be stored within the experiences of millions of displaced refugees, or the realities of homelessness where Irish families languish in privatised emergency accommodation. What about the cruelty of a pensioner waiting 24 hours in a plastic chair to be assessed in an Irish hospital? Commonly these experiences are explained away through the logic that no system will ever be perfect, that the poor will always be with us or that, as individuals, we are each responsible for creating our own life chances. As the cultural logic of neoliberalism personalises the symptoms of inequality, these hardships become each person's responsibility to rectify.

I support the argument that these circumstances are not an inevitable feature of human development but are a consequence of how our social, economic and political world is organised. Structures of class, gender, ethnicity and/or perceptions of ability fundamentally shape our lives. To give an example, if a member of the Irish Traveller community attends a community education return-to-work programme she/he will no doubt satisfy the prescribed outcomes including greater confidence and new skills. This does nothing to address the deep discrimination she/he is likely to face when attempting to enter the workforce.

The fight for equality can at times feel hopeless. Anti-capitalist movements such as the occupy movement (est. 2011) and successive green movements that have sought to reverse environmental impacts appear to be making little inroad. Local counter-hegemonic opposition such as the once vibrant community sector has also been neutered. As the logic of free-market economics favours self-financing and, ultimately, profit-generating models, an ensuing culture of permanent rationalisation has resulted in a drought in funding for anything other than employability. Because of this, social activities for the benefit of the public-good, or to advance democracy, are seen as little more than a drain on the public purse or as a threat to the neoliberal logic.

However, cracks are developing within the neoliberal narrative as the contradictions of capitalism are becoming more difficult to explain away. Unlikely opponents to free-market economics are emerging most surprisingly from the neoliberal vanguard of the International Monetary Fund

(IMF). In a recent report from their research department, the IMF openly acknowledges a "neoliberal" agenda, suggests that this ideology has been "oversold" and accepts it has "not delivered as expected" (Ostry et al. 2016: 38). The economists responsible for this report raise three "disquieting conclusions" namely that benefit in terms of growth are difficult to establish, that there are prominent costs in terms of growing inequality and that this inequality is hurting sustainability and growth.

Years of austerity and anger are also fracturing support for traditional neoliberal political parties who persistently present themselves as parties of the people but covertly prioritise the interests of corporations. Sometimes, those disaffected by the neglectful nature of neoliberalism find support through an apparent growth in right-wing, xenophobic politics, a situation fuelled by a mainstream media that sharply dismisses socialist alternatives. Rather than censure the orchestrators of inequality at the top of society, the most oppressed and displaced amongst us are often the target of blame.

Amidst this challenging economic and political terrain, there is no straightforward way to advise community educators on how to proceed and I am not sure that offering advice is a good idea anyway. I would prefer to trust in the capacity of community educators to determine their own futures and find their voice amidst the weight of neoliberal logic. This book hopes to facilitate this process through the previously unavailable landscape of community education it offers. If nothing else, this offers a platform from which we can defend our practice.

My contribution is not neutral and I do make the case for an overtly political approach that does not just create opportunities in a largely unchallenged world, but seeks to change the structural circumstances that cause inequality in the first place. This is by encouraging practitioners not only to take sides but to mistrust ideologies that claims to be apolitical and that seek to isolate *the self*, from the structures of society.

Before expanding this argument further, this final chapter will firstly summarise some key research findings from earlier chapters and will present practitioner's own suggestions for change. Contemporary examples of community education will also be offered that demonstrate a more expansive approach than the limited employability outlook encouraged through policy. Including practitioners voices and sharing examples of practice at this late stage in a publication is congruent with my own philosophical perspective that seeks to create conditions for many voices, and not just a traditional academic voice, to bookend this contribution.

A LANDSCAPE OF COMMUNITY EDUCATION IN IRELAND

Although community education in Ireland encapsulates a gamut of approaches, the radical model of practice I support (see Chapters 2 and 4) is a minority perspective amongst surveyed community educators. Thirty-five percent align themselves with a radical/critical approach, falling to 31% of examples of practice shared. This compares to 56% of surveyed practitioners aligned with humanistic, person-centred philosophies of practice, rising to 62% of examples of practice shared. Twenty one percent rank the radically influenced statement "to encourage the groups that I work with to collaborate with each other and together, take action to address issues that affects their community" as the least accurate way to describe their role.

As well as uncovering philosophical orientations, Fig. 8.1 also reminds the reader of a rich tapestry of practice that is shared within Chapter 3. Women's groups, men's groups, new migrant communities, people unhappy about their literacy skills including IT skills, communities with housing concerns, parents including people parenting alone, older people, young people, people looking for a job and people trying to get into higher education all access community education and are motivated by a

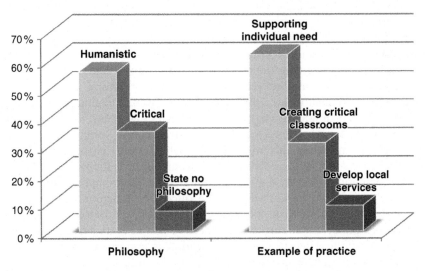

Fig. 8.1   Quantification of philosophies and examples of practice

range of factors. Accredited and non-accredited activities include general studies, arts-based programmes, community gardening, parenting, personal development, health and fitness, community development and leadership, social analysis, coordinating demonstrations, theatre work, workshops on human rights, sex education for young adults and much more.

Earlier chapters have outlined the momentous restructuring of the community sector and of public community education provided through Education and Training Boards (ETBs). These policy-led changes have created a situation where some practitioners work in increasingly precarious jobs that are tightly controlled by each organisation's contract with the State. Forced mergers and the introduction of competitive tendering have wiped away a layer of local control over projects and in doing so, have appropriated assets built up by the community sector over 30 years.

Some wait earnestly for the pendulum of capitalism to swing believing that what we are experiencing is nothing more than a bust period in the usual boom-bust cycle of capitalism. This is not the case as the most pernicious influence of neoliberalism is an injection of business logic into the heart of practice. Given that just 3% interpret their work as primarily about up-skilling for employment, and only 9% of examples of practice sit comfortably within employability discourse, it is not difficult to conclude incongruence between the aspirations of community educators and the will of the neoliberal State. As accreditation is increasingly used to support the production line of standardised measurable outputs, there is also a tension between the rights of the participants of community education to access certification, and a situation where achieving an award becomes the end game to the detriment of everything else. Many practitioners appear powerless to do anything about this colonisation of community education.

Practitioner's Suggestions for Change

Aside from support for critical community education, this book does not offer clear solutions to the difficulties that are reported by practitioners. It does however capture their suggestions for change gathered in part by showing focus-group participants' this image (Fig. 8.2).

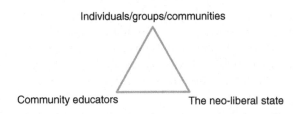

Fig. 8.2   Community education – triangle of involvement

This image depicts three component parts of community education:

1. *Groups/communities* meaning the participants of community education some of whom attend by choice, some as a condition of welfare.
   It also includes communities and groups united by a shared concern
   who are working for change through praxis-oriented practice;
2. *Practitioners*, including the organisers of community education, those
   employed by the public sector, those within once independent community sector spaces, non-governmental organisations (NGOs), higher
   education intuitions and other providers of community education;
3. *The State* who is the primary funder of community education in
   Ireland and the main employer of those working in public provision.

Considering that all three elements will be involved in the future of community education, focus group members were deliberately invited to focus their
attention on the second component part and to think about how *practitioners*
can influence change.

Whilst the dichotomisation suggested in Fig. 8.2 is helpful in taking the
spotlight away from the actions of others, discussion at the Kildare focus group
equally illustrates the limitations of such generalisations. In the midst of
discussion on the reliability of my summation, one participant raises the
following point.

> I am sure there are good people outside the room [the State] as well and we
> are presuming that all tutors are coming from the same place when of course
> they are not, and the same can be said with groups. (Kildare, participant two)

Nonetheless, five clear proposals do emerge across focus groups and one-
to-one interviews. These are to continue to work with the State but in a
more strategic way, to strengthen networks, to re-politicise community

education practice, to become more involved in direct action campaigning and to more deliberately showcase community education. Each will be briefly summarised with the help of some practitioner's words.

Strategising Relationships with the State
Most (not all) community educators support continued engagement with the State as to do otherwise would not be of benefit to the participants of community education. Practitioners acknowledge how financial dependency makes it difficult to renegotiate relationships but equally encourage a continued interpretation of funding as pliable. One contribution captures this point like this:

> Be very creative, hang on to your own style, be true to education, be true to what Paulo Freire talks about, to be meeting people where they are at. (Central Dublin, participant one)

On paper, the State and policymakers continue to support the perspective described above. *Learning for Life, White Paper on Adult Education* (2000) remains the official policy document guiding government interpretations of practice.[1] This supports the notion that community education is separate to Further Education and Training, reaches large numbers of participants "in disadvantaged settings", is pioneering in its approach to teaching and learning, is non-hierarchical and, crucially, takes the lived experience of participants as its starting point (DOES 2000: 110). Despite this rhetoric of social justice, many participants in this study do not describe working conditions that demonstrate support for this viewpoint and the principal reason to engage with the State is a sense that there is no real alternative. One contributor typifies this common justification with the following insight:

> You are going to be completely marginalised and seen as not relevant, not valued ... you can't buy into everything but you need to find out where the niches are within that and you need to find out how to address them. (Limerick, participant two)

The suggestion of finding the cracks or the niches runs through discussion in focus groups in Limerick, Kildare, each of three Dublin groups and Waterford and is a proposal I will return to in the final section of this chapter.

Strengthening Networks

Another theme that emerges is the desire to strengthen networks, a suggestion raised within each of eight focus groups. The functions of these networks are relayed as to give regular information updates, to lobby local politicians, to publically advocate for change and to formalise consultation processes. Some suggest that existing networks require more support with the AONTAS Community Education Network (CEN) named in Waterford, Cork, Limerick, Athlone, South Dublin, Central Dublin and North Dublin. Here is one example of how this is expressed:

> I think AONTAS are very good at lobbying, I think the changes in the legislation that they have initiated were great. It is great to have a voice for community education. I think it is great for community educators to come to a forum like that [the CEN] and actually have it explained to them in plain English what is going on. (North Dublin, Participant three)

Others were less convinced of the suitability of this network, the reason being that AONTAS is itself dependent on State funding. Critics argue this has compromised its willingness to condemn State actions. Alternative networks are also suggested namely grass-roots literacy networks and local networks that combine membership between public and community sector educators.[2] Others suggest more overtly political networks including the Spectacle of Defiance and Hope (named in two focus groups and within some one-to-one interviews). On three occasions, people name these research focus groups as illuminating the importance of practitioners coming together. For example:

> I hear [names participants three and eight] speaking and I am thinking, "Christ I have forgotten that all again"...I need to keep reminding myself that I am doing this [community education] in the context of this huge inequality. (South Dublin, participant five)

Networks help legitimise practice, provide spaces to learn from each other and validate experiences. As they are often not under the same stringent funding control as an organisation, they can be good at creating open spaces for strategising and can support practitioners to work in solidarity. Joining forces can also minimise self-regulatory behaviours such as those linked to accreditation (discussed in Chapter 6). This is because as experiences are shared, we uncover patterns, find allies and grow in confidence in our abilities to instigate change. Notwithstanding these benefits, there is also a danger that networks are offered as an elixir to all ills. This underplays the power-dynamics involved within networks (see Chapter 5) where these amalgams can become a vehicle for accelerating co-option.

*Re-invigorating the Politicised Message with Group
and Other Practitioners*
As well as suggestions to be strategic in our relationships with the State and to strengthen networks, another suggestion is for radical/critical practitioners to reassert the political ambitions of community education amongst the groups they work with. Two excerpts have been chosen to highlight this point.

> For the Sector I suppose, my hope would be that more people would get conscientised [politicised]...I think the more fires that you can light around the place, or even in people's heads and then my hope is that, even in the financial crisis in some ways, my hope is that people will begin to question more. (Interviewee four, community sector)

This second contributor emphasises the importance of practitioners holding a critical analysis in order to do this work.

> I think it is possible for people, if they are really serious about trying to be the change then they have to have a political analysis of what is going on in politics. They have to bring that into the learning environment. So if you want to be the change I think you have got to make the participants be a part of that change. So you have to politicise, you have to give them an analysis of what is going on in terms of how things impact on their lives directly and why they impact on their lives directly. (Tele-interviewee six, community sector)

This type of politicised community education (discussed in detail within Chapter 4) exposes power dynamics in society including the role of discourse in maintaining the hegemonic status quo.

Direct Action and Campaign Work
Given the sociopolitical context and the cracks in capitalism that continue to emerge, the desire for greater involvement in direct action emerges in four focus-group conversations and through some survey

responses. An exchange in Waterford gives us a sense of what a direct action model of community education might involve.

> Interviewer – So what would that look like, that sort of community activism?
>
> Well for me there is no course mentioned, there is no FETAC mentioned, I was taught that community education is a social movement and it is not about having to tick a box or say what you're learning is, it was more a, I mean we are seeing it here, the demonstration on the hospital, you know, that was a mass amount of people challenging that we are not accepting this... In some ways when we put people into systems, FETAC and [names higher education institute] you actually silence their activism, there energy to get out there. (Waterford, participant one)

Another research interviewee puts forward the idea that association with the concept of "community" means community sector organisations are well placed to offer a uniting banner for often disparate activism that is fighting much the same anti-neoliberal fight. I ask, "How can this be done" which evokes the following response:

> The community sector has the potential to play a much bigger role than it does... On its own I think the Community Sector will struggle but the notion of community, and I know it can mean different things to different people, but I think that can be a potentially unifying force in, you know, particularly in the context of all the division we have faced in the last few years. Sort of divide and conquer, public versus private, you know, the deserving poor versus the undeserving poor, the working-class and people who are allegedly middle class and all that. I think community has, is a very powerful notion, and could lead and unite people if it was willing to take a much bigger role and to say that we all live in communities. When I say "we all" I am not talking about the upper echelons of society, but I am talking about the bulk of society. (Interviewee six)

This aspiration – that community can be a unifying anti-neoliberal catalyst for change, is likely to particularly represent the interests and aspirations of radical/critical community educators.

Showcasing Community Education
The final suggestion put forward by numerous practitioners is the idea that we must present a more high-profile, research-based, cohesive and united vision

of the work of community education. During a lengthy conversation at a Limerick focus group, universities are identified as allies that can help community education to raise its profile.

> Relationships with universities could be turned around on its head a little bit. Even what we have been talking about, recording, documenting quality progressions, universities can certainly help, can have the money to do some research, to present the research, to have it brought to the table in education department committee meetings (Limerick, participant three).

These suggestions for change; to strategise relationships with the State, to strengthen networks, to engage in more direct action campaigning and to more deliberatly showcase community education practice, are important in that they focus attention on our own actions as a catalyst for change and not on the actions of others.

FROM THE PERSONAL TO THE POLITICAL – REKINDLING COMMUNITY EDUCATION

As I have already pointed out, a key purpose of this book is to encourage practitioners to embody a more political approach where community education is seen as a democratic process that is part of the struggle for equality. Three possibilites for expanding this interpetation will now be offered; that practitioners, of which I am one, incorporate really useful practice into their work, that practitioners seek out and expand cracks in traditional community education structures, and that the principles of community education are expanded into less traditional community education spaces. Let us look at each of these points individually.

Really Useful Practice, the Integration of Humanism and Radicalism

The prevailing humanistic philosophy captured in this study is a welcome alternative to the behaviourist, banking approach to education that dominates the school system. Many people's lives have been changed for the better through an approach that nurtures and grows intellectual capacities and that often raises a person's self-esteem and self-worth. Person-centred, humanistic education can reduce isolation, enhance community and social engagement and create otherwise impossible opportunities for higher education and employment. We also know from this study that many supporters of humanistic philosophies favour a change in the status quo. Seventy-four percent of those surveyed agree that "the only way equality and social justice can be truly achieved is through a complete overhaul of our political and economic system". This paradox of seeking to preserve learner-led seemingly neutral spaces whilst feeling deep dissatisfaction with political structures raises questions about how to proceed. I suggest a re-emphasis of the notion that *the personal is political* where humanism is seen as a vital component of community education but its person-centeredness is extended to incorporate the criticality of radicalism. Connolly and Hussey (2013) call this educational approach *really useful practice*, a practice that starts where the person is at but locates personal circumstances within collective structures. Drawing from a structural interpretation of gender-based violence, Connolly and Hussey (2013) explain this point clearly.

> Some people think that it's more important to start with the social rather than with the personal. It is to do with the process. For some groups, we start with the social, but for others, the personal. If a woman is in the throes of an abusive relationship, it is not helpful to explain this is patriarchal power. That woman's experience of violence is so visceral, that we start with where she's at. (Connolly and Hussey 2013: 80)

Really useful practice helps us to avoid participatory didacticism where the analysis of the educator, however worthwhile, determines the sequence of events. Instead, the lived experience is the starting point, where a political analysis is self-directed through contextually appropriate problem-posing education.

If we are to effectively embody this approach, practitioners must also evaluate the neoliberal colonisation of community education by interrogating the logic of employability, the limiting nature of accreditation, the surveillance of managerialism and the myth of professionalism amidst precarity. This does not stop with our own individualised analysis but should include our willingness to have open discursive conversations with the participants of community education. Community educators are often reluctant to share their own struggles with groups. This is because, unless interrupted, the cultural norms and societal relations of wider society also determine the norms in an adult learning group (Heron 1999). This includes the location of power with the educator and a professionalist discourse that encourages distanced relationships between dichotomised educators and learners. These conditions make it difficult for educators to feel confident in opening authentic conversions that reveal their own dissatisfaction with the impacts of neoliberalism on community education. Heron (1999) suggests we should disrupt these established patterns in a way that unlocks the potential for groups to become spaces for cultural, educational and psychological openness. This includes naming our own frustrations, trusting each group's capacities to analyse events and supporting them to take actions for change should they choose to do so.

Working in the Cracks

Really useful practice makes community education more meaningful for everyone involved. However, co-option, rationalisation and excessive bureaucracy have closed many traditional spaces for this sort of problem-posing education. Commonly, knowledge is reduced to the silos of subject specialism perceived as relevant for employment or to the obsession with outcomes that push aside unpredictable, needs-based and analytic modes of practice. Many practitioners are likely to feel caught between the need to earn a living and their own frustration with the direction much community education is taking.

In trying to reclaim lost ground, practitioners should seek out spaces for counter-hegemonic actions, and recolonise cracks in neoliberalism to the benefit of a more just and equal society. Politicising seemingly non-political spaces is not a new idea (Kane 2001, 253–256; Thompson 2007; Brookfield and Holst 2011: 129) but it is worth restating in the context of lifelong learning employability discourse (see Chapter 5). One way to emphasis this point is to showcase three examples of practice that successfully integrate political perspectives amidst the traditional structures of contemporary community education.

Healthcare Education in Dublin, Monaghan and Meath

This first example is from my own practice. In 2012, I was working as a community educator in Respond! Voluntary Housing Association, a large NGO with a nationwide presence. I undertook to develop courses on a social housing estate in Tallaght, a working-class South Dublin suburb. The first thing I did was drop flyers through every door inviting people to a coffee morning in an empty house I has spent the previous week revamping. All I had was a flip chart and markers, tea and biscuits, my expertise as a community educator and the fact that the organisation I worked for was a registered

FETAC centre. Ten women showed up and, after we introduced ourselves, we brainstormed ideas. These women wanted to get out of the house, wanted to stimulate their brains and, for some, wanted to get a job. Given my previous experience as a nurse, I suggested a programme in healthcare and, over the next year and a half, 17 people completed a level 5 *Certificate in Healthcare Support* which was delivered from a community building in the middle of the estate.[3] Teaching methodologies were experiential, participatory and very hands-on.

As well as the required skills-based modules, I included an accredited module on social analysis. This module helped develop people's sociological imagination and unveiled the class, gender and ethnic inequalities that were shaping their lives. It also opened the door to discussions on pay and conditions for healthcare workers. When I repeated the same certificate in Carrickmacross, Co. Monaghan, I learnt from this first encounter and more deliberately integrated social analysis within skills-based modules. This enabled discussions to emerge on the social determinants of health, on Ireland's two-tier healthcare system, on patient's rights and on the ongoing closure of rural hospitals. In 2015, I again facilitated the delivery of accredited healthcare awards, this time through the community education section of a publically funded ETB and as part of the national *skillsvec* programme.[4] The dialogic, participatory, critical approach I adopted meant that generative themes were once again allowed to surface. Classes on *Infection Prevention and Control* incorporated discussion on worker's right to vaccination and classes on *Palliative Care* incorporated discussion on inadequate support for families and on the working conditions of carers entering people's homes.

These examples demonstrate how criticality can be infused within accredited, employment related programmes. They also expose a key limitation to politicised practice identified within Chapter 3; where the radical politics of the educator differ from the humanistic politics of the organisation. These courses continue to this day, but whether or not social analysis is included depends on individual decisions by the educators involved.

Community Development and Leadership in Co. Kildare
In 2010 the County Kildare LEADER Partnership (CKLP) initiated a community consultation process to identify needs in the community.[5] What emerged was a plan to attract. a new layer of emerging community activists. This was by offering leadership training that would encourage activists to take up leadership roles in their local communities. The

CKLP decided to offer accreditation for the programme so approached the Department of Adult and Community Education at Maynooth University marking the beginning of an ongoing collaborative relationship. The CKLP placed advertisements for open taster programmes in local papers. Their experience working with marginalised communities for many years had taught them that the people they wanted to reach would not necessarily see these advertisements so they also drew from established relationships with local community groups and individuals. Through these formal and non-formal recruitment methods, 85 people attended taster courses which translated into 45 people who chose to progress to a level 7 *Certificate in Community Development and Leadership*. Acutely aware of financial barriers to education, the CKLP introduced a sliding scale of registration fees up to and including no fees. By 2016, over 100 activists had attended certificate programmes organised by the partnership.[6]

Participant diversity was a key feature of these programmes. Many students were long-term unemployed, members of the Traveller community, asylum seekers living in Direct Provision Centres, Refugees, and individuals granted Humanitarian Leave to Remain in Ireland. Others were actively involved in local LGBT organisations and high proportions were parenting alone. In addition, places were offered to people on community employment schemes who were actively engaged in community and youth work. Despite working to a set curriculum, facilitator's eschewed banking approaches to education and were instead open to emotional and creative expression taking their lead from the different lived experiences shared. Diversity was actively explored creating intercultural over multicultural spaces and spaces where gendered, and class-based dimensions were openly discussed.

In 2016, CKLP carried out an online evaluation with past-participants which had a 50% response rate. Many reported personal growth and improved confidence both in general life terms but also in relation to their community and voluntary work. People also emphasised the power of learning from other learners, how they gained greater understanding of social issues and how the capacity to think critically gave them a new perspective on the world. Many commented the diversity of the groups and the new contacts they made. One-fifth of past-students progressed to further education, almost a half felt their employment prospects were improved as a result of holding a university qualification and two-thirds felt that their role as a community group leader was greatly enhanced, including greater than before involvement in local leadership.

Human Rights-Based Approaches to Housing – The Work
of Community Action Network
Between 2009 and 2014, Community Action Network (CAN), an independent community development project, undertook a programme of human rights awareness in a South Dublin constituency the details of which are recorded in the project's evaluation report *Something inside so Strong* (Pillinger 2015). In the first instance, this project sought to address inadequate housing conditions in a social housing complex called Dolphin House. CAN developed a methodology which focused on four key principles: establishing patterns across people's lives, breaching silence around inequalities, linking experiences to human rights and engaging with duty bearers (Pillinger 2015: 11). An integral part of CAN's work was a programme of critical community education with a specific focus on health and housing, each of which were explored through lived experiences. This process raised participant awareness on their human rights and built community leaderships capacities, thus moving personal difficulties with housing conditions to a level where political awareness of the responsibility of the State as landlord to provide adequate standards of housing was understood. CAN's human rights work demonstrates the centrality of praxis as the process did not begin and end within a classroom but involved the development of a collective complaint which was submitted to the Council of Europe. The process also built many new networks and alliances. In the end, four core impacts of the work are identified as (1) the implementation of an effective model that enabled people affected by rights violations to politically interpret their circumstances through a rights based, framework, (2) evidence of human rights violations by the State, (3) enhanced participation in decision-making and (4) an impact on duty-bearers which has led to real changes in housing conditions for the residents of Dolphin house (Pillinger 2015).

In their own different ways, these three examples demonstrate counter-hegemonic possibilities amidst neoliberal circumstances. Each explicitly deals with dimensions of power and creatively interprets the educational process as a space to instigate social change. However, any suggestions that traditional community education spaces are sufficiently powerful to overturn neoliberalism simply do not stack up. This leads me to a third possibility worth highlighting, that really useful practice and the wider principles of critical community education are nurtured amidst a range of oppositional movements.

Light Many Fires: Extending Practice Beyond Traditional Walls

It will probably come as little surprise that, over the years, my own left-wing leanings have led me to activism outside of traditional community education spaces and within housing-action politics, anti-austerity movements, trade unions, left-wing political parties, pro-Palestinian rights groups and pro-choice groups advocating the reproductive rights of women. Freire (1994: 162) sees these spaces as the real space for learning; where, through struggle, a person can learn more in a week than they may have learnt in a lifetime.

Frequently, I have been struck by the formality of these often locally based movements as they embody polarised discussion through debating and mirror banking approaches to education through traditional question and answer formats; that is assuming there is an incorporation of education in the first place. The structures of social movements can also embody a strongly gendered dimension where patriarchal privilege is unnoticed and under-explored. Critical education was never meant to be locational and the unspoken assumption, even within this book, is that community education only happens within traditionally recognised spaces has to be challenged. I think the principles of critical community education can revitalise a range of oppositional spaces be they local, national or global, can challenge inherent inequalities and can promote a praxis-oriented approach.

IN CONCLUSION

The suggestion that "the end of the world is more imaginable than the end of capitalism" is often attributed to the Slovenian philosopher Slavoj Žižek.[7] The resonance of this slogan is in the way it captures the omnipresence of neoliberal capitalism and the capacity of this socio-economic model to harm our physical world. Ireland is an active participant in pro-market economics and, since its independence; it has always pursued free-trade policies. As the neoliberal agenda has become more radical, successive right-wing governments have intensified efforts to ensure the doctrine of the market invades civil-society spaces – like a runaway train. This invasion is concealed though contradictory language where there is a discourse of equality and official support for community education but a parallel strangulation through bureaucratic managerialist control. Taking its lead from a European labour market activation policy, neoliberalism insidiously introduces an outputs approach to community education that seeks to reduce its very purpose to up-skilling a flexible, mobile, low-paid workforce and dismisses its previous emphasis on what a community and its residents need to create a better, more fulfilling life, both individually and collectively.

As many practitioners work tirelessly to mop up the symptoms of structural inequality, one question to reflect on is who do community educators wish to ally with, corporations and neoliberal policymakers or individuals, groups and communities? Taking sides in this way can been advanced by listening to the suggestions of practitioners involved in this study; to be more strategic within State relationships, more political in practice, more open to working in solidarity through networks and more prepared to showcase practice. Adopting really useful practice in the cracks of colonised spaces and amidst the energy of oppositional social movements can also help to rekindle community education.

I believe the ideas of the Brazilian adult educator Paulo Freire should remain central to our understanding of education; either as an instrument in integrating people into the logic of neoliberalism or as a *practice of freedom* where people can critically, creatively and collectively act to shape their own history. Freire inspires hope through his writings but importantly, this hope is woven into the notion of praxis; a radical union of reflection and action. Freire explains how "hope of liberation does not mean hope already, it is necessary to fight for it within historically favourable conditions" continuing "if they do not exist, we must hopefully labour to create them" (Freire 1998: 44). This is the task for community educators who are led by the principles of equality and social justice; to labour to create the hope Freire inspires. By lighting oppositional fires in as many spaces as possible, the collective glow these create can illuminate the darker recesses of neoliberalism's carnage and can act as a beacon for alternative perspectives. Maybe this can rupture the established world order opening possibilities for a more compassionate and less cruel world.

NOTES

1. There is a direct link to the White Paper on the department of education in skills under the heading adult education and training, http://www.educa tion.ie/en/The-Education-System/Further-Education-Training/ [Accessed 12 June 2016]
2. The Limerick Community Education Network was particularly named as an example.

3. Not all the participants ending up being from the estate as one employee from the housing estate joined us. I also snuck in a man who was seeking asylum in Ireland who I had met on another course and who was keen to quality in healthcare but could not afford to pay.
4. This programme was introduced to support publically employed healthcare workers to work towards a level five healthcare award.
5. Many thanks to Anne Daly from CKLP for providing me with information on this initiative.
6. These include certificates in Community Development and Leadership, one Certificate in Adult and Community Education and one online Certificate in Equality Studies.
7. I first heard this expression used at an address by community activist Dr. John Bissett at a celebration event hosted by the then Lord Mayor of Dublin Críona Ní Dhálaigh who invited the Spectacle of Defiance and Hope to the Mansion House to mark their campaign to save the community sector in May 2016.

BIBLIOGRAPHY

Ali, A. I. (2014). "A threat enfleshed: Muslim college students situate their identities amidst portrayals of Muslim violence and terror". *International Journal of Qualitative Studies in Education, 27*(10), 1243–1261.

Allen, K. (2000). *The Celtic Tiger: The myth of social partnership.* Manchester/NewYork: Manchester University Press.

Allen, K. (2003). "Neither Boston nor Berlin: Class polarisation and neo-liberalism in the Irish republic". In C. Coulter & S. Coleman (Eds.), *The end of Irish history? Critical reflections on the Celtic Tiger.* Manchester/New York: Manchester University Press.

Allen, K. (2007). *The corporate takeover of Ireland.* Dublin: Irish Academic Press.

Allen, K. (2012). "The model pupil who faked the test: Social policy in the Irish crisis". *Critical Social Policy, 32*(3), 422–439.

Allen, K., & O'Boyle, B. (2013). *Austerity Ireland: The failure of Irish capitalism.* London: Pluto Press.

Allias, S. (2007). "Education service delivery: The disastrous case of outcomes-based qualifications frameworks". *Progress in Development Studies, 7*(1), 65–78.

Allman, P. (2001). *Critical education against global capitalism. Karl Marx and revolutionary critical education.* Westport, CT: Bergin and Garvey publisher.

Anderson, G. (2006). "'Assuring quality/resisting quality assurance: Academics' responses to 'quality' in some Australian universities". *Quality in Higher Education, 12*(2), 161–173.

AONTAS. (2001). *Submission to EU Memorandum on lifelong learning.* http://www.aontas.com/download/pdf/eu_submission.pdf. Accessed 10 February 2016.

AONTAS. (2004). *Community education.* Dublin: AONTAS.

© The Author(s) 2017   247
C. Fitzsimons, *Community Education and Neoliberalism,*
DOI 10.1007/978-3-319-45937-0

AONTAS. (2009). *Flower power: AONTAS guide to best practice of women's community education.* Dublin: AONTAS.

AONTAS. (2010). *Response to the report of the further education (Teacher Education Qualification Group) of the teaching council.* http://www.aontas.com/download/pdf/teachcounsub10.pdf. Accessed 18 December 2016.

AONTAS. (2011). *Strategic plan 2011–2013.* Dublin: AONTAS.

AONTAS. (2012a). *AONTAS submission on SOLAS consultation process.* http://www.aontas.com/download/pdf/aontas_submission_on_solas_consultation_process.pdf. Accessed 18 December 2016.

AONTAS. (2012b). *Measuring the outcomes of community education – various models and the role of accreditation.* http://www.aontas.com/download/pdf/meeting_16_report_final.pdf. Accessed 18 December 2016.

AONTAS CEN. (2008). *Community education network, developing a voice for the non-formal adult education sector. A case study of the AONTAS community education network.* http://www.aontas.com/download/pdf/aontas_community_education_network_a_case_study.pdf. Accessed 17 December 2016.

AONTAS CEN. (2014). The QQI re-engagement fee and the case for a waiver for independently managed community education providers. http://www.aontas.com/download/pdf/the_qqi_reengagement_fee_the_case_for_a_waiver_for_independently_managed_community_education_providers.pdf. Accessed July 2014.

Arensman, E., McAuliffe, C., Corcoran, P., Williamson, E., O'Shea, E., & Perry, I. (2012). *First report of the suicide and information system.* Cork: National Suicide Research Foundation.

Aronowitz, S. (1993). "Paulo Freire's radical democratic humanism". In P. McLaren & P. Leonard (Eds.), *Paulo Freire a critical encounter.* London/New York: Routledge.

Bagdikian, B. H. (2004). *The new media monopoly.* Boston: Beakon Press Books.

Bailey, I. (2006). "Overview of the adult literacy system in Ireland and current issues in its implementation". In *Review of adult learning and literacy.* National Centre for the Study of Adult Learning and Literacy. http://www.alm-online.net/images/ALM/conferences/ALM14/proceedings/ALM14-proceedings-p016-033.pdf. Accessed 19 December 2016.

Bailey, N., Breen, J., & Ward, M. (2010). *Community education: More than just a course.* Dublin: AONTAS.

Bailey, N., Ward, M., & Goodrick, M. (2011). *Sowing the seeds of change, the outcomes and impact of a social action model of community education.* Dublin: AONTAS.

Baker, J., Lynch, K., Cantillon, S., & Walsh, J. (2004). *Equality, from theory to action.* Basingstoke: Palgrave MacMillan.

Ball, S. J. (2012). "Performativity, commodification and commitment: An i-spy guide to the neoliberal university". *British Journal of Educational Studies, 60*(1), 17–28.

Ball, R., & Drury, J. (2012). "Representing the riots: The (mis)use of statistics to sustain ideological explanation". *Radical Statistics,* 106. http://www.radstats. org.uk/no106/. Accessed 18 December 2016.

Barbour (2007). Doing focus groups. In *The Sage qualitative research kit.* London: Sage publications.

Barkholt, K. (2005). "The Bologna process and integration theory: Convergence and autonomy". *Higher Education in Europe, 30*(1), 303–312.

Bassett, M. (2007). *Background paper to inform combat poverty submission to department of community rural and Gaeltacht affairs on the development of the community development programme.* Dublin: The Combat Poverty Agency. http://www.combatpoverty.ie/publications/BackgroundPaperOnCDP_ 2007.pdf. Accessed 17 December 2016.

Bassett, M., Brady, B., Ingles, T., & Fleming, T. (1989). *For adults only – A case for adult education in Ireland.* Dublin: AONTAS.

Beck, D., & Purcell, R. (2010). *Popular education practice for youth and community development work.* Exeter: Learning Matters Limited.

Beegle, K., Christiaensen, L., Dabalen, A., & Gaddis, I. (2016). *Poverty in a rising Africa.* World Bank Group. https://openknowledge.worldbank.org/handle/ 10986/22575. Accessed 19 December 2016.

Bell, C., & Newby, H. (1972). *Community studies, an introduction to the sociology of the local community.* London: George Allen and Unwin Limited.

Bennett, M., & Brady, J. (2014). "A Radical Critique of the Learning Outcomes Assessment Model". *Radical Teacher, 100,* 146–152.

Beno, B. A. (2004). "The role of student learning outcomes in accreditation quality review". *New Directions for Community Colleges,* (126), 65–72.

Bhagwati, J. (2004). *In defense of globalization.* New York: Oxford University Press Inc.

Biesta, G. (2010). "Pragmatism and the philosophical foundations of mixed-methods research". In A. Tashakkori & C. Teddlie (Eds.), *The Sage handbook of mixed-methods in social and behavioural research.* Thousand Oaks: Sage Publications.

Birch, K., & Mykhnenko, V. (2010). *The rise and fall of neoliberalism.* London/ New York: Zed Books.

Bissett, J. (2008). *Regeneration public good or private profit.* Dublin: TASC at New Island.

Bissett, J. (2015). "Defiance and hope: Austerity and the community sector in the republic of Ireland". In C. Coulter & A. Nagle (Eds.), *Ireland under Austerity, Neoliberal Crisis, neoliberal solutions.* Manchester and New York: Manchester University Press.

Björnberg, A. (2016). *Euro health consumer index 2015 report.* Health Consumer Powerhouse. http://www.healthpowerhouse.com/files/EHCI_2015/ EHCI_2015_report.pdf. Accessed 18 December 2016.

Blackburn, J. (2000). Understanding Paulo Freire, reflections on the origins, concepts and possible pitfalls of his educational approach. *Community Development Journal*, 35(1), 3–15.

Boldt, S., Devine, B., MacDevitt, D., & Morgan, M. (1998). *Educational Disadvantage and Early School Leaving*. Dublin: The Combat Poverty Agency.

Borg, C., & Mayo, P. (2005). "The EU memorandum on lifelong learning. Old wine in new bottles?". *Globalization, Societies and Education*, 3(2), 203–225.

Boshier, P. (2006). *Perspectives of quality in adult learning*. London: Continuum International Publishing.

Boud, D. (1995). "Assessment and learning: Contradictory or complementary?". In P. Knight (Eds.), *Assessment for learning in higher education*. Oxon: RoutledgeFalmer.

Boughton, B. (2013). "Popular education and the party line". *Globalisation, Societies and Education*, 11(2), 239–257.

Bourdieu, P. (1984). *Distinction: A social critique of the judgment of taste*. Cambridge: Routledge and Kegan Paul Ltd.

Bourke, T., Lidstone, J., & Ryan, M. (2013). "Schooling teachers: Professionalism or disciplinary power?". *Educational Philosophy and Theory*, 47(1), 84–100.

Bowl, M. (2011). "Communities of practice, compliance or resistance? Regional networks in the adult and community education sector in Aotearoa New Zealand". *Community Development Journal*, 46(2), 83–96.

Bowles, S., & Gintis, H. (1976). *Schooling and capitalist America. Educational reform and the contradictions of economic life*. London: Routledge and Kegan Paul Ltd.

Boyce, D. (1995). *Nationalism in Ireland* (3rd Edn.). London: Routledge.

Boyd, P., & Bloxham, S. (2014). "A situative metaphor for teacher learning: The case of university tutors learning to grade student coursework". *British Educational Research Journal*, 40(2), 337–352.

Brady, B. (2003). "Twenty years a-growing". *The Adult Learner, Irish Journal of Adult and Community Education*, 67–72.

Brady, B. (2006). "Developing innovative responses to the education of adults and young people: The Irish experience". *Convergence*, XXXIX(2–3), 39–47.

Brine, J. (2006). "Lifelong learning and the knowledge economy: Those that know and those that do not: The discourse of the European Union". *British Educational Research Journal*, 32(5), 649–665.

Brittingham, B. (2009). "Accreditation in the United States: How did we get to where we are?". *New Directions for Higher Education*, 145, 7–27.

Broaderick, S. (2002). "Community development in Ireland – A policy review". *Community Development Journal*, 37(1), 101–110.

Brookfield, S. (1987). *Developing critical thinkers, challenging adults to explore alternative ways of thinking and acting*. Milton Keynes: Open University Press.

Brookfield, S. D., & Holst, J. D. (2011). *Radicalizing learning: Adult education for a just world*. San Francisco: Jossey-Bass.

Brooks, A. (2006). "Feminist standpoint epistemology, building knowledge and empowerment through women's lived experience". In S. Nagy Hessey-Biber & P. Leavy (Eds.), *Feminist research practice, a primer*. Thousand Oaks: Sage Publications.

Bryman, A. (2004). *Social research methods* (2nd Edn.). Oxford and New York: Oxford University Press.

Butler, S. (2007). "Rabbitte revisited: The first report of the ministerial task force on measures to reduce demand for drugs – ten years on". *Administration, 55*(3), 125–144.

CAN. (2010). *Community development for positive systemic change strategic plan 2010–2015*. Dublin: CAN publications.

Carey, L. (1979)."The history of Aontas". *A review of adult education* 10–15. Dublin: AONTAS.

Carney, G. M., Scharf, T., & Conlon, C. (2014). "Blessed are the young, for they shall inherit the national debt: Solidarity between generations in the Irish crisis". *Critical Social Policy, 34*(3), 312–332.

Carr, J. (2011). "Regulating Islamophobia: The need for collecting disaggregated data on racism in Ireland". *Journal of Muslim Minority Affairs, 31*(4), 574–593.

Carr, J. (2015). *Experiences of Islamophobia living with racism in the Neoliberal Era*. London: Routledge.

Carr, J., & Haynes, A. (2015). "A clash of racializations: The policing of "Race" and of Anti-Muslim Racism in Ireland". *Critical Sociology, 41*(1), 21–40.

CEEU. (2011). *Comprehensive review of expenditure 2011 CEEU cross-cutting paper no.1 rationalising multiple sources of funding to not-for-profit sector*. http://per.gov.ie/wp-content/uploads/Multi-Source-Funding-Cross-Cutting-Paper.pdf. Accessed 17 December 2016.

Central Bank of Ireland. (2015). Household credit market report H1 2015. Retrieved from https://www.centralbank.ie/publications/Documents/HouseholdCreditMarketReport2015H1.pdf. Accessed 18 December 2016.

Cervero, R. (1988). *Effective continuing education for professionals*. San Francisco: Jossey-Bass.

Chanan, G. (2009). "In and not wholly against the state: Widening standards for community development". *Working for Change: The Irish Journal of Community Work, 1*, 52–63.

Chandler, J., Barry, J., & Clark, H. (2002). "Stressing academe: The wear and tear of the new public management". *Human Relations, 55*(9), 1051–1069.

Chesterson, G. (2011). "Britain's love affair with our military is dangerous". *The Guardian*. http://www.theguardian.com/commentisfree/2011/dec/23/military-love-affair-dangerous. Accessed 15 May 2016.

Chomsky, N. (1999). *Profit over people: Neoliberalism and global order*. New York: Seven Stories Press.

Chomsky, N. (2006). *Failed states: The abuse of power and the Assault on democracy*. London: Penguin books.

Choules, K. (2007). "Social change education, context matters". *Adult Education Quarterly, 57*(2), 159–176.

Clancy, P. (1999). "Education policy". In S. Quin, P. Kennedy, A. O'Donnell, & G. Keily (Eds.), *Contemporary Irish social policy*. Dublin: University College Dublin Press.

Clark, D. (1996). *Schools as learning communities. Transforming education*. London: Cassell Education.

Clarke, J. (1989). "Issues arising at the conference". In *Community work in Ireland: Trends in the 80s; options for the 90s*. A report of a conference organised jointly by the Combat Poverty Agency, the Community Worker's Co-Operative and the Community and Youth Work Courses at St. Patrick's College, Maynooth. http://www.combatpoverty.ie/publications/CommunityWorkInIreland_1989.pdf. Dublin: Combat Poverty Agency.

Clarke, J., & Newman, J. (1997). *The Managerial state. Power, politics and ideology in the remaking of social welfare*. London: Sage Publications.

Co. Kildare VEC. (2009). *Community education best practice Guidelines*. http://www.cefa.ie/uploads/1/5/8/8/15883224/co_kildare_vec_-_community_education_best_practice_guidelines.pdf. Accessed 14 January 2016.

Coakley, M. (2012). *Ireland in the world order: A history of uneven development*. London: Pluto Press.

Coffey, A. (2004). *Reconceptualizing social policy*. Berkshire, GBR: McGraw-Hill Education.

Collins, M. (1993). "Critical commentaries on the role of the adult educator: From self-directed learning to postmodernist sensibilities". In M. R. Welton (Eds.), *Defense of the life-world*. New York: State University of New York Press.

Collins, T. (2002). "Community development and state building: A shared project". *Community Development Journal, 37*(1), 91–100.

Collins, M. L., MacMahon, B., Weld, G., & Thornton, R. (2012). *A minimum income standard for Ireland: A consensual budget standards study examining household types across the lifecycle. Studies in public policy* (Edition 27). Dublin: The Policy Institute, Trinity College.

Collision, M., & Ní Chasaide, N. (2008). *Illegitimate debt, a facilitators resource for community education*. Dublin: Debt and development Coalition.

Combat Poverty Agency. (1994). Overview and main recommendations. In B. Harvey (Eds.), *Combating exclusion: Lessons from the third EU poverty programme in Ireland 1989–1994*. Dublin: Combat Poverty Agency.

Combat Poverty Agency. (2003). *Submission to the department of community, rural and Gaeltacht affairs on local and community development structures.* Dublin: The Combat Poverty Agency.

Commission on Adult Education. (1984). *Lifelong learning: Report on the commission on adult education.* Dublin: The Stationary Office.

Committee on Adult Education. (1973). *Adult education in Ireland.* Dublin: Stationary Office.

Community Educators Facilitation Association. (2011). *Community education, enhancing learning, fostering empowerment and contributing to civil society, a position paper by the community education facilitation association,* Ireland: CEFA.

Community Work Ireland. (2016). *All Ireland standards for community work.* Galway: Community Work Ireland.

Community Workers Cooperative. (2014). *Observations on alignment and other recent developments.* www.socialinclusion.ie/documents/alignmentlocalgovlocalDev-AnnIrwinCWCpresentation.pdf. Accessed 17 December 2016.

Community Workers Cooperative. (2008). *Towards standards for quality community work. An all-Ireland statement of values, principles, work standards.* Galway: Community Workers Cooperative.

Community Workers Cooperative. (2013). *Alignment update #2 the second in a series of updates on the CWC alignment project.* http://www.cwc.ie/wp-content/uploads/2013/10/CWC-Alignment-Project-Update-23.pdf. Accessed 15 March 2015.

Connolly, B. (1996). "Community development and adult education: Prospects for change?". In B. Connolly, T. Fleming, D. McCormick, & A. Ryan (Eds.), *Radical learning for liberation.* Maynooth: Centre for Adult and Community Education, St Patrick's College.

Connolly, B. (1999). "Groupwork and facilitation: A feminist evaluation of their role in transformative adult and community education". In B. Connolly & A. B. Ryan (Eds.), *Women in education in Ireland, volume 1.* Kildare: Centre for Adult and Community Education.

Connolly, B. (2001). *Women's community education in Ireland.* AONTAS. http://www.aontas.com/pubsandlinks/publications/womens-community-education-in-ireland-2001/. Accessed 22 July 2012.

Connolly, L. (2002). *The Irish women's movement, from revolution to devolution.* Basingstoke: Palgrave.

Connolly, B. (2003). "Community education: Listening to the voices". *The Adult Learner, the Irish Journal of Adult and Community Education, 10,* 9–19.

Connolly, B. (2005). "Learning from the women's community education movement in Ireland". In I. Crowther, V. Galloway, & J. Martin (Eds.), *Popular education, engaging the academy, international perspectives.* Leicester: NAICE.

Connolly, B. (2006). *Adult and community education, a model for higher education?*. http://eprints.nuim.ie/1064/1/BridConnollyAdEdMPPS.pdf. Accessed 12 October 2014.
Connolly, B. (2007). "Beyond the third way: New challenges for critical adult and community education". In B. Connolly, T. Fleming, D. McCormack, & A. Ryan (Eds.), *Radical learning for liberation 2*. Maynooth: Maynooth Adult and Community Education.
Connolly, B. (2008). *Adult learning in groups*. Berkshire: Open University Press.
Connolly, B. (2010). *Community education: Perspectives from the margins*. http://eprints.maynoothuniversity.ie/3570/1/BC_community_education.pdf. Accessed 29 March 2015.
Connolly, B. (2016). "'Really Useful Research' for real equality in adult community education". *The Adult Learner, the Irish Journal of Adult and Community Education*, 87–99.
Connolly, B. (2014). "Community education: Exploring formative influences within the maelstrom of conflicting social forces". In M. Murray, B. Grummell, & A. Ryan (Eds.), *Further education and training, history politics and practice*. Kildare: MACE Press Publications.
Connolly, B., & Hussey, P. (2013). "The war against people: Adult education practice for critical democracy". *The Adult Learner. The Irish Journal of Adult and Community Education*, 75–89.
Connolly, L., & Hourigan, N. (2006). *Social movements and Ireland*. Manchester/New York: Manchester University Press.
Consedine, M., & Dukelow, F. (2009). *Irish social policy, a critical introduction (chapter eight)*. Dublin: Gill and Macmillan.
Coolahan, J. (1981). *Irish education: Its history and structure*. Dublin: Institute of Public Administration.
Cornelius-White, J. (2007). "Learner-centred teacher-student relationships are effective: A meta-analysis". *Review of Educational Research, 77*(1), 113–143.
Coulter, C. (2003). "The end of Irish history? An introduction to the book". In C. Coulter & S. Coleman (Eds.), *The end of Irish history? Critical reflections on the Celtic Tiger*. Manchester/New York: Manchester University Press.
Coulter, C. (2015). "Ireland under austerity, an introduction to the book". In C. Coulter & A. Nagle (Eds.), *Ireland under Austerity, neoliberal crisis, neoliberal solutions*. Manchester/New York: Manchester University Press.
Council of the European Union. (2008). *Consolidated versions of the treaty on European Union and the treaty on the functioning of the European Union, Brussels*. https://www.consilium.europa.eu/uedocs/cmsUpload/st06655-re01.en08.pdf. Accessed March 2015.
Council of the European Union. (2011). *Council resolution on a renewed European agenda for adult learning*. http://eur-lex.europa.eu/LexUriServ/LexUriServ.do?uri=OJ:C:2011:372:0001:0006:en:PDF. Accessed 18 December 2016.

Craig, G., Popple, K., & Shaw, M. (2008). *Community development theory and practice, an international reader.* London: Coronet Books Inc.

Cranton, P., & Taylor, E. W. (2012). "Transformative learning theory: Seeking a more unified theory". In E. W. Taylor & W. Cranton (Eds.), *The handbook of transformative learning: Theory, research and practice.* San Francisco: Wiley.

Crickley, A., & Devlin, M. (1989). "Community work in 80s an overview" *community work in Ireland, trends in the 80s: Options for 90s."* Dublin: Combat Poverty Agency.

Crickley, A., & Mc Ardle, O. (2009). "Community work, community development: Reflections 2009". *Working for change: The Irish journal of community work,* (1), 14–27.

Croché, S. (2009). "Bologna network: A new sociopolitical area in higher education". *Globalization, Societies and Education, 7*(4), 489–503.

Crowley, N. (1998). "Partnership 2000: Empowerment or co-option?". In P. Kirby & D. Jacobson (Eds.), *In the shadow of the tiger: New approaches to combating social exclusion.* Dublin: Dublin City University Press.

Crowley, N. (2013). "Lost in Austerity. Rethinking the community sector". *Community Development Journal, 48*(1), 151–157.

Crowley, S., Fitzsimons, C., & O'Brien, T. (2015). *The Irish debt crisis, what happened? Workshop template for community education settings.* Dublin: The Spectacle of Defiance and Hope and Debt and Development Coalition. http://www.debtireland.org/download/pdf/the_irish_debt_crisis_community_workshop_final_jan2015.pdf. Accessed 18 December 2016.

Crowther, J., & Shaw, M. (2014). "Adult education, community development and democracy renegotiating the terms of engagement". *Community Development Journal, 49*(3), 390–406.

Crowther, J., Martin, I., & Shaw, M. (1999). *Popular education and social movements in Scotland today.* Leicester: National Institute of Adult Continuing Education.

Crowther, J., Galloway, V., & Martin, I. (2005). *Popular education, engaging the academy, international perspectives.* Leicester: NAICE.

CSO. (2008). *Statistical yearbook of Ireland.* Dublin: Central Statistics Office.

CSO. (2012). *This is Ireland, highlights from Census 2011, part 2.* Dublin: Government Publications, The Stationary Office.

CSO. (2013a). *Quarterly national household survey effect on households of the economic downturn, Quarter 3 2012.* http://www.cso.ie/en/media/csoie/releasespublications/documents/labourmarket/2012/QNHSeconomicdownturnq32012.pdf. Accessed 15 December 2016.

CSO. (2013b). *Survey on income and living conditions (SILC) thematic report on the elderly 2004, 2009, 2010 (revised) and 2011.* http://www.cso.ie/en/media/csoie/releasespublications/documents/silc/2011/elderly040910and11.pdf. Accessed 12 January 2015.

Cullen, B. (1994). *A programme in the making, a review of the community development programme*. Dublin: The Combat Poverty Agency.

Cullen, C. (2009). "The Museum of Irish industry, Robert Kane and education for all in the Dublin of the 1850s and 1860s". *History of Education, 38*(1), 99–113.

Cullen, M. (1987). *Girls don't do honours. Irish women in education in the 19th and 20th centuries*. Dublin: Women's Educational Bureau.

Cullinan, J., Flannery, D., Walsh, S., & McCoy, S. (2013). "Geographic Inequalities in higher education: Accessibility and participation in Ireland". *How equal? Access to higher education in Ireland: Research papers*. Foreward by Trant, M. L. Dublin: Higher Education Authority.

Cullinane, S. (2003). "Community education facilitators – salvation for community education?". *The Adult Learner, the Irish Journal of Adult and Community Education*, 79–86.

Curley, H. (2007). *Finding your way around the community and voluntary sector*. Dublin: The Combat Poverty Agency.

D'alton, E., Fenton, M., Maher, H., & O'Grady, M. (2010). "Grounding higher education in the community: The case of Waterford woman's centre & Waterford institute of technology". *Policy & Practice: A Development Education Review, 10*, 78–88.

De Vaus, D. (2002). *Surveys in social research* (5th Edn.). London: Routledge Taylor and Francis Group.

DDCI. (2015). *Corporate tax secrecy and the state: The apple case in Ireland*. Debt and Development Coalition Ireland Policy Paper. Dublin: Debt and Development Coalition Ireland.

Della Porta, D. (2015). *Social movements in times of Austerity, bringing capitalism back into protest analysis*. Cambridge: Polity Press.

Della Porta, D., & Diani, M. (2006). *Social movements: An introduction* (2nd Edn.). Oxford: Blackwell Publishing.

Denny, K. J., Harmon, C. P., & O'Sullivan, V. (2003). *Education, earnings and skill, a multi-country comparison*. London: The Institute for Fiscal Studies.

Department of Community, Rural and Gealteacht Affairs. (DCRGA). (2009). *National Drugs Strategy (interim) 2009–2016*. http://www.drugsandalcohol.ie/12388/1/DCRGA_Strategy_2009-2016.pdf. Accessed 19 March 2015.

Department of Education and Science (DES). (1997). *International adult literacy survey report, results for Ireland*. Ireland: Department of Education and Science.

Department of Education and Science (DES). (2000). *Learning for life, white paper on adult education*. Dublin: Government Publications.

Department of Education and Science (DES). (2001). *EU Memorandum of lifelong learning response to the Irish consultation process*. Dublin: Department of Education and Science.

Department of Education and Science (DES). (2004). *A brief description of the Irish education system.* Dublin: Communications Unit Department of Education and Science.

Department of Education and Science (DES). (2005). *Literacy and numeracy in disadvantaged schools: Challenges for teachers and learners.* Dublin: Government Publications.

Department of Education and Skills (DOES). (2011). *Evaluation of the labour market activation fund (LMAF) 2010, final report. PA consulting group.* https://www.education.ie/en/Publications/Corporate-Reports/Financial-Reports-List/lmaf_report.pdf. Accessed 18 December 2016.

Department of Education and Skills (DOES). (2012). *Community education programme operational guidelines for providers.* https://www.education.ie/en/Schools-Colleges/Services/Further-Education-and-Training/Adult-Literacy/Community-Education-Operational-Guidelines-to-VECs.pdf. Accessed 10 June 2016.

Department of Environment, Community and Local Government (DECLG). (2012). *Final report of the local government/local development alignment steering group.* Dublin: Government Publications.

Department of Social Protection (DSP). (2011). *Project plan for the development and implementation of the national employment and entitlements service.* http://www.welfare.ie/en/downloads/nees.pdf. Accessed 30 March 2015.

Department of the Environment, Community and Local Government (DECLG). (2007). *Cohesion process.* http://comhshaol.ie/en/Community/LocalCommunityDevelopment/CohesionProcess/. Accessed July 2014.

Department of Environment, Community and Local Government. (2014). Social Housing Strategy 2020, Support, Supply and Reform. Government of Ireland. http://www.housing.gov.ie/sites/default/files/publications/files/social_strategy_document_20141126.pdf. Accessed 6 January 2017.

Dewey, J. (1997). *Experience and education.* New York: Touchstone.

Dockery, T., & Bedeian, A. (1989). "Attitude versus actions: LaPiere's (1934) classic study revisited". *Social Behavior and Personality, 17*(1), 9–16.

Dorgan, J. (2009). *Adult literacy policy, A review for the national adult literacy agency.* Dublin: NALA.

Dorman, P. (2006). *Things can be different, the transformation of Fatima Mansions.* Dublin: CAN publications.

Douthwaite, R. (1999). *The growth illusion. How economic growth had enriched the few, impoverished the many and endangered the planet.* Revised Edition. Devon: Green books ltd.

Drudy, P. J., & Punch, M. (2005). *Out of reach. Inequalities in the Irish housing system.* Dublin: TASC at New Island.

Duckworth, V., & Tummons, J. (2010). *Contemporary issues in lifelong learning.* Berkshire: Open University Press.

Duggan. (1999). *Locally-based interventions to combat poverty and exclusion how effective can they be? A paper presented at the 1999 conference of the Irish social policy* WRC social and economic consultants. http://www.wrc.ie/publica tions/locallyb.pdf. Accessed 18 December 2016.

Duménil, G., & Lévy, D. (2004). "The neoliberal (counter) revolution". In A. Saad-Filho & D. Johnston (Eds.), *The crisis of neoliberalism*. London: Pluto Press.

Duménil, G., & Lévy, D. (2011). *The crisis of neoliberalism*. Cambridge: Harvard College publishers.

Eivers, E., Shiel, G., & Shortt, F. (2004). *Reading literacy in disadvantaged primary schools*. Dublin: Educational Research Centre.

Eivers, E., Shiel, G., Perkins, R., & Cosgrove, J. (2005). *Succeeding in reading? Reading standards in Irish primary schools*. Dublin: Stationery Office.

Eivers, E., Close, S., Shiel, G., Millar, D., Clerkin, A., Gilleece, L., & Kinriy, J. (2010). *The 2009 national assessments of mathematics and English reading*. Dublin: Stationary Office.

Elassey, N. (2015). "The concepts of quality, quality assurance and quality enhancement". *Quality Assurance in Education, 23*(3), 250–261.

Elias, J. L., & Merriam, S. B. (1995). *Philosophical foundations of adult education* (2nd Edn.). Florida: Kreiger Publishing Company.

Entwistle, N. (2005). "Learning outcomes and ways of thinking across contrasting disciplines and settings in higher education". *The Curriculum Journal, 16*(1), 67–82.

Eschle, C. (2001). *Global democracy, social movements, and feminism*. Colorado: Westview Press.

ESRI. (2015). *New Irish research shows that the gap in life expectancy between social groups increased during the boom*. www.esri.ie/newsevents/latestpressreleases/ new-irish-research-shows-/index.xml. Accessed 29 March 2015.

European Commission. (1995). *White paper, teaching and learning: Towards the learning society*. http://europa.eu/documents/comm/white_papers/pdf/ com95_590_en.pdf. Accessed 16 April 2016.

European Commission. (2000). *A memorandum for lifelong learning*. http://pjp-eu.coe.int/documents/1017981/1668227/COM_Sec_2000_1832.pdf/ f79d0e69-b8d3-48a7-9d16-1a065bfe48e5. Accessed 18 December 2016.

European Commission. (2001). *Making a European area of lifelong learning a reality*. http://eur-lex.europa.eu/LexUriServ/LexUriServ.do?uri= COM:2001:0678:FIN:EN:PDF. Accessed March 2015.

European Commission. (2002). *Declaration of the European ministers of vocational education and training, and the European Commission, convened in Copenhagen on 29 and 30 November 2002, on enhanced European cooperation in vocational education and training. "The Copenhagen Declaration"*. http://ec. europa.eu/dgs/education_culture/repository/education/policy/vocational-policy/doc/copenhagen-declaration_en.pdf. Accessed 16 December 2016.

European Commission. (2004). *Success of Lisbon strategy hinges on urgent reforms.* http://eur-lex.europa.eu/legal-content/EN/TXT/HTML/?uri=URISERV: c11071&from=HU. Accessed 17 March 2016.

European Higher Education Area. (1999). *The Bologna declaration.* Retrieved from http://www.magna-charta.org/resources/files/text-of-the-bolognade claration. Accessed 16 December 2016.

European Parliament. (2014). *Directive 2014/24/EU of the European Parliament and of the Council on public procurement and repealing directive 2004/18/EC.* http://eur-lex.europa.eu/legal-content/EN/TXT/?uri=uriserv:OJ.L_.2014. 094.01.0065.01.ENG. Accessed 18 December 2016.

European Universities Association. (2014). *A twenty-year contribution to institution change EUA's institutional evaluation programme.* Brussels: EUA-Institutional Evaluation Programme.

Evans, L. (2008). "Professionalism, professionality and the development of education professionals". *British Journal of Educational Studies, 56*(1), 20–38.

Expert Group on Future Skills Needs (EGFSN). (1998). *Ireland's information skills requirements, technology first report on the expert group on future skills needs.* Retrieved from http://www.skillsireland.ie/Publications/1998/. Accessed 6 December 2016.

Fadiman, A. (2003). "At large and at small, confessions of a literary Hedonist". In A. Fadiman (Ed.), *The best american essays 2003, rereading.* London: Allen Lane. The Penguin Group.

Fahey, T. (1999). *Social housing in Ireland. A study of success, failure and lessons learned.* Dublin: Oak Tree Press.

Fahey, T., Russell, H., & Whelan, C. (2007). *The best of times? The social impact of the Celtic Tiger.* Dublin: Institute of Public Administration.

Fallon, J. (2005). "Targeting disadvantage among young children in the republic of Ireland: An overview". *Child Care in Practice, 11*, 289–311.

Feehan, P. (1979). "Pearse college development". *A review of adult education,* 36–38. Dublin: AONTAS.

Feeley, M. (2007). Redefining literacy from an Egalitarian perspective. *The Adult Learner: The Irish Journal of Adult and Community Education,* 15–27.

Fenwick, T., & Tennant, M. (2004). "Understanding adult learners". In G. Foley (Ed.), *Dimensions of adult learning.* Berkshire: McGraw-Hill Education.

FETAC. (2010). *Quality assuring assessment guidelines for external Authenticators V1.0.* https://www.fetac.ie/fetac/providers/tools/authenticators.htm. Accessed October 2014.

Field, J. (1998). *European dimensions: Education, training and the European Union.* London: Jessica Kingsley Publishers.

Field, J. (2011). "Adult learning, health and wellbeing – changing lives". *The Adult Learner: The Irish Journal of Adult and Community Education,* 13–25.

Field, J., & Leister, M. (2000). *Lifelong learning education across the lifespan.* London: RoutledgeFalmer.

Fitzsimons, C. (2012). "Social change community education, where are we now?". *The Irish Review of Community Economic Development Law and Policy,* 1(4), 26–41.

Fitzsimons, C. (2014). "Worlds apart? The disunity of FET policy directives and community-based education for social change". In M. Murray, B. Grummell, & A. Ryan (Eds.), *Further education and training, history politics and practice.* Kildare: MACE Press Publications.

Fitzsimons, C., & Dorman, P. (2013). "Swimming in the swamp – inquiry into accreditation, community development and social change". *The Adult Learner: The Irish Journal of Adult and Community Education,* 44–58.

Fleming, T. (1989). "Back to the future: Ten years of adult education coordinators". *The Adult Learner. Journal of Adult Education Organisers Association,* 2–7.

Fleming, T. (2004). "The state of adult education". *The Adult Learner, The Journal of Adult and Community Education in Ireland,* 9–17.

Flexnor, A. (2001). "Is social work a profession? ". *Research on Social Work Practice,* 11(2), 152–165.

Foucault, M. (1977). *Discipline and punish: The birth of the prison.* London: Allen Lane, Penguin.

Fraser, N. (2009). "Feminism, capitalism, and the cunning of history". *New Left Review,* 56, 97–121.

Freidson, E. (2004). *Professionalism reborn: Theory, policy and prophecy.* Cambridge: Polity Press.

Freire, P. (1972). *Pedagogy of the oppressed.* Middlesex: Penguin Education.

Freire, P. (1994). *Pedagogy of hope – reliving pedagogy of the oppressed.* London/ New York: Continuum International Publishing Group.

Freire, P. (1998). *Pedagogy of the heart.* New York: The Continuum Publishing Company.

Freire, P. (2001). *Pedagogy of freedom, ethics democracy and civic courage.* Lanham: Rowman and Littlefield Publishers Inc.

Freire, P. (2005). *Teachers as cultural workers, letters to those who dare teach.* Expanded Edition. Colorado: Westview Press.

Freire, P., & Macedo, D. (1987). *Literacy: Reading the word and the world.* Westport: Bergin and Garvey publishers.

Friedman, M. (2002). *Capitalism and freedom. Fortieth anniversary edition.* Chicago/London: The University of Chicago Press.

Gaine, C. (1998). *Gender, race and class in schooling: An introduction for teachers.* London: Falmer Press.

Garner, H. (2006). *Multiple intelligences, new horizons, completely revised and updated.* New York: Basic Books.

Giacinto Garchi, G. (2001). Caught in the nets: A critical examination of the use of the concept of networks in community development studies. *Community Development Journal*, 36(1), 63–71.

Giddens, A. (1998). *The third way. The renewal of social democracy*. Malden: Policy Press.

Giroux, H. A. (1983). *Theory and resistance in education*. Westport, CT: Bergin and Garvey Press.

Giroux, H. A. (2004). Public pedagogy, and the responsibility of intellectuals. *Communication and Critical/Cultural Studies*, 1(1), 59–79.

Giroux, H. A. (2006). *America on the edge: Henry Giroux on politics, culture, and education*. Gordonsville, VA: Palgrave Macmillan.

Giroux, H. A. (2007). "Introduction: Democracy, education and the politics of critical pedagogy". In P. McLaren & J. L. Kincheloe (Eds.), *Critical pedagogy: Where are we now?*. New York: Peter Lang Publishing.

Giroux, H. A. (2009). "Critical theory and educational practice". In A. Darner, M. Baltodano, & R. D. Torres (Eds.), *The critical pedagogy reader* (2nd Edn.). New York/London: Routledge.

Giroux, H. A. (2011). "The disappearing intellectual in the age of economic Darwinism". *Policy Futures in Education*, 9(2), 163–171.

Giroux, H. A. (2013). *America's education deficit and the war on youth*. New York: Monthly Review Press.

Giroux, H. A., & Giroux, S. S. (2006). "Challenging neoliberalism's new world order: The promise of critical pedagogy". *Cultural Studies ↔ Critical Methodologies*, 6(1), 21–32.

Goodson, I. (2003). *Professional knowledge, professional lives*. Berkshire: McGraw-Hill Professional Publishing.

Gore, J. (1993). *The struggles for pedagogies; Critical and feminist discourses as regimes of truth*. New York: Routledge.

Government of Ireland. (1965). *Investment in Education; report of the survey team appointed by the minister for education in 1962*. Dublin: Stationary office.

Government of Ireland. (1996). *First report of the ministerial task force on the measures to reduce the demand for drugs*. Dublin: Government Publications.

Government of Ireland. (1998). *Green paper: Adult education in an era of lifelong learning*. Dublin: Government Publications.

Government of Ireland. (2000). *White paper on a framework for supporting voluntary activity and for developing the relationship between the state and the community and voluntary sector*. Dublin: Government Publications.

Government of Ireland. (2009). *Report of the special group on public service numbers and expenditure programmes, volume two*. Dublin: Government Publications.

Gramsci, A. (1971). *Selections from the prison notebooks*. Eds. Q. Hoare & G. Nowell London: Smith, Lawrence and Wishart.

Granek, L. (2013). "Putting ourselves on the line: The epistemology of the hyphen, intersubjectivity and social responsibility in qualitative research". *International Journal of Qualitative Studies in Education, 26*(2), 178–197.

Greene, J., & Hall, J. (2010). "Dialectics and pragmatism: Being of consequence". In A. Tashakkori & C. Teddlie (Eds.), *Sage handbook of mixed-methods in social and behavioral research* (2nd Edn.). Thousand Oaks, CA: Sage.

Grummell, B. (2008). "The second chance myth: Equality of opportunity in Irish adult education policies". *British Journal of Educational Studies, 55*(2), 182–201.

Grummell, B. (2014). "FET: Responding to community needs or shaping communities to suit a global marketplace in crisis?". In M. Murray, B. Grummell, & A. Ryan (Eds.), *Further education and Training, history politics and practice.* Kildare: MACE Press Publications.

Hadrill, R. (1995). "The NCVQ model of assessment at higher levels". In P. Knight (Ed.), *Assessment for learning in higher education.* Oxon: Routledgefalmer.

Hake, B. J. (1999). Lifelong learning policies in the European union, developments and issues. *Compare: A Journal of Comparative Education, 29*(1), 53–69.

Hanf, G., & Hippach-Sneider, U. (2005). "What purpose do national qualifications frameworks serve? – A look at other countries" *Federal Institute for Vocational and Educational Training, BWP special edition* 9–14. https://www.bibb.de/dokumente/pdf/a1_bwp_special-edition_hanf_hippach-schneider(1).pdf. Accessed 17 March 2016.

Hardiman, N. (2002). "From conflict to co-ordination: Economic governance and political innovation in Ireland". *West European Politics, 25*(4), 1–24.

Harding, S. (1991). *Whose science? Whose knowledge?: Thinking from women's lives.* New York: Cornell University Press.

Harford, J. (2005). The movement for the higher education of women in Ireland: Gender equality or denominational rivalry?. *History of Education, 34*(5), 497–516.

Harvey, B. (1994). *Combating wxclusion: Lessons from the third EU poverty programme in Ireland 1989–1994.* Dublin: The Combat Poverty Agency.

Harvey, B. (1998). *Working for change, a guide to influencing policy.* Dublin: The Combat Poverty Agency.

Harvey, B. (2002). *Working for change, a guide to influencing policy* (2nd Edn.). Dublin: The Combat Poverty Agency.

Harvey, B. (2008). *Working for change, a guide to influencing policy* (3rd Edn, revised and updated). Dublin: The Combat Poverty Agency.

Harvey, B. (2012). *Downsizing the community sector. Changes in employment and services in the voluntary and community sector in Ireland.* Dublin: Irish Congress of Trade Unions, Community Sector Committee.

Harvey, B. (2013). *Travelling with Austerity impacts of cuts on travellers, traveller projects and services.* Dublin: Pavee Point Traveller and Roma Centre.

Harvey, D. (2005). *A brief history of neoliberalism.* New York: Oxford University Press.

Harvey, L. (2004). "The power of accreditation: Views of academics. *Journal of Higher Education Policy and Management, 26*(2), 207–223.

Haug, G. (2003). Quality assurance/accreditation in the emerging European higher education area: A possible scenario for the future. *European Journal of Education, 38*(3), 229–240.

Hawley, J. (1969). "The professional status of community development in the United States". *Community Development Journal, 4*(3), 124–132.

Hayward, K. (2009). *Irish nationalism and European Integration: The official redefinition of the Island of Ireland.* Manchester and New York: Manchester University Press.

Heilmann, A. (2011). "Gender and essentialism: Feminist debates in the twenty-first century". *Critical Quarterly, 53*(4), 78–89.

Hemphill, D. (2001). "Incorporating postmodern perspectives into adult education". In V. Shearad & P. A. Sissel (Eds.), *Merging theory and practice in adult education.* London: Bergin and Garvey.

Henderson, P., & Glen, A. (2006). "From recognition to support, community workers in the United Kingdom". *Community Development Journal, 41*(3), 277–292.

Herman, E. S., & Chomsky, N. (1994). *Manufacturing consent, the political economy and the mass media.* London: Vintage.

Heron, J. (1999). *The complete facilitators handbook.* London: Kogen-page.

Higher Education Authority. (2014). *Consultation paper – Towards the development of a new national plan for equity of access to higher education.* Dublin: HEA.

Hoggett, P., Mayo, M., & Miller, C. (2009). *The Dilemmas of Development work, ethical challenges in regeneration work.* Bristol: Polity Press.

Holloway, J. (2010). *Crack capitalism.* London: Pluto Press.

Holst, J. (2009). "The revolutionary party in Gramsci's pre-prison educational and political theory and practice". *Educational Philosophy and Theory, 41*(6), 622–639.

hooks, B. (1993). "Bell Hooks speaking about Freire: the man, his work". In P. McLaren & P. Leonard (Eds.), *Paulo Freire, A critical encounter.* London/New York: Routledge.

hooks, B. (1994). *Teaching to transgress, education as the practice of freedom.* London/New York: Routledge.

hooks, B. (2003). *Teaching community, a pedagogy of hope.* New York/London: Routledge.

Hope, A., & Timmel, S. (1984). *Training for transformation, A handbook for community workers.* Zimbabwe: Mambo Press.

Hope, A., & Timmel, S. (1995). *Training for transformation, A handbook for community workers book 2.* Zimbabwe: Mambo Press.

Horgan, D. (2001). "Childcare in Ireland, themes and issues". *Journal of Applied Social Studies, 2*(3), 114–118.

Hothersall, S. J. (2012). *Social policy for social work, social care and the caring professions.* Farnham, GB: Ashgate.

Houle, C. (1980). *Continuing learning in the professions.* San Francisco: Jossey-Bass Publishers.

Hurley, K. (2014). "Taking shape, shaping up, changing shape: Equality and human capital". In M. Murray, B. Grummell, & A. Ryan (Eds.), *Further education and training, history politics and practice.* Kildare: MACE Press Publications.

Hussey, T., & Smith, P. (2002). "The trouble with learning outcomes". *Active Learning in Higher Education, 3*(3), 220–233.

Hussey, T., & Smith, P. (2008). "Learning outcomes: A conceptual analysis". *Teaching in Higher Education, 13*(1), 107–115.

Ikeotuonye, F. C. R. A. (2002). "Lateral shades of social engineering: A critical exploration of 'interest representation', 'state' and development". *Community Development Journal, 37*(1), 69–79.

Illeris, K. (2009). "Transfer of learning in the learning society: How can the barriers between different learning spaces be surmounted, and how can the gap between learning inside and outside schools be bridged?". *International Journal of Lifelong Education, 28*(2), 137–148.

Illich, I. (1971). *Deschooling society.* Harmondsworth: Penguin.

Inglis, T. (1998). *Moral Monopoly. The rise and fall of the Catholic church in modern Ireland.* Dublin: University College Dublin Press.

Inglis, T., Bailey, K., & Murray, C. (1993). *Liberating learning: A study of daytime education groups in Ireland.* Dublin: AONTAS.

Irish Congress of Trade Unions. (2012). *The impact of anti-crisis measures and the social and employment situation: Ireland. European economic and social committee workers group.* Dublin: ICTU.

Jackson, S. (1997). "Crossing boarders and changing pedagogies from Giroux and Freire to feminist theories of education". *Gender and Education, 9*(4), 457–468.

Jarvis, P. (2004). *Adult education and lifelong learning theory and practice* (3rd Edn.). London: RoutledgeFalmer.

Jerzack, C. T. (2014). "The EU's democratic deficit and repeated referendums in Ireland". *International Journal of Political Cultural Society, 27,* 367–388.

Jesuits in Ireland. (2012). *Irish Jesuit News, 1*(20), 1–3. http://jesuitcommunication centre.newsweaver.com/Newsletter/jh48ha8b0su?a=6andp=29430205andt= 20449655. Accessed 6 June 2014.

Jickling, M. (2010). *Causes of the financial Crisis.* Congressional Research Service report for Congress. http://www.fas.org/sgp/crs/misc/R40173.pdf. Accessed 9 October 2014.

Johnston, R. (2000). "Community education and lifelong learning, local spice for global fare?". In J. Field & M. Leister (Eds.), *Lifelong learning education across the lifespan.* Leicester: Taylor and Francis.

Jones, I. (2012). *Paulo Freire's philosophy of education origins, developments, impacts and legacies.* London/New York: Continuum International Publishing Group.

Journal of the European Union. (2009). *Council conclusions of 12 may 2009 on a strategic framework for European cooperation in education and training ("ET 2020").* http://eur-lex.europa.eu/legal-content/EN/TXT/PDF/?uri= CELEX:52009XG0528(01)&from=EN. Accessed 18 December 2016.

Kalleberg, A. L. (2009). "Precarious work, insecure workers: Employment relations in transition". *American Sociological Review, 74*(1), 1–22.

Kane, L. (2001). *Popular education and social change in Latin America.* London: Latin American Bureau.

Kane, L. (2010). "Community development: Learning from popular education in Latin America". *Community Development Journal, 45*(3), 276–286.

Keeney, P. (2007). *Liberalism, communitarianism and education.* Hampshire: Ashgate.

Keily, E., Leane, M., & Meade, R. (1999). "It's all changed from here: Women's experiences of community education". In B. Connolly & A. B. Ryan (Eds.), *Women and education in Ireland, volume 1.* Maynooth: The Cardinal Press.

Kelleher, P., & Whelan, M. (1992). *Dublin communities in action.* Dublin: CAN/ Combat Poverty Agency.

Kelly, M. (1994). *Can you credit it? Implications for learners and groups in the community sector.* Dublin: The Combat Poverty Agency.

Kelly, J., & Reilly, A. (2005). "Credit card debt in Ireland: Recent trends". *Central Bank and Financial Services Authority of Ireland, Quarterly Bulletin, 1,* 85–100.

Keogh, H. (2004). "Adult education in Ireland: The implications of developments at European union level". *The Adult Learner, the Irish Journal of Adult and Community Education,* 18–26.

Keyes, D. (2004). "Accreditation within adult education, reflections and views from local tutors". *The Adult Learner, the Irish Journal of Adult and Community Education,* 68–77.

Killeavy, M. (2005). "Practice and procedures regarding accreditation and evaluation in the Irish Republic". In S. Schwartz & D. F. Westerheijden (Eds.), *Accreditation and evaluation in the European higher education area.* The Netherlands: Kluwer Academic Publishers.

Kirby, P. (2002). *The Celtic tiger in distress: Growth with inequality in Ireland.* Basingstoke: Palgrave Macmillan.

Kirby, P. (2010). *Celtic Tiger in collapse: Explaining the weaknesses of the Irish model* (2nd Edn.). London: Palgrave Macmillan.

Kirby, P., & Murphy, M. P. (2011). *Towards a second republic: Irish politics and the Celtic Tiger.* Dublin: Pluto Press.

Kirkwood, G., & Kirkwood, C. (1989). *Living adult education, Freire in Scotland.* Milton Keynes: Open University Press.

Klein, N. (2007). *The Shock Doctrine, the rise of disaster capitalism*. New York: Pan Books Limited.

Klinger, C. (1998). "Essentialism, universalism, and feminist politics". *Constellations*, 5(3), 333–344.

Knowles, M. S. (1980). *The modern practice of adult education: From pedagogy to andragogy*. Englewood. Cliffs: Prentice Hall/Cambridge.

Knowles, M. S. (1984). *Andragogy in action. applying modern principles of adult education*. San Francisco: Jossey Bass.

Knowles, M. S., Holton, E. F., & Swanson, A. R. (2011). *The adult learner, the definitive classic in adult education and human resource development* (11th Edn.). Oxford: Elsevier Inc.

Kohler, J. (2003). "Quality assurance, accreditation, and recognition of qualifications as regulatory mechanisms in the European higher education area". *Higher Education in Europe, XXVIII*(3), 317–330.

Kundnani, A. (2014). *The Muslims are coming! Islamophobia, extremism, and the domestic war on terror*. New York: Verso.

Ladi, S., & Tsarouhas, D. (2014). "The politics of Austerity and public policy reform in the EU". *Political Studies Review, 12*(2), 171–180.

Lapavistas, C. (2004). "Mainstream economics in the Neoliberal Era". In A. Saad-Filho & D. Johnston (Eds.), *Neoliberalism: A critical reader*. London: Pluto Press.

Larraghy. (2006). "Origins and significance of the community and voluntary pillar in Irish social partnership". *The Economic and Social Review, 37*(3), 375–398.

Larraghy. (2014). *Asymmetric engagement*. London: Palgrave Macmillan.

Larson, M. S. (1977). *The rise of professionalism: A sociological analysis*. Berkley/Los Angeles/London: University of California Press.

Larson, M. S. (2014). "Looking back and a little forward: Reflections on professionalism and teaching as a profession". *Radical Teacher, A Socialist, Feminist and Anti-Racist Journal of the Theory and Practice of Teaching, 99*, 7–17.

Lauder, H. (2011). "Education, economic globalisation and national qualifications frameworks". *Journal of Education and Work, 24*(3–4), 213–221.

Lawlor, S. (2005). "Disgusted subjects: The making of middle-class identities". *The Sociological Review, 53*(3), 429–446.

Ledwith, M. (2007). "Reclaiming the radical agenda: A critical approach to community development". *Concept, 17*(2), 8–12. Reproduced in the encyclopaedia of informal education. www.infed.org/community/critical_community_development.htm. Accessed April 2014.

Ledwith, M. (2011). *Community development; A critical approach* (2nd Edn.). Bristol: The Polity Press.

Lee, A. (2003). "Community development in Ireland". *Community Development Journal, 38*(1), 48–58.

Lee, A. (2006). *Community development, current issues and challenges.* Dublin: The Combat Poverty Agency.

Letherby, G. (2003). *Feminist research in theory and practice.* Maidenhead: McGraw-Hill Professional Publishing.

Licqurish, S., & Evans, A. (2015). "Risk or right, a discourse analysis of midwifery and obstetric colleges". *Homebirth Position Statement' Nursing Inquiry, 23,* 86–94.

Licqurish, S., & Evans, A. (2016). "Right or risk? A discourse analysis of midwifery and obstetric colleges' homebirth position statements". *Nursing Enquiry, 23*(1) 86–94.

Linke, U., & Smith, D. T. (2009). *Cultures of fear, A critical reader.* London/ New York: Pluto Press.

Lloyd, A. (2010). "The will of the state and the resilience of the community sector in a time of crisis: Obliteration, compliance or an opportunity for renewal". *The Irish Journal of Community Work,* 43–63.

Lloyd, A., & Lloyd-Hughes, J. (2009). "Building platforms for progression or chasing pie in the sky? Reflections on participatory approaches to social change". *Working for Change: The Irish Journal of Community Work,* Issue 1, 28–51.

Lock, G., & Lorenzo, C. (2007). "Revisiting the university front". *Studies on Philosophical Education, 26,* 405–418.

Lohr, S. (2009). *Sampling, design and analysis* (2nd Edn.). Boston: Brooks/Cole.

Lorenz, C. (2012). "If you're so smart, why are you under surveillance? Universities, neoliberalism, and new public management". *Critical Inquiry, 38*(3), 599–629.

Luke, C., & Gore, J. (1992). *Feminisms and critical pedagogy.* London: Routledge.

Lynch, C. (2015). *The awakening: Empowered by water what are the personal and political implications for female activists in the Irish anti-water charges movement?.* Unpublished Masters in Equality, Community Education and Social Activism. Kildare: Maynooth University.

Lynch, K. (1989). *The hidden curriculum. Reproduction in education and appraisal.* London: The Falmer Press.

Lynch, K. (1999). *Equality in education.* London: Gill and MacMillan.

Lynch, O. (2013). "British Muslim youth: Radicalization, terrorism and the construction of the 'other'". *Critical Studies on Terrorism, 6*(2), 241–261.

Lynch, K., & Baker, J. (2006). "Equality in education: An equality of condition perspective". *Theory and Research in Education, 3*(2), 131–164.

Lynch, K., & Lodge, A. (2002). *Equality and power in schools.* Dublin: RoutledgeFalmer.

Lynch, K., Grummell, B., & Devine, D. (2012). *New managerialism in education, commercialization, carelessness and gender.* Dublin: Palgrave MacMillan.

Lyotard, J. F. (1984). *The postmodern condition: A report on knowledge.* Translated from the French by Geoff Bennington and Brian Massumi. Minneapolis: University of Minnesota.

MacDonald, K. (1995). *The sociology of the professions*. London: Sage.

Malpas, S. (2005). *The postmodern*. New York: Routledge.

Maltone, C., Yvars, B., & Brady, H. (2012). "Globalization and social inequalities in Europe: Assessment and outlook". *Eastern Journal of European Studies, 3*(1), 5–30.

Manfred, B. S., & Roy, R. K. (2010). *Neoliberalism: A very short introduction*. New York: Oxford University Press Inc.

Martin, I. (1987). "Community education, towards a theoretical analysis". In G. Allen, J. Bastiani, I. Martin, & K. Richards (Eds.), *Community education, an agenda for educational reform*. Milton Keynes and Philadelphia: Open University Press.

Martin, I. (1999). "Introductory essay: Popular education and social movements in Scotland today". In J. Crowther, I. Martin, & M. Shaw (Eds.), *Popular education and social movements in Scotland today*. Leicester: National Institute of Adult Continuing Education.

Maunsell, C., Downes, P., & McLoughlin, V. (2008). *National report on lifelong learning in Ireland LLL2010: Sub-project 1: Towards a lifelong learning society in Europe – The contribution of the education system*. Dublin: Educational Disadvantage Centre. https://www4.dcu.ie/edc/eu-project-lll2010-towards-lifelong-learning-society.shtml. Accessed 18 December 2016.

Mayo, M. (1994). *Communities and caring: The mixed economy of welfare*. Basingstoke: Macmillan.

Mayo, P. (1999). *Gramsci, Freire and adult education. Possibilities for transformative action*. London: Zed Books.

Mayo, M. (2000). *Cultures, Communities, Identities: Cultural Strategies for Participation and Empowerment*. Basingstoke: Palgrave.

Mayo, P., & English, L. M. (2013). *Learning with adults, A critical pedagogical introduction*. Rotterdam: Sense Publishers.

Mayo, M., Mendewelso-Bendek, Z., & Packham, C. (2013). *Community research for community development*. Houndmills/Basingstoke: Palgrave and Macmillan.

Mazlow, A. H. (1943). "A theory of human motivation". *Psychological Review, 50*, 370–396.

McCabe, C. (2015). "False economy: The financialisation of Ireland and the roots of austerity". In C. Coulter & A. Nangle (Eds.), *Ireland under Austerity: Neoliberal Crisis, Neoliberal Solutions*. Manchester/New York: Manchester University Press.

McCallion, A. (2009). "An educators Dilemma". *The Adult Learner, the Irish Journal of Adult and Community Education*, 60–73.

McCann, M. (1991). *Ballymun youth action project, ten years on*. Dublin: BYAP.

McCoy, S. (2011). "Higher education expansion and differentiation in the republic of Ireland". *Higher Education, 61*(3), 243–260.

McCoy, S., Smyth, E., & Banks, J. (2012). *The primary classroom: Insights from the growing up in Ireland survey*. Dublin: The Economic and Social Research Institute.

McCoy, S., Smyth, E., Watson, D., & Darmody, M. (2014). *Leaving school in Ireland, a longitudinal study of post-school transitions*. Dublin: ESRI.

McGlynn, L. (2012). *Community educators and the struggle for recognition; theorising meaning, educator and institution in Ireland's community education field using a generative grounded theory approach*. Education Doctorate. http://eprints.nuim.ie/3902/. Accessed 3 December 2012.

McGlynn, L. (2014). *Community education and the labour activation challenge, A literature review on community education in a context of labour market activation, employability and active citizenship in Ireland and the EU*. Ireland: Community Education Facilitators' Association.

McLaren, P. (2000). *Che Guevara, Paulo Freire, and the pedagogy of revolution*. Maryland: Rowman and Littlefield Publishers.

McLaren, P. (2009). "Critical pedagogy: A look at the major concepts". In A. Darder, P. Baltodano, & R. D. Torres (Eds.), *The critical pedagogy reader* (2nd Edn.). London/New York: Routledge.

McLaren, P., & Giroux, H. (1994). *Preface to Gadotti, M. Reading Paulo Freire his life and work*. New York: State University of New York Press.

McNeill, H. (2005). *Connecting communities. A practical guide to using development education in community settings*. Dublin: Lourdes Youth and Community Service Ltd.

McVeigh, R. (2002). "Between reconciliation and pacification: The British state and community relations in the north of Ireland". *Community Development Journal, 37*(1), 47–59.

Meade, R. (2005). "We hate it here, please let us stay! Irish social partnership and the community/voluntary sector's conflicted experiences of recognition". *Critical Social Policy, 25*(3), 349–373.

Meade, R. (2012). "Government and community development in Ireland: The contested subjects of professionalism and expertise". *Antipode, 44*(3), 889–910.

Meade, R., & O'Donovan, O. (2002). "Editorial introduction: Corporatism and the on-going debate about the relationship between the state and community development". *Community Development Journal, 37*(1), 1–9.

Meagher, A. (2014). "Privatising community work, the Genie's out of the bottle – A declining state funding remains a concern". *Ireland: Changing Ireland, Summer*.

Merriam, S. B. (2001). "Androgogy and self-directed learning: Pillars of adult learning theory". *New Directions for Adult and Continuing Education, 89*, 3–14.

Merriam, S. B., & Brockett, R. G. (1997). *The profession and practice of adult education, an introduction*. San Francisco: Jossey-Bass.

Mertens, D. (2012). "What comes first? The Paradigm or the approach?". *Journal of Mixed-Methods Research*, 6(4), 255–257.

Mezirow, J. (1978). "Perspective transformation". *Adult Education Quarterly*, 28(2), 100–110.

Mezirow, J. (2000). *Learning as transformation: Critical perspectives on a theory in progress*. The Jossey-Bass Higher and Adult Education Series. San Francisco: Jossey-Bass Publishers.

Mezirow, J. (2012). "Learning to think like and adult: Core concepts of transformative theory". In E. W. Taylor & W. Cranton (Eds.), *The handbook of transformative learning: Theory, research and practice*. San Francisco: Wiley.

Micari, M. (2003). "Against the Norm: Liberal adult education in an age of vocationalism". *The Journal of Continuing Higher Education*, 51(3), 27–34.

Milana, M. (2012). "Globalisation, transnational policies and adult education". *International Review of Education*, 58(6), 777–797.

Moraes, M. (2003). "The path of dissent, an interview with Peter McLaren". *Journal of Transformative Education*, 1(2), 117–134.

Motherway, B. (2006). *The role of community development in Tackling poverty in Ireland, A literature review for the combat poverty agency*. Dublin: The Combat Poverty Agency.

Mullins, M. (1991). "Representations of history, Irish feminism, and the politics of difference". *Feminist Studies*, 17(1), 29–43.

Murphy, M. (2002). "Social partnership, is it the only game in town?". *Community Development Journal*, 37(1), 80–90.

Murphy, M. P. (2012). "The politics of Irish labour activation: 1980 to 2010". *Administration*, 60(2), 27–49.

Murphy, M., & Fleming, T. (2000). "Between common and college knowledge: Exploring the boundaries between adult and higher education". *Studies in Continuing Education*, 22(1), 77–94.

Murray, M. (2013). "What happens in the classroom stays in the classroom – The limits to the transformative approach to education for political citizenship". *The Adult Learner: The Irish Journal of Adult and Community Education*, 15–28.

Murray, M. (2014). "What's in a name? Terminology, power and contestation". In M. Murray, B. Grummell, & A. Ryan (Eds.), *Further education and training, history politics and practice*. Kildare: MACE Press Publications.

Murtagh. (2009). *The Irish education policy process since 1997: Some lessons for the future*, unpublished PhD. thesis. http://eprints.nuim.ie/1488/. Accessed 28 July 2014.

Murtagh. (2014). "1973-2-13: From membership of the EEC to the establishment of SOLAS and the ETBS". In M. Murray, B. Grummell, & A. Ryan (Eds,), *Further education and training, history politics and practice*. Kildare: MACE Press Publications.

Nagle, A. (2015). "Ireland and the new economy". In C. Coulter & A. Nagle (Eds.), *Ireland under Austerity. Neoliberal crisis, neoliberal solutions*. Manchester/ New York: Manchester University Press.

National Adult Literacy Agency. (2010). *NALA A living history 1980–2010.* Dublin: NALA.

National Archives. (nd). *Hilda Tweedy papers*. http://www.nationalarchives.ie/ topics/womens_history/Tweedy.pdf. Accessed 17 March 2015.

National Economic and Social Forum. (2003). *The policy implications of social capital, Forum Report No. 28*. http://files.nesc.ie/nesf_archive/nesf_reports/ NESF_28.pdf. Accessed December 2015.

National Framework of Qualifications (NFQ). (2003a). *Policies and criteria for the establishment of the national framework of qualifications*. Dublin: National Qualifications Authority of Ireland.

National Framework of Qualifications. (2003b). *Qualifications matter, a brief guide to the national framework of qualifications*. Dublin: National Qualifications Authority of Ireland.

National Framework of Qualifications. (2003c). Grid of indicators. http://www. nfq.ie.webhosting.heanet.ie/nfq/en/documents/NFQLevelindicators.pdf. Accessed 17 March 2015.

National Framework of Qualifications. (2006a). *Verification of compatibility of Irish national framework of qualifications with the framework for qualifications of the European higher education area*. Dublin: National Qualifications Authority of Ireland.

National Framework of Qualifications. (2006b). *Principles and operations guidelines for the implementation of a national approach to credit in Irish higher education and training*. Dublin: National Qualification Authority of Ireland.

Naughton, F. (2002). *Training for transformation: Utopian hope or practical reality*. Unpublished MPhil thesis. Birmingham: University of Birmingham.

Neville, P., O'Dwyer, M., & Power, M. J. (2014). "The social value of community-based adult education in Limerick city". *The Adult Learner, the Irish Journal of Adult and Community Education*, 42–56.

Newton, J. (2000). "Feeding the beast or improving quality?: Academics" perceptions of quality assurance and quality monitoring". *Quality in Higher Education, 6*(2), 153–163.

Nexus. (2002). *Evaluation of the community development programme, main report*. Dublin: Department of Social, Community and Family Affairs (Government Publications).

Noble, S. (2015). "Promoting homebirth, intermediate homebirth report". *British Journal of Midwifery, 23*(4), 276–280.

Norris, M., & Redmond, D. (2005). *Housing contemporary Ireland, policy society and shelter*. Dublin: The Institute of Public Administration.

Nye, M. (2001). "Managing the boom: Negotiating social partnership in an expanding economy". *Irish Political Studies, 16*, 191–199.

Ó Cinnéide S. (1998/1999). "Democracy and the constitution". *Administration, 46*(4), 41–58.

Ó Cinnéide, S., & Walsh, J. (1990). "Multiplication and divisions: Trends in community development in Ireland since the 1960's". *Community Development Journal, 25*(4), 326–336.

O'Brien, M. (2003). "Girls and transition to second-level schooling in Ireland: 'moving on' and 'moving out'". *Gender and Education, 15*(3), 85–96.

O'Brien, T. (2007). "Is there a way out of this clinic? An adult and community education perspective on Methadone and the absence of rehabilitation". *The Adult Learner, the Irish Journal of Adult and Community Education*, 40–55.

O'Byrne, D. (2012). "Investigating the de-politicisation of community development: What happened? Where do we go now?". In A. Jackson & C. O'Doherty (Eds.), *Community development in Ireland, theory, policy and practice*. Dublin: Gill and MacMillan.

O'Connell, P., McCoy, S., & Clancy, D. (2006). "Who went to college? Socio-economic inequality in entry to higher education in the republic of Ireland in 2004". *Higher Education Quarterly, 60*(4), 312–332.

O'Connor, F. (2010). "Institutional racism in Irish adult education: Fact or fiction? ". *The Irish Journal of Adult and Community Education*, 29–52.

O'Connor, N., & Staunton, C. (2015). *Cherishing all equally, economic inequality in Ireland*. Dublin: TASC.

Ó Fathaigh, M. (1998). "Universities, partnership and the promotion of social inclusion: Some issues and developments in Ireland". *Journal of Education through Partnership, 2*(2), 2–17.

Office of the Attorney General. (1986). Combat Poverty Agency Act 1986. Retrieved from http://www.irishstatutebook.ie/eli/1986/act/14/enacted/en/print.html. Accessed 14 December 2016.

O'Flynn, M., Monaghan, L. F., & Power, M. J. (2014). "Scapegoating during a Ttime of crisis: A critique of postCeltic Tiger Ireland". *Sociology, 48*(5), 921–937.

O'Grady, A. (2008). *Choosing to learn or chosen to learn: A qualitative case study of skills for life learners, PhD thesis*. Nottingham: University of Nottingham. http://eprints.nottingham.ac.uk/12070/. Accessed 17 March 2015.

O'Shea, M. and Collins, C. (2016). Access to Diagnostics Used to Detect Cancer. Irish College of General Practitioners/Irish Cancer Society. https://www.cancer.ie/sites/default/files/content-attachments/icgp_irish_cancer_society_report_-_access_to_diagnostics_to_detect_cancer.pdf. Accessed 6 January 2017.

O'Hearn, D. (1998). *Inside the Celtic Tiger. The Irish economy and the Asian model*. London: Pluto Press.

Ó'Muircheartaigh, L. (2004). "Planning for the future of the adult education service: A challenge for VECs". *The Adult Learner: The Irish Journal of Adult and Community Education*, 42–55.

O'Neill, J. (2014). "In search of a clearing, the potential of narrative spaces for adult educator growth". In M. Murray, B. Grummell, & A. Ryan (Eds.), *Further education and training history, politics, practice*. Maynooth: MACE Press.

O'Reilly, N. (2014). "Principles and pragmatism – advocating for adult and community education within a neoliberal policy framework". In M. Murray, B. Grummell & A. Ryan (Eds.), *Further education and training, history, politics, practice*. Kildare: MACE Press Publications.

O'Sullivan, D. (2005). *Culture, politics and Irish education since the 1950s policy paradigms and power*. Dublin: The Institute of Public Administration.

O'Sullivan, S. (2012). "All changed, changed Utterly? Gender role attitudes and the feminisation of the Irish labour force". *Women's Studies International Forum*, 35(4), 223–232.

Oakley, A. (1999). "Paradigm wars: Some thoughts on a personal and public trajectory". *International Journal of Social Research Methodology*, 2(3), 247–254.

OECD. (2001). *The Wellbeing of nations: The role of human and social capital, centre for educational research and innovation*. Paris: OECD.

OECD. (2011). *Divided we stand, why inequality keeps rising. An overview of growing income inequalities in OECD countries: Main findings*. http://www.oecd.org/els/soc/49499779.pdf. Accessed 18 December 2016.

OECD. (2014). *Focus on equality and growth*. https://www.oecd.org/social/Focus-Inequality-and-Growth-2014.pdf. Accessed 18 December 2016.

Óhidy, A. (2008). *Lifelong learning: Interpretations of an education policy in Europe*. Wiesbaden, DEU: Springer.

Oleson, V. (2005). "Early Millennial feminist qualitative research, challenges and contours". In N. K. Denzin & Y. S. Lincoln (Eds.), *The Sage handbook of qualitative research* (3rd Edn.). London: Sage Publications.

Orr, S. (2007). "Assessment moderation: Constructing the marks and constructing the students". *Assessment and Evaluation in Higher Education*, 32(6), 645–656.

Ostry, J. D., Longani, P., & Furceri, D. (2016). "Neoliberalism oversold? ". *Finance and Development*, 53(2), 38–41.

Oxfam (2014). *Working for the few, political capture and economic inequality*. https://www.oxfam.org/sites/www.oxfam.org/files/file_attachments/bp-working-for-few-political-capture-economic-inequality-200114-en_3.pdf. Accessed 19 December 2016.

Paterson, L. (1999). "Social movements and the politics of educational change". In J. Crowther, I. Martin, & M. Shaw (Eds.), *Popular education and social movements in Scotland today*. Leicester: National Institute of Adult Continuing Education.

Pearson, E. M., & Podeschi, R. L. (1999). "Humanism and Individualism: Maslow and his critics". *Adult Education Quarterly November, 50*(3), 41–55.

Philo, G., Hewitt, J., & Beharrell, P. (1995). "'And now they're out again': Industrial news". In *Glasgow media group reader, volume 2: industry, economy, war and politics.* London: Routledge.

Pillinger, J. (2011). *National collective of community based woman's networks, review and evaluation.* Dublin: NWCCN.

Pillinger, J. (2015). *Something inside so strong.* Dublin: CAN Publications.

Platt, L. (2011). *Understanding inequalities, stratification and difference.* Cambridge: Polity Press.

Pobail. (2015). *SICAP mid-term review (1st April–31st August 2015).* Dublin: Pobail.

Powell, F., & Geoghegan, M. (2004). *The politics of community development, reclaiming civil society or reinventing governance?.* Dublin: A and A Falmer.

Powell, F. & Geoghegan, M. (2009). "Community development and the contested politics of the late modern agora: of, alongside or against neoliberalism?" *Community Development Journal, 44*(4), 430–447.

Preston, J., & Hammond, C. (2003). "Practitioner views on the wider benefits of further education". *Journal of Further and Higher Education, 27*(2), 211–222.

Putnam, R. D. (2000). *Bowling alone, the collapse and revival of American community.* New York: Simon and Schuster.

Qualifications and Quality Ireland (QQI). (2013a). "*Green paper on the comprehensive implementation of the functions of quality and qualifications Ireland – for consultation*". http://www.qqi.ie/Downloads/Consultation/Green%20Papers/Green%20Paper-Section%201%20version%202.pdf. Accessed 20 July 2014.

Quality and Qualifications Ireland (QQI). (2013b). *Comprehensive policy development programme – submissions.* Dublin: QQI.

Quality and Qualification Ireland (QQI). (2015). *Effective practice guidelines for external examining revised February 2015.* Dublin: QQI.

Quilty, A. (2003). "Towards a pedagogy of demystification". *The Adult Learner, the Irish Journal of Adult and Community Education,* 57–66.

Radner, H., Koshy, V., & Taylor, A. (2007). "Gifts, talents and meritocracy". *Journal of Education Policy, 22*(3), 283–299.

Ramazanoglu, C. (1989). *Feminism and the contradictions of oppression.* London: Routledge.

Ratcliffe, P. (2012). Community cohesion: Reflections on a flawed paradigm. *Critical Social Policy, 32*(2), 262–281.

Rees, N., Quinn, B., & Connaughton, B. (2010). *Europeanisation and new patterns of governance in Ireland.* Manchester/New York: Manchester University Press.

Riana, V. (2011). "Between behaviourism and constructivism". *Cultural Studies, 25*(1), 9–24.

Ridell, S., & Tett, L. (2010). "Gender balance in teaching debate: Tensions between gender theory and equality policy". *International Journal of Inclusive Education, 14*(5), 463–477.

Roberts, P. (1998). "Extending literate horizons: Paulo Freire and the multidimensional word". *Educational Review, 50*(2), 322–349.

Roberts, P. (2000). *Education, literacy, and humanization: Exploring the work of Paulo Freire.* Westport: Greenwood Press.

Rogers, A. (2002). *Teaching adults* (3rd Edn.). Berkshire: Open University Press.

Rogers, C. (1969). *Freedom to learn, a view of what education might become.* Columbus: C. E. Merrill Publishing Company.

Rogers, C. (1989). *The Carl Rogers reader, selections from the lifetime work of America's Preeminent Psychologist, author of on becoming a person and a way of being.* Ed. H. Kirshenbaum & V. Henderson. Boston: Houghton Mifflin Harcourt.

Rogers, J. (2007). *Adults learning* (5th Edn.). Buckingham: Open University Press.

Rogers, A., & Horrocks, N. (2010). *Teaching adults* (4th Edn.). Maidenhead: Open University Press, McGraw-Hill publications.

Rosenau, P. M. (1991). *Post-modernism and the social sciences: Insights, inroads, and intrusions.* New Jersey: Princeton University Press.

Rourke, S. (2005). *Citywide, A decade of achievement.* Dublin: Citywide.

Ryan, A. (2014). Further education and training, the Trojan Horse. In M. Murray, B. Grummell, & A. Ryan (Eds.), *Further education and training, history politics and practice.* Kildare: MACE Press Publications.

Ryan, A. B. (2001). *Feminist ways of knowing, towards theorising the person for radical adult education.* Leicester: National Institute of Adult Continuing Education.

Saad-Filo, A. (2004). "From Washington to post-Washington consensus: Neoliberal agendas for economic development". In A. Saad-Filho & D. Johnston (Eds.), *Neoliberalism: A critical reader.* London: Pluto Press.

Saarinen, T., & Ala-Va¨Ha¨ La¨, T. (2007). "Accreditation, the Bologna process and national reactions: Accreditation as concept and action". *Higher Education in Europe, 32*(4), 333–345.

Sabel, C. (1996). *Local development in Ireland, partnership, Innovation and Social Justice.* OECD. http://www2.law.columbia.edu/sabel/papers/IrelandFinal.pdf. Accessed 19 December 2016.

Sandelowski, M., Voils, C., & Knafl, G. (2009). "On quantitizing". *Journal of Mixed-methods Research, 3*(3), 208–222.

Sarantakos, S. (2005). *Social research* (3rd Edn.). Hampshire: Palgrave MacMillan.

Save the Children. (2014). *Ending newborn deaths; ensuring every baby survives.* London: Save the Children.

Scheele, K. (2004). "Licence to kill: About accreditation issues and James Bond". *Quality in Higher Education, 10*(3), 285–293.

Schneider, A., & Ingram, L. (2005). *Deserving and entitled: Social constructions and public policy.* Albany: State University of New York Press.

Schultz, T. W. (1961). "Investment in human capital". *The American Economic Review*, 51(1), 1–17.

Scott, M. (2011). "Reflections on the big society". *Community Development Journal*, 46(1), 132–137.

Seltzer-Kelly, D., Westwood, S., & Peña-Guzman, D. M. (2012). "Methodological self-study of quantitizing: Negotiating meaning and revealing multiplicity". *Journal of Mixed-methods Research*, 6(4), 258–274.

Share, P., Tovey, H., & Corcoran, M. (2007). *A sociology of Ireland*. Dublin: Gill and Macmillan.

Shaw, M. (2008). "Community development and the politics of community". *Community Development Journal*, 43(1), 24–36.

Shaw, M. (2009). "Repoliticising democracy, community and the state". *Concept*, 1(1), 1–9.

Shaw, M., & Crowther, J. (2014). "Adult education, community development and democracy: Renegotiating the terms of engagement". *Community Development Journal*, 49(3), 390–406.

Shearad, V., & Sissel, P. A. (2001). *Making space, merging theory and practice in adult education*. Westport: Greenwood Press.

Sheehy, M. (2001). *Partners companion to training for transformation*. Dublin: Partners Training For Transformation.

Sheehy, M., Naughton, F., & O'Regan, C. (2007). *Partners intercultural companion to training for transformation*. Dublin: Partners Training for Transformation.

Shor, I. (1996). *When students have power: Negotiating authority in a critical Pedagogy*. Chicago/London: University of Chicago Press.

Shor, I., & Freire, P. (1987). *A Pedagogy for liberation, dialogues on transforming education*. Westport: Bergin and Garvey Publishers.

Slevin, A. (2009). "Up here it's different: Community education in rural east Donegal". *The Adult Learner, the Irish Journal of Adult and Community Education*, 47–59.

Slowey, M. (1979). "Aspects of women's participation in adult education". *A review of adult education*, 16–24. Dublin: AONTAS.

Smyth, A. (1988). "The contemporary women's movement in the republic of Ireland". *Women's Studies International Forum*, 11(4), 331–341.

Smith, M. K. (2006). "Community work". The Encyclopaedia of InformalEducation. www.infed.org/community/b-comwrk.htm. Accessed May 2016.

Smyth, E. (2009). "Buying your way into college? Private tuition and the transition to higher education in Ireland". *Oxford Review of Education*, 35(1), 1–22.

Smyth, E., & McCoy, S. (2011). "Higher education expansion and differentiation in the Republic of Ireland". *High Education*, 61, 243–260.

Smyth, E., & Hannon, C. (2007). "School processes and the transition to higher education". *Oxford Review of Education, 33*(2), 303–327.

Social Justice Ireland. (2014). *National social monitor 2014.* Dublin: Social Justice Ireland.

Soederberg, S. (2013). "The US Debtfare state and the credit card industry: Forging spaces of dispossession". *Antipode, 45*(2), 493–512.

SOLAS. (2014a). *Further education and training strategy, the department of education and skills.* Dublin: Government Publications.

SOLAS. (2014b). *SOLAS corporate plan 2014–2016.* http://www.solas.ie/docs/ SOLASCorporatePlan.pdf. Accessed 21 July 2014.

Somers, J., & Bradford, S. (2006). "Discourses of partnership in multi-agency working in the community and voluntary sectors in Ireland". *Irish Journal of Sociology, 15*(2), 67–85.

Speeden, S. (2012). "Mainstreaming equality into public management, challenges and opportunities". In J. Diamond & J. Liddle (Eds.), *Critical perspectives on international public sector management, volume 1: Emerging and potential trends in public management: An age of Austerity.* Bingley: GBR: Emerald Group Publishing Ltd.

Spillane, A. (2015). "The impact of the Crisis on Irish women". In C. Coulter & A. Nagle (Eds.), *Ireland under Austerity, neoliberal crisis, neoliberal solutions.* Manchester/New York: Manchester University Press.

Stafford, P. (2011). "The rise and fall of social partnership: Its impact on interest group lobbying in Ireland". *Journal of Public Affairs, 11*(2), 74–79.

Stammers, N. (2009). *Human rights and social movements.* New York: Pluto Press.

Steger, M. B., & Roy, R. K. (2010). *Neoliberalism: A very short introduction.* GBR: Oxford University Press.

Stephen, A. (2006). *The Americanisation of Europe: Culture, diplomacy and Anti-Americanism.* New York: Berghahn Books.

Steyn, I. (2012). "The state and social movements: Autonomy and its Pitfalls". *Politikon: South African Journal of Political Studies, 39*(3), 331–351.

Storey, J. (2010). *Culture and power in cultural studies: The politics of significa-tion.* Edinburgh: Edinburgh University Press.

Tashakkori, A., & Teddie, C. (2010). *Sage handbook of mixed-methods in social and behavioral research.* Thousand Oaks, CA: SAGE.

Taylor, J. (1998). "Feminist tactics and friendly fire in the Irish women's movement". *Gender and Society, 12*(6), 674–691.

Teague, P., & Murphy, M. C. (2004). *Social partnership and local development in Ireland: The limits to deliberation.* Geneva: International Labour Organization (International Institute for Labour Studies.

Tennant, M. (2005). "Transforming selves. *Journal of Transformative Education"*, *3*(2), 102–115.

Tett, L. (2006). *Community education, lifelong learning and social inclusion* (2nd Edn.). Edinburgh: Dunedin Academic Press.

The Teaching Council. (2009). *The teaching council [registration] regulations.* http://www.teachingcouncil.ie/_fileupload/Registration/Overview/Registration_Regulations_2009_90665047.pdf. Accessed September 2012.

Thompson, D. (2001). *Radical feminism today.* London: Sage Publications.

Thompson, G. (2003). *Education, a very short introduction.* New York: Oxford University Press.

Thompson, J. (2000). *Women, class and education.* London: Routledge.

Thompson, J. (2007). "The road to hell...". In B. Connolly, T. Fleming, D. McCormack, & A. Ryan (Eds.), *Radical Learning for Liberation 2.* Kildare: MACE publications.

Tisdell, E. J. (2007). "Popular culture and critical media literacy in adult education: Theory and practice". *New Directions for Adult and Continuing Education, 115,* 5–13.

Tisdell, E. J., & Taylor, E. W. (2001). "Adult education philosophy informs practice". *Adult Learning, Bringing Our Philosophies into Practice, 11*(2), 6–10.

Tobin, D. (2010). *A crisis of Ethics, moral hazard and banking regulation in Ireland,* TASC Think Pieces. http://issuu.com/tascpublications/docs/tobin_250310. Accessed 30 November 2010.

Tobin, P. (1989). "Women in community work". In *Community work in Ireland, trends for the 80's options for the 90's.* Dublin: The Combat Poverty Agency.

Tönnies, F. (2002). *Community and society.* Newton Abbot: David and Charles.

Torres, C. A. (1993). "From the Pedagogy of the oppressed to a Luta Continua". In P. McLaren & P. Leonard (Eds.), *Paulo Freire, a critical encounter.* London/New York: Routledge.

Twelvetrees, A. (2008). *Community work* (4th Edn.). Basingstoke: Palgrave-Macmillan.

United Nations. (2014). *United nations human development report: Sustaining human progress: Reducing Vulnerabilities and building resilience.* United Nations Publications. http://hdr.undp.org/sites/default/files/hrd14-report-en-1.pdf. Accessed 19 December 2016.

United Nations. (2015). *The Millennium development goals report.* New York: United Nations. http://mdgs.un.org/unsd/mdg/Resources/Static/Products/Progress2015/English2015.pdf. Accessed 11 January 2016.

Valsiner, J. (2000). "Data as representations: Contextualizing qualitative and quantitative research strategies". *Social Science Information, 39,* 99–113.

Van Der Wende, M. C. (2000). "The Bologna declaration: Enhancing the transparency and competitiveness of European higher education". *Higher Education in Europe, XXV*(3), 305–310.

Walsh, J. (1996a). "Challenge of corporate governance for community directors". *Poverty Today, 32,* 8–9.

Walsh, J. (1996b). "Review highlights need for partnership reforms". *Poverty today, 33,* 12–13.

Walsh, P. (2006). "Narrowed horizons and the impoverishment of educational discourse: Teaching, learning and performing under the new educational bureaucracies". *Journal of Education Policy, 21*(1), 95–117.

Walsh, T. (2005). "Constructions of childhood in Ireland in the twentieth century: A view from the primary school curriculum 1900–1999". *Child Care in Practice, 11*(2), 253–269.

Walsh, J., Craig, S., & McCafferty, D. (1998). *Local partnerships for social inclusion?.* Dublin: Combat Poverty Agency.

Watson, D., McCoy, S., & Gorby, S. (2006). *The post-leaving certificate sector in Ireland: A multivariate analysis of educational and employment outcomes.* Dublin: Department of Education and Science and ESRI.

Weber, J. (2014). "Humanism within globalisation". *Adult Learning, 25*(2), 66–68.

Weiler. (1991). "Freire and a feminist pedagogy of difference". *Harvard Educational Review, 61*(4), 449–474.

West, J. (2006). "Patrolling the boarders: Accreditation in further and higher education in England". *Journal of Further and Higher Education, 30*(1), 12–26.

Westerman, W. (2009). "Folk schools, popular education, and a Pedagogy of community action". In A. Darder, P. Baltodano, & R. D. Torres (Eds.), *The critical Pedagogy reader* (2nd Edn.). London/New York: Routledge.

Whelan, M. (1989). "Training and professionalisation in community work". In *Community work in Ireland: Trends in the 80s; Options for the 90s.* Dublin: Combat Poverty Agency.

Whitehead, P., & Crawshaw, P. (2012). *Organising Neoliberalism: Markets, privatisation and justice.* London: Anthem Press.

Wiggins, N. (2011). "Critical pedagogy and popular education, towards a unity of theory and practice". *Studies in the Education of Adults, 43*(1), 34–49.

Wildemeersch, D. (2014). "Adult and community education in complex societies: Reconsidering critical perspectives". *International Journal of Lifelong Education, 33*(6), 821–831.

Wilkinson, R., & Pickett, K. (2009). *The spirit level, why more equal societies almost always to better.* London: Penguin Books.

Williams, J., Greene, S., Doyle, E., Harris, E., Layte, R., McCoy, S., McCrory, C., Murray, A., Nixon, E., O'Dowd, T., O'Moore, M., Quail, A., Smyth, E., Swords, L., & Thornton, M. (2009). *The lives of 9-yr-olds, growing up in Ireland, national longitudinal study of children.* Dublin: Office of the Minister for Health and Children.

Wilson, A. (1995). "The common concern: Controlling the professionalization of adult education". In S. B. Merriam (Ed.), *Selected writings on philosophy and adult education*. Florida: Krieger Publishing Company.

Winch, C., & Gringell, J. (1999). *Key concepts in the philosophy of education*. London/New York: Routledge.

Windebank, J., & Whitworth, A. (2014). "Social welfare and the ethics of Austerity in Europe: Justice, ideology and equality". *Journal of Contemporary European Studies, 22*(2), 99–103.

Young, M. (2007). "National frameworks, some conceptual issues". *European Journal of Education, 42*(4), 445–457.

Zappone, K. (1998). "Top-down or bottom-up: The involvement of the community sector in partnerships in the shadow of the Tiger". In P. Kirby & D. Jacobson (Eds.), *New approaches to combating social exclusion*. Dublin: Dublin City University Press.

Žižek, S. (2009a). *First as tragedy, then as Farce*. London/New York: Verso.

Žižek, S. (2009b). "Welcome to the Desert of the real!". In U. Linke & D. T. Smith (Eds.), *Cultures of fear, A critical reader*. London/New York: Pluto Press.

INDEX

A

Accreditation, 31, 32, 47, 98, 105,
129, 131, 140, 161, 163–193,
231, 234, 238, 241
Adult Education Organisers/
AEOs, 75, 87
Adulthood, 109
Ahern, Bertie, 16, 33n8
All Ireland Endorsement Body/
AIEB, 203
Allen, K., 6, 8, 11, 12, 13, 19, 23, 227
Anti-globalisation protesters, 25
Anti-intellectualism, 106, 122, 123
AONTAS
community education network/
CEN, 2, 5, 32n2, 92–93, 135,
161n2, 178, 234
history of, 73, 92
Apple Inc, 12, 24
Assessment of learning, 164, 165,
172–173
Austerity, 2–3, 16, 19–23, 25, 60, 70,
99, 146, 151, 229

B

Ballymun, 33n9, 151
Bank guarantee, 20, 149

Boards of management (Community
Sector), 83, 86, 148
Behaviourism, 107, 170
Bissett, john, 14, 60, 135, 147,
157, 245n7
Bologna Declaration, 166, 168, 169
Bourdieu, P., 45
Brexit, 27–28
Brookfield, S., 29, 29,
107, 111, 239

C

Capitalism, 5, 6, 9, 12, 13, 16, 17, 20,
29, 38, 45, 111, 116, 117, 122,
207, 227, 228, 243
Celtic Tiger, 11, 12, 33n14, 136, 143
Childcare courses, 213
City and Guilds, 167
Citywide, 86, 87, 93
Civil society, 13–15, 25, 42, 59, 60,
82, 142, 144, 147, 149, 218
Codes (as used in Freirean
practice), 128
College knowledge, 214
Combat Poverty Agency, 13, 83, 84,
135, 167, 211

© The Author(s) 2017
C. Fitzsimons, *Community Education and Neoliberalism*,
DOI 10.1007/978-3-319-45937-0

Common Awards System/CAS,
  177, 184
Communities against cuts, 28
Community Action Network, 82,
  225n5, 242
Community Development
  definition of, 98
  development fund, 83, 102n10
  development programme, 2, 15, 21,
    33n6, 62, 76, 83–84, 86, 90,
    102n6, 148
  development projects, 13, 83, 84,
    86, 102n10, 148, 196, 242
  development support
    programme, 13, 33n6, 85,
    87, 156
  as a process, 5, 31, 59, 77, 86, 142,
    148, 150, 240
Community Education
  core principles, 3, 32, 63, 84,
    146, 189
  definitions of, 3–6
  history of, 4, 60, 71–90, 112, 131
  landscape of provision in
    Ireland, 73, 230–237
Community Education Facilitators, 6,
  49, 77, 93, 135, 142
Community Education Facilitator's
  Network/CEFA, 5, 77, 135, 159
Community Pillar, 12, 14
Community Sector
  cuts to, 2, 19, 28, 99
  history of, 23
Community Workers Cooperative, 22,
  93, 135, 201
Community Work Ireland, 22, 93,
  135, 203
Conditionality of welfare, 146, 153
Connolly, Brid, 4, 5, 29, 45, 58, 59,
  78, 80, 87, 110, 112, 125, 140,
  147, 167, 238
Constitution of Ireland, 134

Constructivism, 105
Continuous professional
  development, 94,
  198, 205
Copenhagen Declaration, 166, 168
Corbyn, Jeremy, 28
Council for the Status of Women, 78
Critical
  group-work, 124, 129
  pedagogy, 30, 104, 110–112, 117
  thinking, 57, 111, 139
Culture of Fear, 18
Curriculum, 45, 52, 57, 98, 129, 165,
  170–171, 196, 241

D
Debtfare States, 10
Department of Adult and Community
  Education, Maynooth
  University, 87, 241
Department of Community, Rural and
  Gealteacht Affairs, 13, 147,
  161n5
Department of Education and Science
  (DES), 142
Department of Education and Science
  (DOES), 5, 76, 135, 142, 154,
  159, 204, 233
Department of Enterprise, Trade and
  Employment, 142
Department of Environment,
  Community and Local
  Government, 21, 41, 149
Department of Social Protection, 222
Development Education, 92, 93, 98,
  193n1, 203
Dewey, John, 105, 107
Direct Provision, 19, 241
Disability, 20, 95,
  97, 139

Disadvantage, 4, 41, 42, 44, 47, 51, 53, 57, 61–64, 70, 77, 84, 89, 95, 97, 98, 100, 148, 150, 151, 153, 167, 182, 183, 196, 211–212, 215, 216
Disciplinary power, 188

E
Education and Training Boards/ ETBS, 23, 30, 55, 90–92, 97, 145, 187, 206, 220, 231
Employability, 32, 49, 55, 57, 65, 131, 133–161, 171, 228, 229, 231, 238, 239
Equality, 4–6, 8, 13, 29, 31–32, 42, 43, 49, 53, 54, 57, 58, 66, 79, 80, 81, 83, 89, 92, 97, 101, 110, 113, 114, 131, 134, 136, 141, 150, 151, 152, 160, 167, 168, 173, 203, 217, 228, 229, 243
EU poverty programme, 83
European Credit Transfer System, 169
European Union, 15, 81, 136, 140–141
External Authentication, 164, 179

F
Family Resource Centres, 13, 33n6, 49, 84, 85
Family Support Agency, 85
FÁS, 15, 22, 30, 55, 84, 145, 146, 167, 193n4
Feminism
    and popular culture, 80
    second-wave feminism, 80
    third wave feminism, 208
Feminist pedagogy, 32, 118–129
FETAC, 31, 34n22, 174, 175, 177, 178, 183, 186, 193n4, 211, 240
Fianna Fail, 41, 66n2, 79, 148

Fine Gael, 27
First Report of the Ministerial Task Force on the Measures to Reduce the Demand for Drugs, 86
Focus-groups, 46, 94, 127, 135, 153, 159, 186, 189, 209, 210, 221, 231, 232, 235
Foucault, Michel, 180–181, 188
Free Market Economics, 3, 6, 9, 19, 24, 131, 228
Freire, Paulo, 28, 32, 34n19, 43, 58, 82, 102n5, 102n7, 104, 105, 111–119, 122, 124, 125, 127, 129, 130n2, 170, 196, 206, 243, 244
Further Education
    Further Education and Training/ FET, 23, 34n22, 56, 135, 145–146, 174, 178, 205, 224n4, 233
    Further Education and Training Strategy, 145, 178
    relationship with community education, 178

G
Gates, Bill, 8
Giddens, Anthony, 12–13
Globalisation, *see* Neoliberalism
Gramsci, Antonio
    on organic intellectuals, 207
    on hegemony, 10, 113, 207
Green Paper, Adult Education in an Era of Learning, 5, 142, 204, 208
Group work, 32, 58, 76, 81, 99, 104, 124, 125, 129, 175

H
Healthcare courses, 180, 193n7
Health Service Executive, 23

Hegemony, 10, 17, 33, 113, 207
HETAC, 31, 34n22, 174, 177, 193n2
Highlander school, 112
History of community education, *see*
    Community education
Homelessness, 19, 23, 228
Home Sweet Home (social
    movement), 26
Hooks, bell, 29, 58, 105, 106, 114,
    116, 118, 122, 129, 217
Hope, Anne, 81–82, 102n8, 122, 124,
    126, 127, 244
Housing policy, 135, 136, 164
Human capital, 137–139
Humanistic adult education, 104

I
Individualism, 42, 84, 110, 111,
    113, 117
Internal Verification, 178
'*International Adult Literacy Survey*'
    Report, 75
International Monetary Fund, 7, 228
Intreo, 147
'*Investment in Education*' Report,
    43–44
Irish congress of Trade Unions, 28,
    33n8, 72, 148
Irish Women's Liberation
    Movement, 78

K
Kane, L., 29, 59, 60, 111,
    128, 239
Kenny Report, 75
Kildare LEADER Partnership, 240
Knowledge economy, 9, 137, 139,
    219
Knowles, Malcolm, 109, 119

L
Labour Market Activation, 32, 70, 146,
    147, 152–154, 176,
    185, 193
LEADER programme, 15, 33n7
*Learning for Life; White Paper on
    Adult Education*, 4, 76, 135, 142,
    204, 233
Learning outcomes, 32, 165, 166,
    171–173, 175, 177,
    179, 184
Liberal, 12, 84, 105–107,
    134, 193
Liberation theology, 73, 81–82,
    102n7
Lifelong Learning, 32, 53–55, 75,
    136–143, 166, 239
Literacy movement, 73–77, 82, 88
Local Area Partnerships, 15, 86, 148
Local and Community Development
    Programme, 62, 90,
    102n6, 148

M
*Making a European Area of Lifelong
    Learning a Reality*, 140
Managerialism, *see* New public
    managerialism
Marx, Karl, 113, 122
McCarthy report, 148
McDonald, Mary-Lou, 27
McLaren, Peter, 30, 110, 111, 117
McVerry, Peter, 23
*Memorandum on Lifelong
    learning*, 138, 140, 142
Mezirow, Jack, 105, 122
Militarisation of society, 17, 18
Millennium Development Goals, 8
Mixed-methods research, 46
Murphy Report, 74–76

N

National Adult Literacy Agency/
NALA, 73–78, 88, 93, 102n3,
144, 216
National Assets Management Agency
(NAMA), 26
National Collective of Community
Based Women's Networks, 81
National Council for Vocational
Awards, 166
National Development Plan, 143
National Framework of
Qualifications/NFQ, 169, 170,
175, 177, 178
National Qualifications
Frameworks, 164, 165, 169–174
National Skills Strategy, 178
National Women's Education
Initiative, 81
Neoliberalism
and globalisation, 3, 11
impacts of, 29, 219, 239
meaning of, 11, 70
neoliberal logic anti-neoliberal
movements, 228
Networking, 81, 203
New Opportunities for Women
(NOW) programme, 80
New public managerialism
in the community sector, 13
in Ireland, 23
meaning of, 11
No class without crèche, 79
Non-governmental organisations/
NGOs, 12, 46, 91, 92, 97, 102,
155, 197, 232

O

Oakley, Ann, 30
Occupy Wall Street
in Ireland, 25
the occupy movement, 25
Organisation for Economic Co-
operation and Development
(OECD), 6, 8, 23, 43, 44, 74–76,
137, 139, 227
Outputs, 11, 13, 21, 85, 101, 139,
144, 145, 148, 150, 152, 155,
172, 185, 208, 231, 243

P

Participation, 5, 6, 12, 16, 57, 59, 77,
79, 85, 102, 109, 110, 117, 138,
141, 143, 147, 159–161, 203, 242
Participatory banking (as an approach
to education), 128, 129
Partners in Faith, 82
Partners Training for
Transformation, 81
Patriarchy, 30, 56, 118
Popular education, 111–112
Post-leaving certificate programmes/
PLCs, *see* Vocational Preparation
and Training Programme
Poststructuralism, 116
Praxis, 4, 29, 58, 59, 81, 105,
115, 139, 207, 232, 242, 243
Precarious employment
and managerialism, 208
meaning of, 207
precariat, and working
conditions, 219
Privatisation, 7, 11
of the community sector, 147
Professionalisation
of community development, 197,
201–202
of community education, 195–223
meaning of professional, 197–207
professionalism, 196–198
Progressive education, 107
Public-Private Partnerships, 135

Q
Qualifications (education and training)
    Act, 174
Quality Assurance
    meaning of, 173,
        178–181
    use in Ireland, 176
*Quality Assurance and Qualifications
    (Education and Training)
    Act)*, 176
Quality and Qualifications Ireland/
    QQI, 31, 56, 165, 177

R
Radical education, 104
    See also Critical
Really Useful Research, 29
Respond! Voluntary Housing
    Association, 239
Right to read movement, 74
Rogers, Carl, 108–110, 119

S
St Patricks College, Maynooth, 87
Social Inclusion and Community
    Activation Programme/
    SICAP, 22, 28, 86, 150–151
Social partnership, 12–16, 21, 175
Social policy, 134–136, 152
SOLAS, 2, 23, 57, 135, 145–146,
    178, 205–206
Specialist knowledge, 198
Spectacle of Defiance and Hope, 28,
    94, 99, 149, 234

T
Teaching Council of Ireland, 33, 94,
    204, 205, 209
Theories of learning, 104–105
The third way, 12
*Towards Standards for Quality
    Community Work*, 203
Training for Transformation, 31, 73,
    81–82, 127, 196
Traveller Training Centres, 76
Troika, 20, 21, 25, 127
Trump, Donald, 24, 27
Twitter, 26

U
Unemployment, 10, 15, 20, 33n9,
    57, 82, 95, 115, 141,
    147, 150
University College Dublin, 88, 167

V
Vocational Educational Committees/
    VECs, 13, 22, 30, 31, 46, 73–77,
    80, 87–88, 90–92, 97, 99
*Vocational Preparation and Training
    Programme*, 166
Vocational Training and
    Opportunities Scheme, 75

W
Washington consensus, 6
Waterford Institute of
    Technology, 167, 224n3

White Paper on a Framework for Supporting Voluntary Activity, 143
Women's community education
conscious-raising practice, 80
history of, 77
Women's movement, 31, 58, 73, 78–80, 112

World Bank, 7, 9, 25, 227
World Trade Organisation, 7

Z
Žižek, S., 16, 18, 25, 243

Printed by Printforce, the Netherlands